IELTS
Speaking

雅思口语
核心话题精讲精练

宋鹏昊　主编

（英）奥利弗·戴维斯（Oliver Davies）　齐小霞　郑楚楠　编著

音频

浙江教育出版社·杭州

图书在版编目(CIP)数据

雅思口语核心话题精讲精练 / 宋鹏昊主编 ；(英)
奥利弗·戴维斯 (Oliver Davies)，齐小霞，郑楚楠编
著. -- 杭州 ：浙江教育出版社，2023.2（2024.8重印）
ISBN 978-7-5722-4727-9

Ⅰ．①雅… Ⅱ．①宋… ②奥… ③齐… ④郑… Ⅲ.
①IELTS－口语－自学参考资料 Ⅳ．①H319.9

中国版本图书馆CIP数据核字(2022)第212091号

雅思口语核心话题精讲精练
YASI KOUYU HEXIN HUATI JING JIANG JING LIAN
宋鹏昊　主编　（英）奥利弗·戴维斯（Oliver Davies）齐小霞　郑楚楠　编著

责任编辑　赵清刚
美术编辑　韩　波
责任校对　马立改
责任印务　时小娟
封面设计　李　倩
出版发行　浙江教育出版社
　　　　　地址：杭州市环城北路177号
　　　　　邮编：310005
　　　　　电话：0571-88900883
　　　　　邮箱：dywh@xdf.cn
印　　刷　大厂回族自治县彩虹印刷有限公司
开　　本　787mm×1092mm　1/16
成品尺寸　185mm×260mm
印　　张　14
字　　数　256 000
版　　次　2023年2月第1版
印　　次　2024年8月第7次印刷
标准书号　ISBN 978-7-5722-4727-9
定　　价　58.00元

雅思考试的四个科目中，口语和写作往往更令考生头疼，其原因在于"在这件事上花的时间不足"。这里说的花时间，包含了三方面的因素：一是知识的学习，也就是首先要有足够的输入；二是技能的练习，也就是要不断地开口回答问题，让回答雅思口语问题变成自己"非常熟悉"的事；三是心态的适应，慢慢适应答题过程中可能存在的紧张感，以及学会在答题非常顺利或非常不顺利时进行即时调整，保证自己发挥平稳。在这三个方面花足够的时间，是获得高分的前提。在本书中，我们为大家提供的便是"花时间的对象"，也就是把时间花在这本书上。如果能把这本书吃透，相信你会成为雅思口语的一个"行家"，并取得理想的分数。

本书的主要内容

这本书的编写团队由资深前雅思考官、雅思研发人员、雅思教师等不同角色的人员组成，并且这些人员均具有十几年的从业经验。我们结合当前考试的特点和大量的考生案例，最终完成了一本包括方法、问题、回答、解析、音频等在内的雅思口语复习用书，以下是本书的主要内容。

雅思口语学习 30 问：这部分内容从备考、评分、答题的角度精选了 30 个考生关注的问题，并给出了明确的解答。问答的形式可以增强考生在学习过程中的"代入感"，相信对这 30 个问题有了足够的理解后，考生能够对雅思口语考试建立正确的认知，而这无疑是高效备考的前提。

雅思口语 Part 1 核心话题：这部分精选 30 个 Part 1 的核心话题，每个话题后有 3~4 个具体的问题，针对这些问题给出了示例回答，并且配有对回答要点的讲解。这些讲解中既包括了重要的单词、短语，也提示了如何实现好的衔接以及其他需要考生掌握的语言点。这部分内容希望考生可以全部掌握。

雅思口语 Part 2 & 3 核心话题：这部分精选 50 个 Part 2 & 3 的核心话题，同样提供了示例回答和语言点讲解，这部分内容依然希望考生可以全部掌握。对于 Part 1、Part 2 和 Part 3 话题的选择，我们主要遵循"高频 + 可复用 + 覆盖面"的原则，也就是重点选择那些考试频率高的话题，选择那些回答可以复用到其他题目的话题，以及选择足够全面的、不同类型的、能覆盖考试范围的话题。

雅思口语补充练习话题：在完成前面的学习后，本书针对 Part 1 和 Part 2 & 3 分别提供了一部分练习话题，考生可以使用前面学习的素材进行练习，也可以将这些练习话题作为对自己备考情况的检验，测试一下如果自己遇到这些没有完全复习过的题目，能不能自如地回答问题。

备考建议

结合我自身学习和教学中的反思，以及与大量雅思考生的交流，以下建议对大家会有所帮助。

第一，先有足够的输入，再输出。对于刚刚开始备考的考生而言，最大的问题就是"无话可说"。这种时候不要着急表达，先仔仔细细、认认真真吃透我们给出的示例回答，然后自己做些修改和调整，该背就背，再慢慢达到可以自如表达和交流的程度，即先僵化再灵活。

第二，靠时间取胜，靠遍数取胜。任何技能最后都是靠时间和遍数取胜，比如弹钢琴，比如画画，比如打篮球，再比如雅思口语。同一首曲子，弹过 100 遍的人必定比弹过 10 遍的人更熟练。我常说，考生在雅思备考中遇到的几乎所有问题，都是练习量不够以及学习时间太少造成的，所以不要急于求成。学 1 个小时有 1 个小时的效果，学 10 个小时的人怎么会比学 100 个小时的人分数高呢？

第三，找到适合自己的学习方法。学习方法是否高效主要看是否适合学习者。每个人的学习风格各不相同，有的人擅长听别人说话和口头表达，有的人擅长看文字，用文字和别人交流，有的人看一遍就能记住，听五遍才能记住，有的人看五遍都记不住，听一遍就记住了，所以考生们要多了解自己，不要怕自己的方法"土"，我们的最终目的是能够灵活地进行口语表达。在这之前，不管是列提纲自己说，跟读录音，完全自由发挥，还是背答案，都是通向灵活表达的路径，建议考生找到一种或几种适合自己的学习方法。

这本书中的内容，尤其是涉及的语言点，我认为对备考雅思口语而言都是必需的，希望考生可以尽可能地学会、练熟，让自己多花一些时间在雅思口语上，以获得优秀的口语成绩。

宋鹏昊

Dear readers,

This book is the result of our many years' experience helping students achieve higher band scores in their IELTS tests.

The book provides you with the language and skills you need to excel in all three parts of the Speaking test, including:

* Familiarising you with the topic areas and key vocabulary that commonly arise.
* Improving the way you structure your answers & learning the logic of quality high-scoring responses.
* Learning common vocabulary in context, and collocations and lexical structures used by educated native speakers.
* Introducing simple and complex grammatical structures into your conversations naturally, accurately and intelligently.

Covering over 80 topic areas (30 in part 1, 50 in part 2&3), with over 200 examples of model answers, the book is the ultimate resource in achieving higher scores in your speaking test and developing greater confidence in structuring your answers.

Designed through collaboration with ex-IELTS examiners with decades of experience, and our extensive research and analysis of key question types, patterns and structures common in IELTS Speaking, the book offers a concise language focus after each model answer.

How to Use the Book

The central approach of the book is to give you high-scoring model answers to typical IELTS questions, with key vocabulary, grammatical items and language that will enable you to put together your own answers like a native speaker.

We suggest you approach personal study in the following way:

* Read the questions carefully and cover up the model answer.
* Ask yourself: how would I answer this question?
* Write down your answer on paper — check it and revise it.
* Read it out loud to yourself, as if you were in the speaking test.
* Then read our model answer slowly and carefully.
* Read our model answer again, loudly.
* Pick out and highlight any vocabulary, phrases or language points that strike you as new, interesting or useful.
* Consider the context of these language items in the answer.
* Then look at the language items we have noted.
* Ask yourself: how could you incorporate these language items into your answers?
* Write your own answer that applies to you, using the key vocabulary and language from the model answer.
* Read your answer out loud, as if you were in the speaking test.

If you follow these steps, you will learn to internalise language and develop greater fluency and accuracy in a way that sounds natural and native.

Do not simply memorise our model answers hoping the exact questions will come up in your speaking test!

Make the most of the examples and language items we have carefully put together to help you speak more like a native and gain high speaking test scores!

Oliver Lyn Davies

目录

第一章 雅思口语学习 30 问

考试流程及备考篇 ▶▶▶

1 雅思口语有几个部分？考试时间多长？

雅思口语考试由三部分组成，即 Part 1，Part 2 和 Part 3，考试总时长为 11~14 分钟。其中 Part 1 时长为 4~5 分钟，Part 2 时长为 3~4 分钟。Part 3 时长为 4~5 分钟。

2 每个部分的考试流程是怎样的？有多少个问题？

在 Part 1 中考官会就考生熟悉的话题进行提问。该部分考查考生就日常性的观点和信息、常见的生活经历或情形以回答问题的形式进行交流的能力。此部分一般涉及三个话题，考官针对每个话题提出 3~4 个相关的小问题。因此该部分平均有 10 个小问题左右。

在 Part 2 中考官将以"话题卡"的方式给考生提供一个熟悉的话题。考生有一分钟的准备时间，其间可以用考场上提供的纸和笔记笔记，然后就此话题进行 1~2 分钟的陈述。考官会在 2 分钟后打断考生，并在最后提 1~2 个问题。该部分考查考生就一个特定话题进行较长时间陈述的能力，并关注考生是否能恰当地运用语言并连贯地组织自己的观点。

在 Part 3 中考官将基于 Part 2 中出现的话题进行延伸，并和考生就相关且较为抽象的话题进行双向讨论。该部分考查考生表达和论述看法、分析和讨论问题的能力。另外，该部分的问题数量和具体的讨论情况有关系，平均有 5~7 个问题。

3 考试时如果没听清考官的问题怎么办？会影响分数吗？

如果在 Part 1 中出现该情况，考生可立即向考官提出，并礼貌地请考官重复一遍问题，例如可以说"Sorry, can you say that again?"或者"Could you repeat the question, please?"。

如果在 Part 3 中出现该情况，考生同样可礼貌地请考官重复一遍问题，或请考官改述、解释问题，以便进一步理解问题，例如可以说"Sorry, could you explain the question? I don't really understand it."。

因此，偶尔出现没听清或没听懂问题的情况，考生无须紧张，及时向考官提出即可，同时要避免回答的内容和问题毫不相关的情况。只要考生不是每个问题或者大量问题都需要考官重复或解释，分数就不受影响。

但请注意，在考官重复和解释后，如果考生还是不太理解问题的具体意思，可尝试回答一些和问题相关的内容，避免什么都不回答的情况。同时也建议考生先和考官进行简单说明，例如"Well, I haven't thought about the question before, but I think...", 再回答相关内容。

4 口语考试时被考官打断要紧吗？会影响分数吗？

考官在雅思口语考试中打断考生的回答，主要有两个原因。

第一，考官需要严格把控口语考试时间。因此考生如果某个问题回答时间过长，会被考官适时打断。

第二，考官需要预留时间以便提问考生不同的话题。因为考官需要引导考生全面地展示英文水平，如词汇、语法在不同情况下的应用。如果考生始终只谈论一个话题，就很难全面地展现自己的语言能力。

因此，口语考试时考生如果被考官打断往往不会影响分数。考生只要确保仔细听问题，正确理解问题，并回答和问题相关的内容即可。如果偶尔出现了被考官打断的情况，不要慌张，注意听好下一个问题，继续冷静回答即可。

5 本书中话题选取的标准是什么？每个话题都要准备吗？

本书选取话题主要遵循三个原则。第一，在过去 5~8 年的考试中出现的高频话题，这种话题大概率也会出现在以后的题库中。第二，通用性较强的话题，例如 Part 2 物品类话题中收录了描述"过去收到的一件礼物"，之后遇到描述"自己丢掉的一件物品"以及描述"想买一直没买的一件物品"，实际上都可以使用同一个物品，因此我们会选择可复用性比较强的话题。第三，尽可能覆盖不同的题目类型，例如人物类话题中，会覆盖"身边的人"和"有名的人"；物品类话题中，会覆盖"具体的某个物品"和"抽象的事物或现象"，以保证能全面覆盖考试中可能遇到的话题。

这样做的目的是尽可能帮助考生提升备考效率。比如，当季雅思口语题库中如果出现了"Describe a gift you would like to buy for a child"这一 Part 2 的话题，直接结合本书中的"Describe a toy you got in your childhood"这一题目进行迁移延展即可，这样就比从零开始思考某个题目答案的效率高得多。

因此，对于语言或口语基础较弱且备考时间有半年以上的考生，我们建议练习本书中的所有话题。除了模仿回答思路，也可有效积累口语表达，夯实基础，以便之后应对当季雅思口语题库中的各种话题。对于有一定的语言基础但备考时间较短的考生来说，则可以结合当季雅思口语题库，寻找本书中可以进行迁移延展的话题，进行适当修改后再练习，以便提升练习和备考效率，并积累相关语料。

6 雅思口语题库的换题规律是什么？几月报考比较好？

雅思口语考试中所使用的话题都是从一个事先拟定的范围内抽取的，特别是考试的 Part 1 和 Part 2 两部分。因此这些话题往往会根据考生的考试回忆被整理成一个话题库，即雅思口语题库。

　　口语题库中的话题不是一成不变的。每一季的题库可连续使用四个月，并在每年的1月初、5月初、9月初进行部分更新和调整。

　　有考生担心题库调整会影响自己的备考，实际上对大多数考生而言不用过于担心。第一，从换题月的第三场考试开始，其实新题出现的比例已经非常低，因此报名当月的后两场考试实际上不太会受到换题库的影响。第二，换题月的首场考试实际上也只有一部分题目会被调整，比如保留三分之二，调整三分之一。题库中出现的新题很可能是将之前使用过的题目进行了微调，并不影响考生的作答，即使出现全新的题目，考生也可以根据自己复习过的答题内容进行迁移和延展。因此在报名时，考生只需要多多关注自己的时间安排、复习进度、对出分时间的需求等因素，不必过于担心口语的题库调整。

7 备考雅思口语能不能背句子或者背答案？

　　如果考生基础较弱，在前期练习时，可首先适当背诵或者跟读一些句子，让自己有足够的"输入"，并以此学习如何组织语言，例如让自己能够在口头上使用和话题相关的词汇或者常见句型，清晰有效地表达意思。本书中也提供了大量的口语回答供考生学习和模仿。

　　需要注意的是，考生如果提升了语言基础，在后期口语练习中就应当以表达和交流为主，避免背诵答案，并且练习时也要尝试直接回答不同的问题，让自己的表达更加自然、灵活、准确。

　　如果考生在实际考试中还是使用背诵的方式回答问题，很容易被考官发现，并影响最终口语分数。例如考官可在 Part 3 的讨论中提问考生没有事先准备过的问题，通过考生口语流利性的稳定度、发音特征是否自然等因素，判断考生是在背诵，或是在进行自然交流。一旦考官判定考生是在背诵，考生将无法得到理想的口语成绩。

8 备考中可以把口语答案都写下来再练习吗？

　　如果考生基础较弱，无法有效的组织语言或者延展话题，在前期练习中可尝试把回答内容先写下来，之后朗读熟练，再尝试转化为口语表达。

　　同理，如果考生在回答口语话题时始终无法意识到自己频繁出现的某些语法错误，也可尝试写下部分内容，检查是否存在问题之后，再继续进行口语练习。

　　在考生的基础能力得到提升之后，就不再建议把口语答案都写下来再练习，考生可以通过列出提纲和关键词再组织语言的方式进行练习。口语应该通过多说而得到提升，而不是通过多写来提升。当然这也要考虑题目的情况，如果考生已经具备了不需要写答案就可以回答问题的能力，但在回答部分话题时有明显的困难，或者遇到的话题非常不熟悉，那么可以使用先写出提纲，或者写出完整答案再进行练习的方法。

9 如何自己一个人进行练习？如何独自备考雅思口语？

理想的状态是考生可以找到一名伙伴，例如同样需要参加雅思口语的考生，一同备考。除了互相监督之外，也可以在练习部分话题后，相互提问，模拟考试中的问答情况并测试自己连续回答问题的能力。当然还有更重要的一点在于，我们自己说错的句子，自己是不太容易识别的，这时候互相问答就成了发现错误、纠正错误的好时机。

如果是自己独自备考和练习，那么录音就成了必不可少的环节，考生可将自己的回答内容录音保存，并进行播放和分析，总结之后再进行练习。考生可以在录音中发现词汇错误、语法错误，以及是否存在过于单一的词汇和语法表达，另外也可以重点关注回答中有明显犹豫的部分，总是重复的部分，以及可能导致他人理解困难的部分。

10 词汇和语法在口语中如何提高？需要背诵口语词汇吗？

考生需要结合话题和语境进行词汇和句型的积累。本书根据不同话题的答案整理出的内容亮点，包括了常用词组和句型等相关语言点，把这些内容全部掌握，已经足够在一场雅思口语考试中取得不错的分数。

如果考生基础较弱，在前期备考和练习时，可直接背诵本书中的口语话题答案，以便打好词汇和语法基础。

在后期结合当季题库练习和备考时，考生需要能够独立使用从本书中学习到的相关词汇和句型。只有结合口语话题开口练习，才能有效提升使用词汇和语法的熟练度。

考试评分标准篇 ▶▶▶

1 考官会对雅思口语考试的每个 Part 分别打分吗？

考官不会分别打分，而是根据考生在口语考试三个部分的总体表现进行打分。打分涉及四个维度，分别是流利性与连贯性、词汇多样性、语法多样性及准确性以及发音。

针对每个维度，考官会根据考生在三个部分的总体表现，在 0~9 分的打分范围中给出一个整数分，再对四项打分取平均数得出考生口语的最终分数。

2 有创意和特别的回答会帮助我拿到更好的分数吗？

这种回答不会帮助考生获得更好的分数。

首先雅思考试考查的是语言能力和交流能力，因此评分依据只关乎语言水平，如发音、流利度、连贯性等。

其次，在评分标准中，并没有涉及"内容"这一项，也就是说是否有创意，是否很特别，并不在评分的考虑范围之内。

因此，考生只需要在问题的框架内进行合理的内容延展即可。考生也不一定要说完全符合自己真实生活的内容，只要回答合理、有条理，同时可以体现流利性等语言能力即可。

3 考官如何识别我的回答中是否使用了很好的衔接？

考官除了根据考生的回答是否易于理解这一因素判断外，还会留意考生是否能够有效且合理地使用一系列的连接词和语篇标记。

连接词的使用涉及是否能合理地使用并列、因果、转折等逻辑连接词串联句子，而不是仅仅把句子罗列出来。因此考生需要使用例如 and、also、the reason why、however 等一系列的连接词。

同时考生也需要使用语篇标记，指出下一步所要回答的内容。例如，考生如果说"So the next thing we did... "，考官就清楚考生要说"接下去发生的事情"。这对于体现"好的衔接"也是有帮助的。

本书也对不同的衔接方式进行了具体说明，供考生学习和参考。

4 回答问题时，语速是不是越快越好？

并不是语速越快就越好。

语速快并不等于流利。考生如果说得很快，有可能反应不出接下去需要说的内容，这反而会导致流利度的下降。同时，语速快也可能导致发音的清晰度下降，进而导致考官出现理解困难。

当然，很多时候考生语速快，实际上是不自信的表现，由于对自己的用词和语法准确性不够自信，一些考生会快速地说完，感觉这样似乎能掩盖自己可能的语言错误。

因此建议考生用适中且合理的语速进行回答即可。适中的语速除了能保证稳定的流利度和发音清晰度之外，也有助于更好地体现发音特征，比如语调的变化，意群的划分等。

5 积累一些"高级词汇"是不是对拿高分有帮助？

积累所谓的"高级词汇"对获得更高分数有一定帮助。

但准确来说，考生如果想获得口语高分，需要使用的是一些能体现一定英语水平的词汇及习语，同时需要对合理的词汇搭配有所认识。根据雅思考试口语评分标准，在词汇多样性这一打分维度中，7 分及以上的标准对考生有上述词汇能力的要求。

因此，考生如果想获得 7 分以上的口语分数，需要尝试多使用例如 tedious 这样的非常见词汇，而非全篇都使用 boring 一词；需要多使用例如 break something down 这类习语；也需要多使用例如 technological innovation 这类词汇搭配。

本书在口语回答的内容亮点中整理和总结了大量词组和习语，供考生学习和参考。

6 词汇和语法出现了错误会不会影响分数?

这类错误需要视情况而定。

根据口语评分标准,词汇和语法的使用是有一定容错度的。但是考生需要体现对于错误的控制能力,同时要避免因为错误而导致理解困难的情况。换言之,如果考生的词汇和语法错误出现较频繁,且导致理解困难,就会影响口语分数。

例如,在语法多样性及准确性这一评分维度中,5分的标准指出"考生能使用有限的复杂句式结构,但通常会出错且会造成理解困难"。而6分的标准则指出"考生使用复杂结构时经常出现错误,但这些错误极少造成理解困难"。

7 使用复杂的句式是不是可以帮助拿高分?

正确使用复杂句式会有助于考生得到更高的分数。

考生需要注意句式和语法的多样性,例如,语法多样性及准确性这一评分维度提到,6分标准的考生能结合使用简单与复杂的句型。如果考生前期练习时无法使用复杂的句子,建议可先从简单句型入手,确保自己能够清晰表达意思,然后再逐步过渡到使用复杂句型,提升语法的多样性。

本书在口语回答的内容亮点中整理和总结了多种常见句型,供考生学习和参考。

8 对发音而言,用英音还是美音回答问题更好?

实际上两种发音在考试中都可以使用。

雅思口语评分标准对于口音没有明确的要求,发音只需要清晰即可。换言之,即便考生的口音混杂了英音、美音或者其他口音,只要发音正确、清晰且不影响考官理解,都不会影响分数。

因此在练习或模仿本书中的口语回答时,建议考生进行朗读,以便确认自己是否有不确定的词汇发音或者发音反应速度较慢的情况。

9 口音很重会不会影响口语分数?

口音对分数的影响主要取决于是否影响考官理解。

如果口音不会严重影响发音的清晰度或考官的理解,就不会影响口语分数,建议考生可以自信地回答口语问题。但如果口音会导致考官有明显的理解困难,甚至导致误解或清晰度下降,就会影响口语分数。例如,考生如果把 neighbour 说成了 /ˈleɪbə(r)/(labour),把 smile 说成了 /smel/(smell),就可能会导致理解困难,这种情况需要加以纠正。

10　体现连读等特征是不是可以帮助拿高分？

符合连读等发音规则的回答更容易得到较高的分数。

口语评分标准在发音这一维度中，对使用多种发音特点做出了明确要求。连读只是多种发音特征中的一项，考生还需要注意合理体现语调、句中重音、意群划分等发音特征。在练习或模仿本书中的口语回答时，建议考生听录音，大声朗读并录音，回听确认自己是否体现了上述的发音特征。如果考生不清楚如何体现以上发音特征，可寻求专业雅思老师的帮助。

考试答题策略篇 ▶▶▶

1　雅思口语每个 Part 要回答多长时间？回答几句话比较好？

Part 1 每个问题建议流利地回答 15~25 秒，平均 3~4 句话。Part 2 建议流利地讲满 2 分钟，体现持续表达的能力。Part 3 每个问题建议流利地回答 30~60 秒，平均 6~8 句话。如果偶尔回答内容较短也是可以接受的，只要确保能体现论述自己观点的能力，或者能灵活应对考官随后提出的追问即可。

2　口语考试中哪个 Part 最简单，哪个最难？

Part 1 的话题相对简单，因为大部分话题都和考生的生活相关，而且也均是考生熟悉的话题。另外，该部分也不需要提供很长的回答，平均 3~4 句话即可。因此刚开始备考的考生可以先从该部分入手，练习简单的回答和思路的延展。

前期练习时大部分考生会认为 Part 2 最难，因为需要就一个话题持续讲满 2 分钟，这对刚刚开始准备的考生而言并不轻松。本书中的口语回答提供了多种思路延展的方向，考生可以模仿书中的回答方式和内容。

后期练习时，考生会认为 Part 3 最难，因为问题本身比较抽象，且部分话题在举例分析时，考生也会感到明显的困难。同时大量考生因为缺少对 Part 3 的练习和思考，也会觉得这部分很难回答。本书同样提供了大量 Part 3 的例子，考生可以学习和模仿如何就某个观点进行解释举例，这也可以帮助考生熟悉 Part 3 常见的提问方式。

3　在 Part 1 中如果遇到了自己不熟悉的话题怎么办？

在实际考试中，这类情况并不常见。

首先，从内容方面看，Part 1 的话题围绕考生的日常生活展开，所以不太会出现考生无话可说的情况。其次，从语言方面看，Part 1 往往是考生首先准备的一部分，并且可以使用雅思口语题库进行参考和练习。

因此，考生是了解 Part 1 话题的大致方向，并且可以进行充分练习和准备的。

4 在 Part 2 中做准备时打草稿有哪些注意事项？

首先，建议平时用英文整理思路和关键词。如果习惯用中文写提示思路，在备考过程中要及时调整为英文，以免影响考试时的流利度。其次，确保所写内容有条理，并清晰易读。考生可以使用列要点或画思维导图的方式进行准备，确保回答时逻辑和思路不会混乱。

另外，考试时 Part 2 只有 1 分钟的准备时间，因此考生需要留意考前练习时所写关键词的数量，对于大部分考生来说，如果能在 1 分钟的准备时间内写出 10~15 个关键词就已经足够了。

最后，考试中的回答在内容上不必追求完美，口语评分也不会针对内容进行打分，因此只要列出的提纲简单明了、容易理解、内容合理、逻辑清晰即可。

5 Part 2 话题卡上的提示点都要提到吗？顺序可以调整吗？

实际上，不完全提到或者顺序有调整都不会影响分数，但多数情况下考生会按照顺序来回答，原因是话题卡上给出的提示点本身就符合正常的思维逻辑，按照顺序回答是最简单和安全的一种选择。

话题卡给出的要求是 "you should say"，而不是 "you must say"。考生可根据实际的回答内容进行灵活调整，只要确保在话题的框架内合理拓展即可。如果 2 分钟到了但是四个提示点没说完，或者考生没有提到某个提示点，都不会成为扣分的原因。

因此，可以根据实际情况灵活处理，但最简单和安全的选择是按照顺序提及所有提示点。

6 Part 2 的回答一定要讲满 2 分钟吗？

备考时，建议考生讲满 2 分钟，或者至少接近 2 分钟，以便锻炼持续表达的能力。在实际考试中，出于控制时间的要求，考官有可能在 2 分钟未到的情况下提前打断考生。这种情况下，考生如果未说完自己的内容，分数不受影响。

如果考官要求考生讲满 2 分钟，但考生只说了大约 1 分多钟，且在考官提示之后仍无法继续陈述，则分数可能受影响，因为考官可能认定考生不具备持续表达的能力。

7 在 Part 2 中可以使用事先准备好的回答吗？

可以使用事先准备好的回答，但要"表达和交流"，而非"背诵"。

部分 Part 2 话题有一定难度，需要考生结合口语题库提前进行练习和准备。本书中也包含了部分难点话题供考生学习和参考。在实际考试中，如果考生使用准备的内容回答 Part 2，需要注意自然合理地进行陈述，避免机械性表达。例如注意使用适中的语速，体现合理的语调，突出句中重音，展现合理意群划分，以及面部表情自然等。

8 在 Part 3 中能不能用自己的例子举例?

需要根据问题的具体要求来决定能否使用自己的例子。

在考试中,大部分 Part 3 问题关注的是多数人的情况,比如"people in your country""old people"或者"children"。

因此,虽然考官会询问考生对某些事情的个人观点或看法,但考生依旧需要通过大多数人的情况进行解释举例。如果考生用了和自己相关的例子,考官可能会提示并告诉考生"We're talking about general situation."。如果出现这种情况,考生也无须慌张,回到多数人的角度并继续回答即可。

如果在 Part 3 中考官问到和考生个人生活相关的问题,考生可以使用个人的例子进行回答,但这种情况在 Part 3 中出现的较少。

9 为什么考官在 Part 3 部分一直追问我 why?

大部分情况下是因为考生在回答 Part 3 问题时仅仅在罗列观点,没有就自己表达的观点进行足够的解释举例,这时考官就会追问考生 why。

考生需要注意的是,Part 3 重点考查考生表达和论述看法、分析和讨论问题的能力,而原因分析无疑是非常必要的答题要素,在备考中需要进行针对性的练习。考试中如果考生被追问了 why,也不需要慌张,可以就已提出的观点进行详尽的解释举例。

本书中提供了很多 Part 3 的问题和回答供考生参考和学习,可以多关注和学习示例回答如何就所提出的观点进行解释举例。

10 前两个 Part 表现不错,但 Part 3 表现不好,会影响分数吗?

这种情况会影响分数,因为考官会根据考生的总体表现进行打分。当然,这种情况也需要结合考生的口语目标分数来看。

如果考生只需要 5 分左右的口语分数,可以把重点放在 Part 1 和 Part 2。Part 3 只要争取听懂问题,并能简略并清楚的回答问题,即便无法进行详尽的解释举例,考生也可以拿到基本的口语分数。

如果考生希望获得至少 6 分或更高的口语成绩,在保证 Part 1 和 Part 2 表现的前提下,需要在 Part 3 和考官的开放性问答中,展现多种语言能力。例如稳定的流利性、词汇和语法的多样性、详尽回答并分析讨论问题的能力等等。考生可以根据自己的口语目标分数,制定相应的备考策略。

学习或工作（Study or work）▶▶▶

话题介绍

  雅思口语考试 Part 1一开始，考官往往会从三个必考话题中选取一个进行提问，而"学习或工作"就是其中之一。比如考官会通过问 "Do you work or are you a student?" 来确认考生的情况，然后再根据考生的回答，进行拓展提问。如果考生一开始回答该问题时答案比较简短，是完全可以接受的。但对于同一个话题中的其他相关问题，还是建议考生进行适当的细节补充。比如可以说明工作的具体性质和内容，学某个科目和专业日常要做什么，或者为什么选择这个工作和专业等内容。

★ Part 1

1 Do you work or are you a student?

示例回答

Currently I am a student and I am studying at Peking Normal University, but *as it's the summer holiday I'm not actually attending any classes*. I'm studying at home, *going out with friends*, and *doing a bit of part-time work tutoring a friend* of a nephew a few evenings each week.

内容亮点

- currently *adv.* 现在

  使用 currently 而非常用的 now，可以增加连接词的多样性。

- as it's the summer holiday... 使用 as 替换常用的 because 说明原因

- I'm not actually attending any classes... 我实际上没有上课

  actually 作为副词在回答中可重读以体现发音特征，同时表达"上课"用了 attend classes，而非基础的表达 go to classes。

- go out with friends 和朋友出去玩

- do a bit of part-time work 做一点兼职

- tutor a friend 辅导一位朋友

- 示例回答并没有只简单地描述"不用上课"，而是结合具体做的事情延伸到了假期安排等内容。

2 What subject are you studying?

示例回答

I am studying *civil engineering*. It's *quite a good field* today in China, as there are a lot of *construction projects and developments* that require civil engineers. My father was a *civil engineer*, so *that's what inspired my interest* in the subject area.

内容亮点

- civil engineering 土木工程
- quite a good field 相当不错的领域

  回答时可重读 quite，体现发音特征。
- construction projects and developments 建筑项目和开发
- civil engineer 土木工程师
- that's what inspired my interest 这激发了我的兴趣

  注意 that's 使用现在时表示个人当下的看法，inspired 使用过去时表示"激发兴趣"发生在过去。
- 示例回答中提到选择土木工程是因为"这是一个相当不错的领域"，之后也补充了具体的原因。同时在考官没有问到相关问题时，也可以简单说明为什么选择了这个专业，这些都是符合题目要求的拓展。

3 Why did you choose that subject?

示例回答

I chose the subject because I have *both an interest in and an aptitude for things related to engineering*. I am good at maths. *I'm fascinated by urban design and development*. Also my father *worked in the field* until he retired, and he inspired me.

内容亮点

- I chose the subject...使用的是过去时，因为题目问的是 why did you choose。
- both an interest in and an aptitude for things related to engineering 对与工程有关的事情既感兴趣又有天赋

  使用 both...and...连接了两个词组，即 have an interest in things related to engineering（对工程相关的事情感兴趣）以及 have an aptitude for things related to engineering（对工程相关的事情有天赋）。
- I'm fascinated by urban design and development

  I'm fascinated by sth. 表示"我对某事很感兴趣"，同时词组 urban design and development 表示"城市设计及发展"。
- work in the field 在该领域工作

11

4 Do you think it's important to choose a subject you like?

示例回答

I think it's important *to some extent*, yes. I don't think a person should choose a subject that they *strongly dislike*, but also you can never like everything about the subject you choose – there's always going to be *modules and courses* you don't like so much. But *generally*, yes, I think it's important.

内容亮点

- to some extent 在一定程度上
- strongly dislike 表示"极度不喜欢"，注意 strongly 作为副词可重读以体现发音特征。
- modules and courses （课程）模块和科目
- generally *adv.* 通常，大体上
- 示例回答提到"你不会喜欢所选专业中的所有内容"的原因是"总会有一些你不喜欢的课程内容"，这是一个考生可参考的拓展思路。

5 What work do you do?

示例回答

I work in an office in *a large education company designing and creating online adverts, graphics and marketing materials*. I studied *computer design*, and that's how I got *a position in my current company* with the *design and marketing team*.

内容亮点

- a large education company 一家大型教育公司
- design and create online adverts, graphics and marketing materials 设计和制作线上广告、图表和市场营销材料
- computer design 计算机设计
- a position in my current company 我目前所在公司的一个职位
- design and marketing team 设计和市场营销团队
- 示例回答除了简单描述工作内容之外，还介绍了专业背景作为选择这份工作的原因，是一个不错的答案拓展思路。

6 Why did you choose to do that type of job?

示例回答

I studied *art and design*, with *a course in illustration*, and *I'm really proficient with basic computer use and some programming*. *I also have a keen interest in* business – so *all these things combined* inspired me to *look for work* in *a marketing department of a company*.

内容亮点

- art and design 艺术与设计
- a course in illustration 插图课程

- I'm really proficient with... 常用句型，表示 "我对……很精通" 或 "我对……很熟练"

- basic computer use and some programming 基本的电脑操作和一些编程技能

- I also have a keen interest in... 常用句型，表示 "我同样对……也有浓厚的兴趣"

- all these things combined 所有这些事情（因素）结合在一起

- look for work 找工作

- a marketing department of a company 一家公司的市场营销部门

7 Do you like your job?

示例回答

I *quite* like it, yes. I'd like to *move on to more challenging work though*, *to be honest*. I think my talents *are* not really *exploited to the maximum* in *my current role* and I'd like to *develop my career a bit more*. But, yes, I like it.

内容亮点

- quite *adv.* 相当

- move on to 转向至，更换

- more challenging work 更有挑战性的工作

- though *adv.* 然而，虽然

  可用在句末，也有补充说明，使语气减弱的效果。

- to be honest 说实在的，老实说

  可用于句首，也可用于句末。

- be exploited to the maximum 被最大限度地利用

- my current role 我当前的角色（职位）

- develop my career a bit more 再进一步发展我的事业

- 示例回答使用了让步的思路，即用 "觉得目前这份工作可能还不够具有挑战性" 作为拓展，这是考生可参考的回答方向。

家乡（Hometown） ▶▶▶

话题介绍

　　该话题也是雅思口语 Part 1 的必考话题之一。考官常在 "家乡"、"学习或工作" 以及 "住宿" 这三个话题中随机选择一个，作为 Part 1 的第一个话题向考生进行提问。如果考生在介绍家乡时需要用到一些中文名词，建议不要默认考官懂中文就只用中文去表达某个名词。正确的方式是至少用英文简单解释相关词汇的基本意思，否则就可能导致无法建立沟通。比如在介绍家乡有名的食物的时候，不要只是给出食物的中文名字，可以至少加一句 "It's a kind of tasty local cuisine." 或者 "It's a kind of seafood that you should try at least once." 这类对英语母语者而言有意义的内容。

★ Part 1

1 **Is your hometown a big city or a small place?**

示例回答

My hometown is a pretty big city. Actually, I think it's one of the largest cities in China. It's *very developed*, very popular and *the traffic is crazy*. So, yes, it's a big place! *A bit too big and overwhelming really*. But it's exciting and *there's a lot to do and see*.

内容亮点

- very developed 非常发达
- the traffic is crazy 交通十分拥堵
- A bit too big and overwhelming really 城市有点太大了而且让人的确难以承受
  overwhelming 表示"让人难以承受，让人难以应付"的含义，同时 really 作为副词也可以放在句末修饰程度。
- there's a lot to do and see 有很多可做，可参观的事情
- 示例回答使用了各种细节描述城市的规模，比如城市高度发展，交通拥堵等。同时也提到了对于城市规模的感受，以及城市规模所带来的好处等内容。

2 **How long have you been living there?**

示例回答

I've lived there all my life. I was born and brought up in this city, and I *went to university* in this city! *Apart from* holidays and some trips, I've never been anywhere else or lived anywhere else!

内容亮点

- I've lived there all my life 我一直在那里生活
- go to university 上大学
- Apart from... 除了……之外
- 示例回答没有仅单纯描述"我一直在那里生活"，而是补充了在那期间具体经历的事情。同时也描述了"除了假期和旅行之外"作为特殊情况的补充，进而突出一直在家乡生活的情况，这些都是可参考的拓展思路。

3 **What do you like most about your hometown?**

示例回答

I like the fact that it's cosmopolitan and diverse. *There's* a lot of *work opportunities* and *a lot of different things going on in terms of* entertainment, restaurants, and art and culture.

内容亮点

- I like the fact that... 我喜欢的事情（事实）是……
- it's cosmopolitan and diverse 它是国际化且多样的

- work opportunities 工作机会
- There's a lot of different things going on 有很多事情正在发生
- in terms of... 在……方面
- 示例回答在提到城市里"有很多事情正在发生"时也补充了例如娱乐、餐饮、艺术文化等内容，对答案进行了适当拓展。

4 Is there anything you dislike about your hometown?

示例回答

Two things *stand out* that I really dislike about my hometown: *the traffic jams and the prices*! The traffic is *horrendous* and there are just too many cars on the roads and *it makes travelling about very frustrating*. *It's also getting increasingly expensive to do* or buy anything in my city.

内容亮点

- stand out 突出
- the traffic jams and the prices 交通堵塞和物价
- horrendous *adj.* 可怕的；惊人的
- it makes travelling about very frustrating 这让出行变得非常崩溃
- It's also getting increasingly expensive to do... 做……的费用变得越来越高
- 示例回答补充了具体例子，如提到"路上有很多车辆并且让人觉得很崩溃"等内容说明交通堵塞的严重性，这是可参考的拓展思路。

住宿（Accommodation）▶▶▶

话题介绍

该话题也是雅思口语 Part 1 的必考话题之一。考官常在"家乡"、"学习或工作"以及"住宿"这三个话题中随机选择一个，作为 Part 1 的第一个话题向考生进行提问。该话题问的范围主要是你的住所以及所在社区的情况，而不是你所住的城市的总体情况，所以要注意和家乡这个话题进行区分。考生在回答时需要适当添加细节进行拓展，比如一般会在自己的住处做什么事情，而不是简单地罗列住处有哪些房间和物品。

★ Part 1

1 Do you live in a house or a flat?

示例回答

I live in a flat. Most people in China live in flats, apartments or in big *apartment blocks*. Houses *are more common* in the countryside, or possible in *old areas or districts of cities* like Shanghai. So, like most people, I live in a flat, a *fairly* small, comfortable flat in *a large residential community* in the city.

内容亮点

- apartment blocks 公寓楼
- be more common 更普遍
- old areas or districts of cities 城市中的老城区
- fairly *adv.* 相当地
- a large residential community 一处大型住宅社区

2 How long have you lived there?

示例回答

I've lived in my current apartment for about 3 years. Before that, I lived with my parents in our house *in the west of the city*. I *moved out* after I got my job *after finishing university*.

内容亮点

- in the west of the city 在城市的西部
- move out 搬走
- after finishing university 表示"毕业之后"，可替换 after I graduated from my university。
- 示例回答提到了搬到目前居所之前的情况，这是可参考的拓展思路。

3 What do you usually do in your house / flat / room?

示例回答

I usually sleep there! *I mean*, I'm very busy. I get up, go to work, *come back quite late*, maybe *have a snack* or *make some quick dinner*, and then I go to bed. *My routine is pretty busy*, so I don't really do much there, to be honest.

内容亮点

- I mean...为连接词，表示"我的意思是……"，可引出进一步的解释。
- come back quite late 回家很晚
- have a snack 吃零食，吃点心
- make some quick dinner 简单做点饭
- my routine is pretty busy 我的日常工作很忙
- 示例回答没有单纯地表述"我只是睡觉"或者"没有做什么其他的事情"，而是补充说明会这么做的原因，即"日程很忙碌"，这是可参考的拓展方向。

4 What's the difference between where you are living now and where you lived in the past?

示例回答

Well, where I'm living now is in a much more *cosmopolitan* and interesting area of the city. I live in a smaller apartment, but it's *a much more lively area* to live in. *Beforehand*, I lived with my parents *in the far east of the city*, in *a quieter*, *more residential neighbourhood*, which was not very interesting and *didn't have much going on*.

内容亮点

- cosmopolitan *adj.* 国际性的

- a much more lively area 一个更热闹的区域

- beforehand *adv.* 事先

- in the far east of the city 在城市东边较远处

- a quieter, more residential neighbourhood 一个更安静，更适合居住的社区

- didn't have much going on 没有什么活动

朋友（Friends）▶▶▶

话题介绍

该话题是基础的 Part 1 话题。除了参考示例回答的思路之外，也可以结合细节和具体的场景进行答案的拓展。例如，在描述一个好朋友应有的品质时，你可以说 they are willing to help me out。然后补充具体需要朋友帮忙的场景，比如 when I fail an important exam。也可以说朋友的帮助有哪些作用，比如 they can always try to reassure me 等相关内容。

★ Part 1

1 **What makes a good friend?**

示例回答

A good friend is someone who *is fun to be with*, who you *have some key things in common with*, and who understands you. A good friend is also someone who is prepared to listen, and also *not scared to disagree with you* and *be direct and honest with you* – even when you might not want to hear it.

内容亮点

- be fun to be with 待在一起是有趣的

- have some key things in common with 有一些重要的共同点

- not scared to disagree with you 不害怕否定你

- be direct and honest with you 对你直接和诚实

- 示例回答列举了多个 "好的朋友" 应有的特征。回答此题时，也可尝试选择其中某个特征进行解释举例。比如 some key things in common 可以说有共同的爱好，即都喜欢 outdoor activities，因此经常 go hiking in our spare time 等等。

2 What do you usually do with your friends?

示例回答

We usually *hang around* in cafés, go shopping a little bit, try new restaurants and bars, and occasionally play sports. *Things like this*. *At times* I go to the cinema with a friend, or maybe *go for a long walk* in spring or summer.

内容亮点

* hang around 闲逛；出去玩
* Things like this. 类似这样的事情。
* at times 有时
* go for a long walk 出去散个步
* 示例回答提到了 usually 和 at times 两种频率下做的不同事情，这是可参考的拓展方向。

3 How do you make friends?

示例回答

Well, I make friends quite easily. I am *a very social person* and I am not shy, so *I seem to meet people quite easily*, *through other friends*, *through activities on campus...*things like this. I think most people make friends in the same way. *Though* today it is popular to meet people online – not just *online dating* to meet *a potential girlfriend or boyfriend*, but today people also join different *interest groups online*, *through apps*, and *things like this*. This is *a new and quite acceptable way* of meeting new people today, and *I can see that* it's pretty effective. I don't really use this method myself *though*.

内容亮点

* a very social person 一个非常善于社交的人
* I seem to meet people quite easily 我似乎很容易结识人
* through other friends 通过其他朋友
* through activities on campus 通过校园活动
* though *conj.* 虽然，尽管；不过
* online dating 在线交友（约会）
* a potential girlfriend or boyfriend 一个潜在的女朋友或男朋友
* interest groups online 线上兴趣小组
* through apps 通过应用程序
* things like this 类似这样的事情
* a new and quite acceptable way 一种新颖又很受欢迎的方法
* I can see that... 我明白……；我能懂……
* though 可用于句末，表示"然而，虽然"，也有补充说明、使语气减弱的用法。
* 示例回答较长，提供了较多的参考思路。实际考试中只需回答三句话左右即可。以此题为例，在前半部分的"传统交友方式"和后半部分的"线上交友方式"中选择一个方面来说即可。

4 Do you have many friends?

示例回答

I have lots of friends. I think, *talking of* "real friends", I *mainly* have 3 or 4. But I have lots of other friends. *You'd maybe call them acquaintances*. So, yes, *I'd say* I have many friends – I'm a really social person. But *I am also very aware that* we can only have *a few genuinely close friends in life* – people that we really *click with*, who also will *support us through thick and thin*.

内容亮点

- talking of... 谈到……，说到……
- mainly *adv.* 主要地
- You'd maybe call them 你可能会称呼他们……（等于 You would maybe call them）
- acquaintance [əˈkweɪntəns] *n.* 相识的人；泛泛之交
- I'd say...表示"我会说……""我觉得……"等含义，可以替换 I think。
- I am also very aware that... 我也很清楚……
- a few genuinely close friends in life 一些生活中真正亲密的朋友
- click with 与……产生共鸣；与……合拍；与……建立积极联系或友好关系
- support us through thick and thin 在任何情况下都支持我们
- 示例回答把朋友分类成"泛泛之交"和"真正亲密的朋友"两种类型来进行回答，是可参考的拓展思路。

5 Are you a good friend to others?

示例回答

I think so. I *mess up* sometimes, *like all of us do* – I can be a bit selfish sometimes, *talk about* my own problems and *concerns above those of others*. *But in general*, I think I'm *a good friend to others*. I *try to be there for my friends*, listen to their problems, give good advice and give them support. So, in general I think I'm a good friend.

内容亮点

- mess up 搞糟
- like all of us do 就像我们所有人一样
- talk about concerns above those of others 谈论自己的烦恼，把自己的烦恼至于别人的问题之上
- but in general 但总的来说
- a good friend to others 其他人的好朋友
- try to be there for my friends 尽量陪着我的朋友
- 示例回答使用了让步的思路，提到"虽然有时有点自私"，但觉得还是个"好的朋友"。同时分别使用了具体的例子说明，比如会聊什么，或者怎么做，这些都是可参考的拓展思路。

公共交通（Public transport）▶▶▶

话题介绍

　　该话题是基础的 Part 1 话题，可以和 city 或者 the area you live in 等话题进行关联和拓展，比如你可能因为便利的公共交通才住在某个地方等。注意依旧要多提供细节信息以便进行拓展，不要只用 convenient 或者 arrive on time 描述公共交通，可以补充说明所在城市有专门的 bus lane 等设施，从而避免了堵车等情况的发生。

★ Part 1

1 **Do you often use public transportation?**

示例回答

Yes, I take the subway every day to work. I hate it. It's *packed*, really crowded, and I have to *change lines* twice. I really dislike using public transport, but if you take a taxi or *go by private car* then you *face horrific traffic jams*, so it's a *nightmare either way*! I really don't like living in such *a big overcrowded city*.

内容亮点

- packed *adj.* 拥挤的，挤满人的
- change lines 换乘
- go by private car 乘坐私家车出行
- face horrific traffic jams 面临严重的交通堵塞
- nightmare *n.* 噩梦；可怕的经历
- either way 不管怎样；无论哪种方式（用于句末）
- a big overcrowded city 拥挤的大城市

2 **Do people in your country take the bus?**

示例回答

Yes, a lot of people take the bus. For some destinations in the city, it's more convenient, and it's really cheap. *Depending on where you're going to and from*, it can be more comfortable than taking the subway, and you at least can *see out of the window*! There are also some places, especially in *suburbs*, where there is no *train service*, so you have to take the bus. *Anyway*, yes, buses are still popular in cities, also *to and from some locations outside cities*.

内容亮点

- Depending on where you're going to and from 这取决于你要去哪里和从哪里来

  depending on 可用于句首，意为"根据，取决于"，在一句话中表示前提或条件。
- see out of the window 看窗外

- suburb ['sʌbɜːb] *n.* 城郊，近郊
- train service 列车服务
- anyway 好吧（用于转换话题或回到前一个话题）
- to and from some locations outside cities 往返于城市以外的一些地方

3 What kind(s) of transport do you usually use?

示例回答

I usually take the subway, or walk if I'm going *somewhere nearby*. *At times* I take one of those *hire-bikes you see around the city*. They're pretty convenient and there's a lot of *fairly safe bike lanes* in my city, so that's a good way to *get around*, especially in spring, summer or autumn *when it's not too cold or wet*.

内容亮点

- somewhere nearby 附近某处
- at times 有时；偶尔
- hire-bikes you see around the city 城市里随处可见的租赁自行车
- fairly safe bike lanes 很安全的自行车道
- get around 到处逛逛
- when it's not too cold or wet 天气不太冷也不太潮湿的时候
- 示例回答解释选择自行车出行的原因时，提到了租赁单车和自行车道等细节，并和天气结合进行说明，是可参考的拓展思路。

4 How often do you take the bus?

示例回答

I take the bus about once or twice a week. I usually go to work on the subway, *you see*, so I only take the bus on weekends if sometimes I want to go to visit a park or a friend who *lives in another district*. The *bus routes* are pleasant and *buses have their own lanes* on the street, so they are usually efficient and on time.

内容亮点

- you see 表示"你瞧"的含义，可以替换 you know 作为口语语气填充词使用。
- live in another district 住在另外一个区域
- bus routes 公交线路
- buses have their own lanes 公交车有自己的专用车道
- 示例回答说明乘坐公交车的频率之后，还补充了乘坐公交车的时间、目的以及感受，均是可参考的拓展思路。

购物（Shopping）▶▶▶

话题介绍

　　该话题是基础的 Part 1 话题，可以和 weekends、holiday、relaxation 等话题进行关联和拓展，因为购物对于很多人来说都是重要的休闲方式之一。如果考生觉得话题难度不大且好拓展，可以尝试多使用词汇搭配，比如 go around stores 或者 domestic items 等描述购物的方式以及经常购买的物品。

★ Part 1

① Do you like shopping?

示例回答

Not really. I find shopping *a bit of a drag to be honest*. I don't like *going around stores and shops looking at clothes and things*. I *much prefer* to *look at things casually on my phone and order things online*, *but even then*, I don't really enjoy it much. I'm not someone who *gets much pleasure from shopping* really.

内容亮点

- not really 表示"不完全是，并不"，可在回答问题时替换 no。
- a bit of a drag 有点累人

  drag 作为名词表示"拖累；令人不快的事；无聊的事"等含义。
- to be honest 表示"老实说"，也可用于句末。
- go around stores and shops 逛商店
- look at clothes and things 看看衣服和其他东西
- much prefer 表示"更喜欢"，much 作为副词可适当重读，体现发音特征。
- look at things casually on my phone and order things online 在手机上随便看看东西并在网上订购
- but even then 但即使是这样
- get much pleasure from shopping 从购物中获得很多乐趣
- 示例回答中提及了"逛街"和"网购"的操作细节，作为不喜欢购物的原因，均是可参考的拓展思路。

② How often do you go shopping?

示例回答

About once every couple of weeks, I think. Of course, to buy food, I will go to the supermarket or a market about once a week, that's just to buy some *essentials* – but *clothes shopping or shopping for pleasure*, I don't do that often. Yes, about *once a fortnight* I'd say, *on average*.

内容亮点

- about once every couple of weeks 大约每两（几）周一次
- essential [ɪˈsenʃl] *n.* 必需品

- clothes shopping or shopping for pleasure 买衣服或消遣式购物
- once a fortnight 意为 "每两周一次"，其中 fortnight 表示 "两星期"。
- on average 平均；通常
- 示例回答把购买的物品进行分类，然后分别说明购买频率，这是可参考的拓展思路。

3 Is price important to you when you buy something?

示例回答

It totally depends on what I want to buy! I usually compare prices of the same items I want to buy online, then *choose the best value item*. There's *a lot of sales at certain times of year online* in China too, like the *now-famous* 11-11 day, *and things like this*. 11-11 is basically the 11th day of the 11th month, and it is *a big day for online sales* in China.

内容亮点

- It totally depends on... 这完全取决于……
- choose the best value item 选择最具价值的商品
- a lot of sales at certain times of year online 每年的某些时候网上都会有大量的降价（打折）优惠
- now-famous *adj.* 现在著名的
- and things like this 和像这样的事
- a big day for online sales 线上销售的大日子
- 示例回答中提到和打折降价相关的内容，补充说明了价格的重要性，是可参考的拓展思路。

4 Do old people and young people have different shopping habits?

示例回答

Most definitely. Older people usually just buy essentials like food and *domestic items*, but younger people *are often into fashion and trends*, so they enjoy buying clothes, *accessories* and sometimes *famous brand names* that *are on sale in the high streets or online*. Younger people are also more *frivolous* with money, *it seems*, so they *indulge in the latest fashions* without thinking so much about their *longer-term value*.

内容亮点

- most definitely 明确地；肯定地
- domestic items 家用物品
- be often into fashion and trends 经常关注时尚和潮流
  be into sth. 喜欢某事
- accessory [ək'sesəri] *n.* 配件；装饰品
- famous brand names 著名的品牌
- be on sale in the high streets or online 在商业街或者网上打折
- frivolous ['frɪvələs] *adj.* 轻率的
- it seems + *adv.* 看来是；可用于句中表示个人看法和感受

- indulge in the latest fashions 沉迷于最新的时尚潮流
- longer-term value 长期价值
- 示例回答中提到年轻人购物时可能比较大手大脚的细节信息，这是重要的参考思路，在回答 Part 3 相关问题时也可使用。

礼物（Gifts）▶▶▶

话题介绍

该话题是基础的 Part 1 话题，可以和 celebration、birthday、festival 等话题进行关联和拓展。不过描述礼物的外观可能有点难，考生可以转而描述收礼物或者送礼物的具体场景和对应感受，比如 it was a complete surprise for me，或者送礼物的原因等相关内容。

★ Part 1

1 What's the best present or gift you have ever received?

示例回答

Oh, *let me think...*emmm...I think the best gift I received was a new bike, when I was a kid. I was so excited about this! I was about 6 years old, and all my friends had cool bikes, and then *my birthday came around* and I got a really amazing bike. I was so happy about this. So, at least *at that time in my life*, it was *definitely* the best present!

内容亮点

- let me think... 让我想想……
  回答时如果需要思考回答的内容，可使用这样的句式合理地争取思考时间，但也请注意使用合理的语调。
- my birthday came around 我的生日到了
- at that time in my life 表示"在我生命中的那刻"，可在回忆过去的事情时使用。
- definitely 表示"肯定地；确定地"，可适当使用重读以体现发音特征。
- 示例回答提到了当时收到礼物的很多细节，比如背景、感受等，均是可参考的拓展思路。

2 Do you give expensive gifts?

示例回答

It depends, but I *occasionally* do, yes. Sometimes for a friend's birthday, a few of us *club together*, put some money together and get *a really nice pair of fancy sunglasses* or an accessory or something for the person. But usually I think *it's the thought that counts*, and many people *put too much emphasis on the price of gifts* and this isn't a good thing.

内容亮点

- occasionally [əˈkeɪʒnəli] *adv.* 偶尔地
- club together 凑钱；出份子；club *v.* 募集
- a really nice pair of fancy sunglasses 一副非常漂亮且时髦的太阳镜
- it's the thought that counts 心意更重要；count *v.* 重要
- put too much emphasis on the price of gifts 过于强调礼物的价格

3 What do you often choose as gifts?

示例回答

It depends on who the gift is for! I usually *get some ideas from the person's friends* if I don't already know the kind of things they like or need. A choice of gift could *range from a small desk-toy* for an office, like *a cute cartoon figure*, *to a pair of designer sunglasses* or a book. It *completely* depends on the person.

内容亮点

- get some ideas from the person's friends 从对方的朋友那里得到一些想法
- range from...to... 范围从……到……
- a small desk-toy 一个小桌面摆件
- a cute cartoon figure 一个可爱的卡通人物
- a pair of designer sunglasses 一副名牌太阳镜

  designer 在此作为形容词表示"由设计师设计的；时尚的"。
- completely [kəmˈpliːtli] *adv.* 完全地；彻底地

4 What kinds of gifts are popular in your country?

示例回答

Popular gifts today are perhaps *small fashion accessories*. Cute bags for girls, maybe a football or basketball T-shirt for boys. If you go to someone's house for dinner then it's *customary* to take some fruits, some juice, a bottle of wine, maybe some snacks and cakes. *Things like this*.

内容亮点

- small fashion accessories 小型的时尚配饰
- customary [ˈkʌstəməri] *adj.* 习惯的；习俗的
- things like this 表示"类似这样的事情"，可用于句末作为一段话的结语。
- 示例回答提到"饰品"和"到别人家做客时的礼物"两个方面时都补充了很多例子，是可参考的拓展思路。

周末（Weekends）▶▶▶

话题介绍

　　该话题是基础的 Part 1 话题，可以和 cinema、restaurant、housework、plan 等话题进行关联和拓展，总体难度不大。回答这类话题时可以结合周末具体会做的事情，并补充原因，比如想要 wind down 等。另外也要注意此话题除了用一般现在时提问之外，也会经常要求考生使用一般过去时和一般将来时表达上周末的安排和下周末的计划，所以需要考生合理使用对应的时态。

★ Part 1

1 **What do you usually do on weekends?**

示例回答

On weekends I do *a variety of things*. I rest, read, go out with friends to a park or go to the cinema. Occasionally I go have dinner in a restaurant – *there are lots of new restaurants opening up in my city* so I often go with *a group of friends* to a restaurant, usually *a hotpot restaurant*. I like *eating out* with friends and family – it's a popular *communal activity* in my country, *actually*.

内容亮点

- a variety of things 各种各样的事情
- there are lots of new restaurants opening up in my city 我的城市里有很多新开业的餐馆；open up 开业
- a group of friends 一群朋友
- a hotpot restaurant 一家火锅店
- eat out 出去吃；下饭馆
- communal activity 群体活动；communal [kəˈmjuːnl] *adj.* 群体的；团体的
- actually 表示"实际上，事实上"，也可放于句末使用。
- 示例回答先列举了一些活动，之后选了其中的一个活动进行细节描述（即"出去吃饭"），是可参考的回答框架。

2 **Would you say weekends are important to us?**

示例回答

I think they're very important. *It's when we get time to* spend with family and friends, and *kick back*, relax, forget about work or *the hassles of daily life*. Weekends are when we can *wind down*, *recharge our batteries* and relax a bit *after a working week*. I think everyone should have free weekends.

内容亮点

- it's when we get time to do sth. 是我们有时间做某事的时候
- kick back 平静下来
- the hassles of daily life 日常生活的烦恼；hassle [ˈhæsl] *n.* 麻烦；困难

- wind down 平静下来；放松一下（注意此处 wind 的发音是 [waɪnd]）
- recharge our batteries 给电池充电；恢复体力
- after a working week 在工作了一周之后

3 Do you often go to the cinema on weekends?

示例回答

From time to time, depending on *what's on*. I wouldn't say I go that often, perhaps *once every couple of months*. But *when I do go*, I enjoy it *immensely*. I love seeing a film on the big screen and eating popcorn and maybe going to dinner *afterwards* and discussing the movie with my friends.

内容亮点

- from time to time 有时
- what's on （此语境中）有什么电影
- once every couple of months 每两（几）个月一次
- when I do go 当我去（电影院）的时候
- immensely [ɪ'mensli] *adv.* 极其地；非常地
- afterwards *adv.* 过后；后来
- 示例回答说明了频率之后，还补充了看电影时的具体行为和感受，都是可参考的拓展思路。

4 What do you plan to do for next weekend?

示例回答

I have no plans next weekend. In fact, I've got some work to *catch up on* so I will *work half of the time* and *the other half of the time*, I'll *do odd jobs around the house*, *run some errands in town* and then just *get an early night*. These days I don't go out much on weekends really. *It's been* a few busy months for me and I've got *all sorts of random things to do by the time* the weekend *comes around*.

内容亮点

- catch up on 赶上
- work half of the time 花一半的时间工作
- the other half of the time 另一半的时间
- do odd jobs around the house 在家里干些杂活
- run some errands in town 去城里办点事；errand ['erənd] *n.* 差事
- get an early night 早点睡觉
- It's been 是 It has been 的缩写，现在完成时表示最近发生或者经历的事情。类似用法还有 "It's been a while." 表示"已经有一段时间了"。
- all sorts of random things to do 各种要做的事情
- by the time 等到；到……的时候
- come around 来；靠近

- 示例回答中提到的 no plans 指的是没有"出去玩的计划"，之后提到还有很多工作和杂事要处理，以及近期的忙碌程度。这些内容均是可参考的拓展思路。

唱歌（Singing）▶▶▶

话题介绍

　　该话题是基础的 Part 1 话题，可以和 weekend、relaxation、leisure activities 等话题进行关联。如果不太会描述喜欢唱的歌的内容或者风格，可以选择描述唱歌的水平，比如"I can sing in tune."。或者说会在什么地方和什么情况下唱歌，比如 when I'm taking a shower。同样也可以说唱歌的感受以及为什么想要唱歌，比如是为了 chill out 等。

★ Part 1

1 Do you like singing?

示例回答

I love singing. I *thoroughly* enjoy going to KTVs and singing *on my own* at home to music, too. *I don't think I'm that good at singing*, to be honest, but *I'm not bad either*. I can *belt out a good tune* at KTV if I'm already familiar with it, and I *get a lot of pleasure from* that if I'm with *a bunch of good friends*.

内容亮点

- thoroughly ['θʌrəli] *adv.* 完全地；极度地
- on my own 独自一人
- I don't think I'm that good at singing 我觉得我不太会唱歌

  that 作为副词修饰 good，表示程度，即"那么"。
- I'm not bad either. 我也（做的）不差。
- belt out a good tune 大声演唱一段好的曲调；belt out 大声演唱
- get a lot of pleasure from... 从……中得到很多乐趣
- a bunch of good friends 一群好朋友
- 示例回答提到了唱歌的地点、方式、感受、以及一起唱歌的人，均是可参考的拓展思路。

2 Did you enjoy singing when you were younger?

示例回答

Yes, I loved singing when I was a kid, and I still love singing now. I think singing is really good for people, and often, when I was a child, we would sing songs together in *playgroup*. Singing songs with other people is a great feeling and really *brings people together* and gives you *an uplifting feeling of unity and positivity*. This is something that especially younger people enjoy – I *certainly* did!

【内容亮点】

- playgroup *n.* 托儿所

- bring people together 让人们聚在一起

- an uplifting feeling of unity and positivity 一种振奋人心的团结和积极向上的感觉

  uplifting *adj.* 令人振奋的；unity *n.* 团结；positivity *n.* 积极性

- certainly *adv.* 无疑地；肯定地

3 How often do you sing now?

【示例回答】

I sing quite often on my own. ***I mean***, I ***sing along to songs*** I am listening to at home or on my ***headphones***. I also sing at KTV with my friends about once a month, too. I'm ***a fan of singing***, though I'm not sure if I'm that good at it really. I can ***sing in tune*** though, ***that's the main thing***.

【内容亮点】

- I mean 表示"我是说，我的意思是"，可作为连接词在回答中使用。

- sing along to songs 跟着歌一起唱

- headphone *n.* 耳机

- a fan of singing 喜欢唱歌的人

- sing in tune 唱歌不跑调

- that's the main thing 这是最重要的

- 示例回答提到具体会做的事情，以及自己是否擅长唱歌，对唱歌的频率进行了补充说明，是可以参考的拓展思路。

4 Will you take singing lessons in the future?

【示例回答】

I would quite like to ***take singing lessons***, yes. To be honest I've never really thought about it, but why not? It would be nice to be able to sing more professionally, I think. I don't think I would take a lot of singing lessons, or ***do it very seriously***, but I think it would be nice to take ***a short weekend course or something***. At least it would help me to sing better at ***company gala events*** at Spring Festival!

【内容亮点】

- take singing lessons 上音乐（歌唱）课

- do it very seriously 认真对待

- a short weekend course or something 一个周末短期课程之类的

- company gala events 公司庆典活动（年会）

- 示例回答提到如果要上课会选择什么类型的课程，以及学习唱歌的目的，都是可参考的拓展思路。

驾车出游（Car trips）▶▶▶

话题介绍

　　该话题是和 travelling 以及 transport 相关的基础的 Part 1 话题，但也有可能在 Part 2 中见到类似话题。如果题目问的是和 travel by car 相关的内容，需要注意问题的语境是和远途旅行相关，即 a car journey，还是和日常通勤相关，即 daily commute。如果不确定，也可以从两个方面都说一下自己的想法，或者先和考官说一些自己理解这个问题的角度，比如 if you're talking about a car journey 等。

★ Part 1

1 Do you like to travel by car?

示例回答

Sometimes, it really depends. If I am *going on a trip out of the city*, I enjoy being in a car *out on the open roads*. But, in city like Beijing, no, I don't enjoy it at all, the traffic is a nightmare. *In this case* I prefer to take a bus or the subway, it's easier and more efficient and *you're guaranteed to arrive* at your destination on time.

内容亮点

- go on a trip out of the city 出城旅行
- out on the open roads 在开阔的道路上
- in this case 这种情况下；既然这样

  作为连接词可以替换 therefore、so 等等。
- be guaranteed to do 保证能做到某事
- 示例回答通过分情况讨论的方式，结合城内城外的路况进行了说明，是可参考的拓展思路。

2 Where is the farthest place you've travelled to by car?

示例回答

The farthest I've been by car is *probably* to Gu Bei water town, which is about 2 or 3 hours *outside of Beijing*. It's *a lovely drive* actually, and *is especially nice to do* that trip in summer. So, I haven't been that far in a car really, at least as far as I can remember.

内容亮点

- probably ['prɒbəbli] *adv.* 大概；也许
- outside of somewhere 某地之外的地方
- a lovely drive 一次令人愉快的车程
- be especially nice to do sth. 表示"做某事是尤其好的"，其中 especially 作为副词可重读，体现发音特征。

3 **Do you like to sit in the front or back when travelling by car?**

示例回答

I enjoy sitting in the front, in ***the passenger seat***. I like to ***see the road ahead*** and you ***get a better view*** if you're ***travelling through a picturesque area*** where there are mountains or ***rolling hills***. Also, for some reason, I don't know why, I tend to ***get a little car sick*** if I sit in the back, but if I sit in the front, then I usually ***feel fine***.

内容亮点

- the passenger seat 副驾驶位
- see the road ahead 看见前方的道路
- get a better view 视野更好
- travel through a picturesque area 在风景如画的地方旅行
- rolling hills 起伏的群山
- get a little car sick 有点晕车
- feel fine（身体）感觉很好
- 示例回答提到喜欢坐在前排的原因之后，接着用对比思路提及坐在后排不舒服的原因，是可参考的对比思路。

语言（Languages）▶▶▶

话题介绍

　　该话题虽然比较难和其他话题进行关联，但是拓展并不难。依旧建议考生给出的答案不宜太过空洞，需要补充对应的细节。比如会说一门语言的原因是这是自己的母语，即 native language，还是出于个人兴趣才去学的。另外，在说明学习一门语言的难度时，依旧可以补充具体的例子，比如这门语言的文字书写，即 writing system，是比较简单还是比较难等。

★ Part 1

1 **What languages do you speak?**

示例回答

I speak English, Chinese and a little Japanese. I studied all three languages in school ***from a very early age***. Of course, Chinese is my ***native language*** so I also ***learned to speak at home***, as a child, like most children. English, I learned in school, and I ***took a module of Japanese language*** in university.

内容亮点

- from a very early age 从很小的时候开始
- native language 母语

- learn to speak at home 在家学习怎么说
- take a module of Japanese language 学习了日语的课程；module ['mɒdjuːl] *n.* 课程的单元；模块
- 示例回答除了提及自己会说的语言之外，也补充了不同语言的习得方式，是可以参考的拓展思路。

② Why do you learn English?

示例回答

Everyone from where I'm from learns English, and it's *the international language of business and politics* too, so I think it's important and useful to speak, read and write English. That's why most people I know here learn English. I think it's quite easy to learn English at first, to *a basic level*, but to speak and understand it at a very high level, *it's more challenging for sure*.

内容亮点

- everyone from where I'm from 我所在地方的所有人
- the international language of business and politics 商务和政治的国际语言
- a basic level 一个基本水平
- it's more challenging for sure 这当然更具挑战性
- 示例回答中除了提及学习英语是因为其重要性之外，也提到了不同水平的学习难度，是可参考的拓展思路。

③ Do you think it's difficult to learn a new language?

示例回答

I think it *honestly* depends on what the language is, and whether you are familiar with *the language family* or not. I mean, if you are Chinese then it might be easier to learn Japanese than, *say*, German or Russian, because they *share some characteristics in common*, at least in the *written form*. So, it really depends.

内容亮点

- honestly ['ɒnɪstli] *adv.* （强调信念或情感）的确；（强调所说的是事实）真的
- the language family 语系
- say 表示"比如"，类似用法还有 let's say，都有举例的意思。
- share some characteristics in common 有一些共同的特点
- written form 书写形式
- 示例回答中提到的语系和相似语言的一些特征，是可参考的重要拓展思路。

④ Will you learn another language in the future?

示例回答

To be honest, I hope not. I don't really like learning languages much. I think that 3 languages are enough and I would like to focus on *speaking those as well as possible*, and then *focus my energy on* my *master's degree studies* – in *international relations*. So, it's not a *priority* for me to study any new languages, at least not in *the foreseeable future*.

内容亮点

- speak those as well as possible 尽可能把这些都讲好

  those 等于 those languages，用于指代上文提及的语言，避免语言重复，提升回答的自然度。

- focus my energy on sth. 把精力集中在某件事上

- master's degree studies 硕士学位学习

- international relations 国际关系

- priority [praɪˈɒrəti] n. 优先事项；最重要的事

- the foreseeable future 可预见的未来；foreseeable [fɔːˈsiːəbl] adj. 可预知的；可预料的

风景（Scenery）▶▶▶

话题介绍

　　该话题是基础的 Part 1 话题，也是可以和各种旅行、甚至休闲活动进行关联的话题。除了依旧可以讲感受之外，也可以说在这些景区，即 a scenic spot，具体能做的事情，比如 take a long country walk 甚至 go fishing。之后还可以补充这样做是可以让人休息和放松的，即 put work or study aside。考生还可以借鉴和 Relaxation 相关的话题思路。

★ Part 1

1 **What kinds of beautiful scenery are there around your hometown?**

示例回答

Around my hometown there are *mainly mountains and fields*. They're quite beautiful, especially in the spring and autumn. There are also a number of rivers and small *woodland areas* which are great for *long country walks*, hiking, fishing and outdoor activities. So, there is quite a bit of beautiful scenery around my hometown, actually.

内容亮点

- mainly mountains and fields 以山野为主

- woodland areas 森林地区

- long country walk 乡村漫步

- 示例回答中把 scenery 和 outdoor activities 相结合进行解释举例，是可参考的重要拓展思路。

2 **When you travel, do you like to stay in hotels with scenic views?**

示例回答

Yes, of course. It's much better to have *a hotel room with a nice view*. I think most people prefer this. However, sometimes, if I *go somewhere touristy* and choose a cheap hotel or *guest house*, *I don't really mind not having a great view* – because I am going to *be out sightseeing and doing things* most of the time anyway, and just using the hotel to *spend the night*, to sleep – so *in these cases* I don't really mind much if the hotel has a good view or not.

内容亮点

- a hotel room with a nice view 一间风景优美的酒店房间
- go somewhere touristy 去某个地方旅游；touristy ['tʊərɪsti] *adj.* 适宜游览的
- guest house 廉价宾馆；小型旅馆
- I don't really mind not having a great view 我真的不介意风景不好；mind doing sth. 介意做某事
- be out sightseeing and doing things 出去观光和做一些事情；sightsee ['saɪtsiː] *v.* 观光；游览
- spend the night 过夜
- in these cases 连接词，表示"在这些情况下"

❸ Do people like to take photos of beautiful scenery?

示例回答

Yes, everyone likes to take photos of beautiful scenery, I think. Especially today when everyone can take great photos using their *smartphones*, it's very common that people take photos of pretty much everything they do and see to *put on their WeChat moments* and *social media sites*. In China people often post photos of their food, their weekend activities, and their holidays – lots of things – usually positive things that they are happy, excited, or *proud about*.

内容亮点

- smartphone 智能手机
- put on WeChat moments 发到微信朋友圈
- social media site 社交媒体网站
- proud about 自豪；骄傲
- 示例回答中具体描述了人们拍了什么，以及拍照之后如何处理照片的很多相关细节，均是重要的拓展思路。

❹ Why do people prefer to take photos of beautiful scenery with smartphones?

示例回答

Today everyone *takes photos of everything with their phones*. Camera phones now have really *excellent quality*, they take *fantastic photographs* and also lots of phone cameras now have *all sorts of software filters* to make photographs more beautiful, brighter or darker or *richer in colour* – they can even *make* people's faces look younger, their *skins smoother*, and their *lips redder*! So, yes, people take lots of photos of everything with their smartphones today, not just beautiful scenery – *literally* everything.

内容亮点

- take photos of everything with their phones 用手机拍下一切

- excellent quality 质量过硬
- fantastic photograph 很棒的照片
- all sorts of software filters 各种各样的软件滤镜；filter ['fɪltə] *n.* 过滤器；滤镜
- richer in colour 颜色更丰富
- make skins smoother 使皮肤更光滑
- make lips redder 使嘴唇更红润
- literally ['lɪtərəli] *adv.* （强调事实可能令人惊讶）真正地，确实地；简直
- 示例回答并没有简单提及手机拍照效果更好，而是补充了很多和功能效果相关的细节，是可参考的重要拓展思路。

艺术（Arts）▶▶▶

话题介绍

　　该话题属于 Part 1 的难点话题，主要因为艺术类的词汇较难，比如 sculpture、abstract art、calligraphy 等。考生可以尝试从简单的内容入手，比如 painting 或者 performance art，然后说明会在哪里看到这些表演，是在博物馆还是在街头？也就是通过结合具体场景的方式进行拓展，这样也能有效地帮助考生降低话题的难度。

★ Part 1

1 Do you like art?

示例回答

Yes, I love art. I like many different types of art, actually. I love *traditional Chinese paintings and calligraphy*, but I also really enjoy looking at *western art*, *art from different periods in history*, as well as *abstract art*, *sculpture* and even *performance art*. I'm a big fan of *all aspects of culture* and so I enjoy visiting museums and *art galleries* when I go to another country or when I visit another city in China. Art is an important part of life, and children who learn about art usually *end up being thoughtful*, *creative and innovative people* when they get older.

内容亮点

- traditional Chinese paintings and calligraphy 中国传统绘画和书法
- western art 西方艺术
- art from different periods in history 历史上不同时期的艺术
- abstract art 抽象艺术；抽象派
- sculpture ['skʌlptʃə] *n.* 雕像；雕塑
- performance art 表演艺术；行为艺术

- all aspects of culture 文化的各个方面
- art gallery 美术馆；画廊
- end up being thoughtful, creative and innovative people 最终成为有思想、有创造力、有创新精神的人

  end up doing 以……告终；thoughtful ['θɔːtfl] *adj.* 有思想的，深思的，思考的；creative [kri'eɪtɪv] *adj.* 有创造力的，有想象力的；innovative ['ɪnəveɪtɪv] *adj.* 革新的；创新的

2 Have you ever visited an art gallery?

示例回答

I've visited lots of art galleries, in my city, Beijing, *as well as* in other cities. I enjoy *modern art galleries* the most, but I also like to see *painting and artwork from history* as well. There are quite a few different art galleries in my city and I sometimes go to the *temporary exhibitions* at one gallery in particular that is in the famous *art district*, 798. I know the manager of that gallery too, so I enjoy going there, chatting to her and perhaps *having a coffee* at one of the *boutique arty coffee shops* nearby.

内容亮点

- as well as 表示"也"，可作为连接词串联两个句子或者名词词组。
- modern art gallery 现代艺术画廊
- painting and artwork from history 历史上的绘画和艺术品
- temporary exhibition 临时展览；exhibition [ˌɛksɪ'bɪʃən] *n.* 展览
- art district 艺术区
- have a coffee 喝杯咖啡

  口语中可以不需要说 a cup of coffee，直接使用 a coffee 表示"一杯咖啡"。
- boutique arty coffee shops 精品艺术咖啡馆

  boutique [buː'tiːk] *n.* 精品店，时装店；arty ['ɑːti] *adj.* 艺术的，附庸风雅的
- 示例回答除了提及去艺术画廊会看到的内容之外，还提到了在画廊周边能做的事情，均是可参考的拓展思路。

3 Is there any art work on the wall in your room?

示例回答

Yes, I have a couple of pictures. They are *prints* actually – of course they are not *originals*. One is the famous picture of the Great Wave, by the Japanese artist, Hokusai, and the other is a painting by Salvador Dali, the *eccentric Spanish painter* who painted quite strange and *abstract works*. I can't remember the name of the Dali painting, but it's a painting of a stone man looking at his *own reflection in the water*. It's quite *mysterious* and *evocative*. I think it is good to have art work in the house – it helps us *reflect on life* as well as *creating a certain atmosphere*.

内容亮点

- print *n.* 印刷品；版画；（冲印出的）照片
- original [ə'rɪdʒənl] *n.* （艺术作品或文件的）原件

- eccentric Spanish painter 古怪的西班牙画家；eccentric [ɪk'sentrɪk] *adj.* 古怪的
- abstract work 抽象的作品
- own reflection in the water 自己在水中的倒影；reflection [rɪ'flekʃn] *n.* 反射；倒影
- mysterious [mɪ'stɪəriəs] *adj.* 神秘的；奇怪的；不易解释的
- evocative [ɪ'vɒkətɪv] *adj.* 引起记忆的；唤起感情的
- reflect on life 思考人生
- create a certain atmosphere 创造某种氛围
- 如果考生觉得示例回答中提供的参考思路难度较大，可少说具体的 art work 的内容，多描述作品是哪里买的，或者是谁送的，或是参考示例回答中描述艺术作品对于装饰和创造氛围的作用等相关内容。

科学（Science）▶▶▶

话题介绍

该话题在 Part 1 中略有难度，因为科学以及相关课程的内容涉及的词汇并不常用。建议考生尝试表达科学在日常生活中的作用，比如 "Everything is rooted in science."。同时该话题也可从 science 拓展到 technology，但是在回答前，请考生务必确认自己是否能回答例如 "科技给我们的生活带来了什么便利" 等类似问题，并通过具体的例子或场景进行解释说明。

★ Part 1

1 Did you learn science in primary school?

示例回答

Yes, we all have science lessons in China, in primary school. We learn *the basics of how the planet earth works*, a bit of physics and geography, and a bit of biology and chemistry. Things like this. So, yes, I learned science in primary school. In fact, I really liked studying science. I found it exciting to *gain an understanding of how things worked*, like *why wheels move around*, and how the water in a *bathtub spins around in one direction* as it *goes down the plug hole*, or why water *boils* at less than 100 degrees *Celsius* when on top of a very high mountain! I love all these little *scientific facts* and learning *the reasons behind why things do what they do*! I think it's also very good for children – it teaches them *cause and effect logic* as well, which is a useful *mental skill* that is used in other studies too.

内容亮点

- the basics of how the planet earth works 地球运行的基本原理
- gain an understanding of how things worked 了解事物是如何运作的
- why wheels move around 为什么轮子会转动

- bathtub ['bɑːθtʌb] *n.* 浴缸
- spin around in one direction 朝一个方向旋转
- go down the plug hole 从放水孔流下去
- boil *v.* 沸腾
- Celsius ['selsiəs] *adj.*（温度）摄氏的 *n.* 摄氏温度
- scientific fact 科学真相；科学事实
- the reasons behind why things do what they do 事物之所以这样的原因
- cause and effect logic 因果逻辑
- mental skill 智力技能；脑力技能
- 本题给出的示例回答较长，回答此题时，考生可在"上课所学内容"以及"对科学事实的好奇"两者中选择一个方面进行说明，符合 Part 1 回答的长度要求即可。

2 Do students still learn science when they are in high school?

示例回答

Yes, sure, but in high school you can choose subjects so you choose usually one or two science subjects. I was never very good at maths so I chose biology only. But some students who want to ***go on to study*** science or ***science-related subjects*** choose two or three science subjects in high school. So, yes, students do still learn science but they have ***a certain element of choice as to*** which subjects to choose, to continue to study at high school level.

内容亮点

- go on to do sth. 继续做另一件事
- science-related subject 科学（理科）相关学科
- a certain element of choice 一定的选择因素
- as to 至于，关于；就……而论
- 除了示例回答提到的内容，考生还可以举例说明具体有哪些可以选择的科目。

3 Is there any technology that you think is helpful in daily life?

示例回答

Sure, computers, smartphones...these are the main types of technology that ***are most widely used*** today. In fact, they are ***indispensable*** – we ***couldn't live our daily lives or work without them***. They are not just "helpful", but in many cases they ***are absolutely necessary to communicate and get work done***, and even ***complete financial transactions and all sorts of stuff***. So, ***there was a time***, maybe over ten years from now, when information technology helped us do things. But now, this kind of technology ***is absolutely essential for us*** to ***get almost everything done***!

内容亮点

- be most widely used 应用最广泛；使用最广泛

- indispensable [ˌɪndɪˈspensəbl] *adj.* 不可或缺的，必不可少的
- couldn't live our daily lives or work without them 我们的日常生活和工作都离不开他们
- be absolutely necessary to communicate and get work done 对于沟通和完成工作是绝对必要的
- complete financial transactions 完成金融交易
- and all sorts of stuff 还有各种各样的事情
- there was a time 曾有一段时间
- be absolutely essential for us 对我们来说是绝对必要的
- get almost everything done 完成几乎所有的事情
- 示例回答中使用了 absolutely、almost 等副词，回答时可适当重音，以便体现发音特征。

4 Do you think science classes are important?

示例回答

Science teaches us about our planet, about *the basic laws of nature*, and science forms *the basis of how we construct things*, how we *build human society*, how we *understand the natural world*, how we develop *medicine and medical technology*. *Everything is rooted in science to some extent*. So, science is indispensable to *human development*.

内容亮点

- the basic laws of nature 自然的基本规律
- the basis of how we construct things 我们如何构建事物的基础
- build human society 构建人类社会
- understand the natural world 了解自然世界
- medicine and medical technology 医学与医疗技术
- everything is rooted in science 一切都起源于科学；be rooted in 来源于，起源于
- to some extent 在一定程度上；在某种程度上（可用于句末表示对程度的理解和看法）
- human development 人类发展

睡眠（Sleep）▶▶▶

话题介绍

　　该话题是基础的 Part 1 话题之一，可以和 weekend、relaxation 等话题进行关联。但考生也可能会被问到过去和现在的睡眠习惯是否有改变等问题，所以需要注意正确使用对应的时态。另外话题也可以往 reading before bed，或者小时候的 bedtime story 等方向进行拓展，考生可以描述这些事情对于睡眠是否有帮助，或者自己有何感受等。

★ Part 1

1 How have your sleeping habits changed since you were younger?

示例回答

When I was really young, *I used to sleep loads*. I loved sleeping. My parents used to have to *force me to get out of the bed* in the morning and get ready to go to school. However, like most people, as I got older, and had more responsibilities in life, I learned that it's better to get up early, *simply to make the most of the day* and *get things done*. So, now *I'm in my 30s* and have a full-time job and a family, I don't sleep as much as I used to, and I get up early *as a routine*, almost every day.

内容亮点

- I used to sleep loads 我以前睡眠很多
- force me to get out of the bed 逼我起床
- simply to make the most of the day 只是为了充分利用每一天
- get things done 把事情做好；完成事情
- I'm in my 30s 我 30 多岁了（类似的表达还有 I'm in my 20s 等）
- as a routine 作为一种惯例
- 此题涉及过去和现在的内容，在回答时需要注意时态的合理使用。

2 Do you take naps at noon?

示例回答

Some of my colleagues *take a noon nap* on their desk or in the *cafeteria area* of our office. We have a really nice office actually! *But for some reason*, I don't know why, I can't sleep *during the day*. My mind is always too active *during the daytime* and so I usually take a walk around the office block outside, especially if it's a nice day. This helps me to relax. I've never really had *the habit of taking daytime naps*, except perhaps when I'm on holiday in a sunny place.

内容亮点

- take a noon nap 午休
- cafeteria area 餐厅区域
- But for some reason 表示"但是由于某种原因"，可用作连接词放置于句首。
- during the day / daytime 在白天的时候
- the habit of taking daytime naps 白天小睡的习惯
- 示例回答中将身边人的午休习惯和自己的习惯进行对比，是可参考的拓展思路。

③ Do you like to read before bed?

示例回答

I nearly always **read before bedtime**. In fact, I often read on my phone. I know it's not a good habit – because it **keeps you awake** more than reading a book – and I always **get messages or look at people's WeChat moments** and **distract myself a lot**. It's much better to **put the phone away** and read a book. I should really try to **nurture this habit**, **to be fair**. Although I do read a lot of stuff on my phone – from news to articles online, blogs and even novels and **academic texts**.

内容亮点

- read before bedtime 睡前阅读

- keep you awake 让你保持清醒

- get messages or look at people's WeChat moments 获取信息或刷别人的微信朋友圈

- distract myself a lot 让自己分心；distract [dɪ'strækt] v. 使分心；使转移注意力

- put the phone away 把手机收起来；把手机放到一边

- nurture this habit 培养这个习惯；nurture ['nɜːtʃə] v. 培养

- to be fair 公平地说；说句公道话

- academic texts 学术文献

- 示例回答结合在手机上阅读这一常见方式，补充说明可能让自己无法入睡或者分心的原因，是可参考的拓展思路。

④ How much sleep do you need every night?

示例回答

I sleep around 7 hours a night. I think that's pretty good. I like to go to bed early and wake up pretty early. I heard that experts say that you should get more than 6 hours a day, so I think I have **a fairly healthy sleep habit**. There are nights, however, where I can't sleep well – usually nights when I am worried about something, **stressed out** and so on. My own mind sometimes **keeps me from getting good sleep. Apart from this**, I can **sleep through almost any noise**! I'd say I am **a good sleeper**.

内容亮点

- a fairly healthy sleep habit 一个相当健康的睡眠习惯

- be stressed out 紧张；饱受压力

- keep me from getting good sleep 让我睡不好觉；keep me from doing sth. 阻止我做某事

- apart from this 表示"除此之外"，是口语回答中常用连接词之一。

- sleep through almost any noise 在几乎所有的噪音中都能睡觉

- a good sleeper 睡眠好的人

- 示例回答除了说明日常的睡眠时间之外，也提到偶尔睡不好的情况，这也是可以参考的重要拓展思路。

报纸 & 杂志（Newspapers & Magazines）▶▶▶

话题介绍

该话题是常见的 Part 1 话题，可当作是 reading 这个话题的另一种提问方式。但需要注意报纸和杂志的区别，前者偏向 current affairs，而后者更多偏向例如 fashions and sports 等相关内容。但是有些信息在报纸和杂志上都会出现，比如 economy 等。考生在回答问题的时候需要先说清楚报纸和杂志的类型，然后再补充说明自己更喜欢哪一种。另外如果想要表达喜欢在线阅读新闻和杂志，也不要只是说它们方便，可以结合具体的场景进一步展开，比如 while commuting to work 等。

★ Part 1

1 **Do you prefer to read newspapers or magazines?**

示例回答

I definitely prefer to read magazines. *I'm not so into politics and stuff like this*, so I don't pay a lot of attention to news, newspapers or news apps. However, I do like magazines, or at least *online versions of magazines*. I'm interested in *celebrity gossip stories*, fashion articles, sports...I guess I do sometimes read *the sports section of news apps*, *come to think of it*. But, yes, mainly I'm the kind of person who reads magazines.

内容亮点

- I'm not so into 我不太喜欢
- politics ['pɒlətɪks] *n.* 政治
- and stuff like this 表示 "诸如此类的东西"，可用于替换 and so on。
- online versions of magazines 线上杂志
- celebrity gossip stories 名人的八卦故事
- the sports section of news apps 新闻应用程序的体育板块
- come to think of it 细想一下
- 示例回答结合不喜欢阅读报纸的原因，来说明喜欢阅读杂志的原因，这是可参考的拓展思路和逻辑。

2 **Do you prefer to read news online or in a newspaper?**

示例回答

Online of course. Pretty much every one reads news online these days, maybe *apart from* some older people who *are not really used to mobile technology*. Online news *is regularly updated*, you can *access it at any time*, and it's very convenient – for example, you can read the news while *commuting to work* or sitting in a café or *walking down the street*. Pretty much anywhere!

内容亮点

- apart from 除……之外

- be not really used to mobile technology 真的不习惯移动技术（设备）

- be regularly updated 定期更新

- access it at any time 随时访问

- commute to work 通勤上班

- walk down the street 沿街走，沿街散步

- 示例回答描述了阅读在线新闻的具体场景，是可参考的拓展思路。

3 Do people in your family often read newspapers?

示例回答

Not many people in my family *pay much attention to* the news really, *neither on TV nor in newspapers*. My dad *takes some interest in* international news online, and my brother often reads sports news – football, basketball and so on. *But generally*, we don't really read, watch or listen to the news much.

内容亮点

- pay much attention to 非常注意；很重视

- neither on TV nor in newspapers 电视和报纸上的都没有；neither...nor... 既不是……也不是……

- take some interest in 对……有一些兴趣

- But generally 表示"但一般来说"，可用于句末作为总结。

4 Do you think it's important to read newspapers?

示例回答

Well. I'm not sure. I don't believe most of what I read in the news *anyway*, to be honest. I think the news can be *informative I suppose*. And *it is important to a certain extent*, but *shouldn't be taken too seriously* – like most things, social media, *and so forth*, you should *take all this online stuff with a pinch of salt* and *not think about it too much or too seriously*.

内容亮点

- anyway *adv.* （用于表明某事不重要）反正；至少；总之

- informative [ɪnˈfɔːmətɪv] *adj.* 提供有用信息的；增长见闻的

- I suppose 表示"我想"，可用于替换 I think 等表达。

- it is important to a certain extent 这在一定程度上是重要的

- shouldn't be taken too seriously 不要太当真

- and so forth 表示"等等"，可用于替换 and so on 等表达。

- take all this online stuff with a pinch of salt 对这些网上的东西要有所保留

  pinch [pɪntʃ] *v.* 捏，拧，掐；with a pinch of salt 有所保留地

- not think about it too much or too seriously 不要想得太多或太认真

早晨日常（Morning routine）▶▶▶

话题介绍

　　该话题是 Part 1 的基础话题，指的是"每日早晨的日常"。该话题不难拓展，只需要描述每天早上起床，然后去上班或上课之前会具体做的事情即可。练习时可以重点关注示例回答中如何表达起床、赖床这些生活中常见，但是却不太会用英文表达的内容，比如 snooze、lie-in 等。

★ Part 1

1 Do you like to get up early in the mornings?

示例回答

Not really. I'm not *a morning person*, but I'm not *a night person* either. I guess you could say I'm an afternoon person? *Or more precisely*, a person who "loves to sleep" kind of person? *Either way*, it's *a daily struggle to peel myself out of bed*, so I need all the help I can get.

内容亮点

- a morning person 早起的人
- a night person 一个夜猫子
- Or more precisely 或者更准确地说；precisely [prɪ'saɪsli] *adv.* 准确地；恰好地
- either way 不管怎样；无论哪种方式
- a daily struggle to peel myself out of bed 每天挣扎着从床上爬起来
- 示例回答提到早起困难的细节，是可参考的重要拓展思路。

2 What is your morning routine?

示例回答

I wake up around 6:00 a.m. when *my alarm goes off*, and *snooze* for a few minutes. When I finally *roll out of bed*, I take a shower, quickly *put on my makeup*, and *blend my daily smoothies* – healthy drinks I make from fruits, yoghurt and berries. Then *I am out of the door*. If it's *a non-working day*, I'll *hit the gym*, or I'll just chat with my boyfriend for a bit, before taking a shower.

内容亮点

- my alarm goes off 我的闹钟响了；go off 发出声响
- snooze [snuːz] *v.* 小睡；打盹
- roll out of bed 起床
- put on my makeup 化妆
- blend my daily smoothies 调制我的每日奶昔

  blend *v.* 混合，调制，配制；smoothies ['smuːðɪ] *n.* 奶昔，冰沙

- I am out of the door 我要出门了
- a non-working day 非工作日的一天
- hit the gym 去健身房
- 示例回答把工作日和非工作日进行了区分，是可参考的拓展思路。

3 **Which one is your favorite morning of the week?**

示例回答

My favourite morning is Saturday morning because I don't have to get up for work and I can *lie in bed for hours* reading or watching *TV series*. Saturday morning is *most certainly* my favourite morning and *it always has been*. I think a lot of people *share the same feeling as me* about Saturdays, or at least weekend days. These are usually times when we can *wind down* and *recharge* our *batteries*.

内容亮点

- lie in bed for hours 躺在床上几个小时
- TV series 电视剧
- most certainly 很肯定地
- it always has been 一直都是
- share the same feeling as me 和我有同样的感觉
- wind down 平静下来；放松一下（注意此处 wind 的发音是 [waɪnd]）
- recharge batteries 充电
- 示例回答没有单纯地提到"休息"，而是用具体例子说明了可以做哪些事情，是可参考的拓展思路。

4 **Do you want to change your daily routines in the future?**

示例回答

If there's one thing I could change, it would be *having a lie-in in the morning*. I always wake up really early and get out of bed *as soon as* I wake up which means I never really have a lie-in. Sometimes I *get a bit tired* in the afternoon and I think it's because I get up too early. So yeah, *I'd like to be able to* have a lie-in sometimes.

内容亮点

- have a lie-in in the morning 早上睡个懒觉
- as soon as 一……就……
- get a bit tired 有点累（注意添加副词可表达不同的程度）
- I'd like to be able to... 我希望可以做……

集中力（Concentration）▶▶▶

集中力（Concentration）▶▶▶

话题介绍

该话题是从 study 或者 reading 等话题延伸出来的 Part 1 话题。练习时建议考生思考无法专注的原因，以及如何让自己保持专注的方法。这些都是实际考试中考官经常提问的内容。基于这两点，可以留意示例回答中如何用细节描述相关内容，比如"走神"可以用 my thought start to wander off 表达，"注意力集中的时间段"可以翻译为 concentration span 等。

★ Part 1

1 When do you need to be focused?

示例回答

Usually, I need to concentrate and be focused when I am doing homework. Some people can study when there is a lot of noise around them, but I can't, I have to *be in complete silence*. I must be in a place where there is no music, no *household noise*, no people talking...*total silence*. Maybe I am not good at concentrating and I *get distracted too easily*, but *that's just the way I am*. It's my personality.

内容亮点

- be in complete silence 处于完全安静的环境中
- household noise 家务噪音
- total silence 寂静无声
- get distracted too easily 太容易分心
- that's just the way I am 我就是这样的人
- 示例回答提到了自己和他人相比，比较不容易专注的情况，是回答完 when 之后可参考的相关拓展思路。

2 What may distract you when you are trying to stay focused?

示例回答

When I am trying to stay focused, I can get easily distracted by many things. Firstly, my *own thoughts start to wander off*, and I suddenly realise I am *staring out of the window* thinking about something completely different and not focusing on my studies. Sometimes if I hear music or my parents or friends talking outside the room, I start to *lose my concentration*. Things like that.

内容亮点

- own thoughts start to wander off 自己的思想开始游离
- stare out of the window 凝视窗外
- lose my concentration 失去我的注意力
- 示例回答对可能会让自己走神的原因进行了具体的场景化描述，是可参考的重要拓展思路和方向。

3 **What do you do to help you concentrate?**

示例回答

I put on *noise-cancelling headphones* – you know, those kinds of headphones that play music but do not allow *other external sounds* to enter your ears! I *put on light classical music*, and I make sure I *shut the door* and I tell my friends and family that I need to *study in peace*.

内容亮点

- noise-cancelling headphones 降噪耳机
- other external sounds 其他外部的声音
- put on light classical music 播放轻松的古典音乐
- shut the door 关门
- study in peace 在安静的环境中学习
- 示例回答描述了让自己保持专注的具体做法，是可参考的重要拓展思路。

4 **Is it difficult for you to stay focused on something?**

示例回答

Yes, I've got *a poor concentration span*. Well, *a lot of the time*, anyway. There are times when I can focus really well – when I've *had a good night's sleep*, or when I am *feeling calm and confident*. But if I *am stressed or nervous*, I find it hard to concentrate on things and I am easily distracted.

内容亮点

- a poor concentration span 注意力不集中；span [spæn] *n.* 时间跨度；持续时间
- a lot of the time 很多时候
- have a good night's sleep 睡个好觉
- feel calm and confident 保持冷静和自信
- be stressed or nervous 感到压力或紧张
- 示例回答提到了两种容易和不容易专注的情况，均是可参考的拓展思路。

电视节目（TV program）▶▶▶

话题介绍

　　该话题是常见的 Part 1 话题，并且也可以和其他话题进行关联。当提到喜欢看的 TV series 时，也可以延伸到喜欢的电影类型，比如电视剧和电影都有侦探类型的内容，即 detective series 或者 detective movies。建议考生在回答时选择自己擅长的内容，不一定要把 TV programs 限制在 documentaries 或者 variety shows 的范围内。同时也可以尝试回答自己看这些节目的时候，会不会追剧，即 binge-watch the drama 等具体行为。

★ Part 1

1 **Do you like watching TV programs?**

示例回答

I enjoy watching certain *TV series*, yes. I particularly enjoy *detective series and crime thrillers*, as I enjoy *the sense of mystery* and trying to *solve the crimes* and things like this. Sometimes I watch *comedy series*, because they're *light-hearted* and *cheer me up*. I watch them on my phone or *tablet* at night in bed.

内容亮点

- TV series 电视剧
- detective series and crime thrillers 侦探系列和犯罪惊悚片
  detective [dɪˈtektɪv] *adj.* 刑侦的；thriller [ˈθrɪlə] *n.* 惊悚小说；惊悚电影
- the sense of mystery 神秘感
- solve the crime 破案
- comedy series 喜剧连续剧
- light-hearted *adj.* 轻松的；无忧无虑的
- cheer me up 使我高兴；鼓励我；使我振作起来
- tablet *n.* 平板电脑
- 示例回答描述了观看不同电视节目的感受。如果考生不擅长描述节目的具体内容，可以参考这样的拓展思路。

2 **What types of TV programs do you like to watch?**

示例回答

Generally, I enjoy *documentaries* more than anything else. I like *nature documentaries and documentaries about mysteries*, the *supernatural*, and history. I also enjoy watching some *American thriller dramas*, too.

内容亮点

- documentary [ˌdɒkjuˈmentri] *n.* 纪实节目；纪录片
- nature documentaries and documentaries about mysteries 自然纪录片和神秘纪录片
- supernatural *n.* 超自然现象
- American thriller drama 美国惊悚剧

3 **Do you stick to one type of program all the time?**

示例回答

Not really, it depends on my mood. I have different moods and *phases* in which I watch different kinds of programmes. I also like to watch TV series that my friends are watching, so we can talk about them and *exchange ideas and opinions* about the *characters*, the *plots* and the *atmosphere* they create. So, *I tend to follow those that some of my friends watch*.

内容亮点

- phase [feɪz] *n.* 阶段；时期

- exchange ideas and opinions 交换想法和意见

- character ['kærəktə] *n.* 角色

- plot [plɒt] *n.* 情节

- atmosphere ['ætməsfɪə] *n.* 氛围

- I tend to... 我倾向于……

- follow those that some of my friends watch 关注我的一些朋友看的节目

    those 指代之前出现的 program，避免重复，提升回答的连贯性。

4 Do you talk to your friends about the programs you watched by yourself?

示例回答

Some of them, yes. I have a number of friends who are *following a series* right now, actually. It is *a sort of high-school drama series* set in America, and we often *talk about what goes on in that*, the characters, their *romances*, their *arguments and disputes* and *the things they get up to*. We chat about their lifestyles compared to ours. So, yes, I do chat to friends about TV series quite often.

内容亮点

- follow a series 追剧

- a sort of high-school drama series 一种高中主题的电视剧

- talk about what goes on in that 说说里面发生了什么

- romance [rəʊ'mæns] *n.* 爱情故事

- arguments and disputes 争辩与纠纷

    argument ['ɑːgjumənt] *n.* 争辩；dispute ['dɪspjuːt] *n.* 纠纷

- the things they get up to 他们干的那些事

- 示例回答中具体说明了聊天内容和细节，是可参考的重要拓展思路。

衣服（Clothes）▶▶▶

话题介绍

　　该话题代表了 Part 1 中可能会出现的和服饰相关的话题，类似话题还有 jeans、shoes 等等。如果觉得服饰的外观和设计不好描述，依旧可以结合具体的场景解释需要或者不需要穿某一些服饰的原因。比如，在 workplace 可能需要 formal dress，而参加派对则可以穿 casual clothes。同时也要注意该话题可能会和结合 colour 进行提问，所以也可以描述自己的日常穿搭，即 outfit 是什么，以及自己喜欢的穿搭等内容。

★ Part 1

1 **What kind of clothes do you often wear in daily life?**

示例回答

In my normal, everyday life, I usually wear jeans and a T-shirt, perhaps a skirt or a dress in summer. It really depends. But usually quite *casual clothes* – clean and *presentable*, but *casual attire*, normally.

内容亮点

- casual clothes 休闲服
- presentable [prɪ'zentəbl] *adj.* 像样的；体面的
- casual attire 休闲装；attire [ə'taɪə] *n.* 服装；衣服
- 示例回答提到了衣服的风格，如果考生不擅长描述自己穿着的具体服饰，可以参考示例回答中的思路。

2 **Is there any difference between the clothes you wear on weekends and weekdays?**

示例回答

Perhaps there's *a bit of a difference*, yes. During the week I tend to focus more on wearing *conventional styles*, because I have to go to work and must *look a bit smarter*. On weekends I tend to *be more laid back* and wear more casual clothes, perhaps even *slightly more informal clothes*. For example, if I go to a party or something I might *dress up in heels* and *sort of more striking-looking dresses*, which I don't tend to wear in the office.

内容亮点

- a bit of a difference 有一点不同
- conventional style 日常的风格
- look a bit smarter 看起来更时髦一点；smart *adj.* 时髦的；高档的；整洁而漂亮的；光鲜的
- be more laid back 更放松的
- slightly more informal clothes 稍微随意一点的服饰
- dress up in heels 穿高跟鞋
- sort of more striking-looking dresses 更引人注目的裙子
- 示例回答结合了办公室和派对两种不同的场景进行说明，是可参考的重要拓展思路。

3 **Is there any colour you dislike when buying clothes?**

示例回答

I don't really like yellow. I don't think this colour suits me. Also, *pastel shades* don't really suit me, either. I prefer *plain colours*, *subdued colours* for work, and perhaps more *bold colours* if I go out on the weekend with friends.

【内容亮点】

- pastel shade 轻淡优美的色彩

  pastel ['pæstl] *adj.* 淡的，柔和的；shade *n.* 色度

- plain colour 素色

- subdued colour 柔和的颜色；subdued [səb'djuːd] *adj.* （光线或色彩）柔和的

- bold colour 亮色；bold [bəʊld] *adj.* 大胆的；轮廓突出的

- 示例回答中提到的很多颜色类型的表达是考生备考练习时的常见难点，可多参考和模仿。

家具（Furniture）▶▶▶

【话题介绍】

　　该话题也是 Part 1 中常见的物品类话题。需要注意的是，如果纯粹描述家具样式可能会比较局限，因此建议考生结合具体的某件事进行拓展。比如 a bookshelf 就是一个不错的选择，除了可以和阅读或者自己收藏的书籍相结合之外，如果题目问到了类似 tidiness 的话题，也可以进行关联，即可以说有了书架之后就能整洁地存放书籍等相关内容。

★ Part 1

1 Is there much furniture in your room?

【示例回答】

No, not really, there's only a desk, a small table and a bed really. Oh, and I also have *a bedside table* with a *lamp* on it. I use this to *keep some books on*. I like reading *thriller novels*, you see, and I often read in bed before going to sleep so the bedside table and lamp is quite *handy*.

【内容亮点】

- a bedside table 一个床头柜
- lamp *n.* 台灯
- keep some books on 存放一些书
- thriller novel 惊悚小说；thriller ['θrɪlə] *n.* 惊悚小说
- handy *adj.* 有用的；方便的
- 示例回答主要选择了一件家具（床头桌）进行说明和补充细节，和 reading 相结合也是一个不错的回答，是考生们可参考的重要思路。

② What kind of furniture would you like to buy?

示例回答

I'd really like to buy a bookshelf. I have *a growing collection of books*, *print books*. And I would like to *store them on a proper bookshelf*, rather than just *piling them up in the corner of the room* or on my bedside table which I do *at the moment*. So, yeah, a bookshelf, a nice wooden bookshelf would keep my room a bit more tidy and enable me to *organise my books properly*.

内容亮点

- a growing collection of books 越来越多的藏书
- print book 印刷书；纸质书
- store them on a proper bookshelf 把它们放在合适的书架上
- pile them up in the corner of the room 把它们堆在房间的角落里；pile up 积累；堆放起来
- at the moment 表示"此刻"，是常用连接词，可以用于替换 now。
- organise my books properly 整理好我的书

③ Who has bought or given furniture to you?

示例回答

My parents usually bought furniture for my room, actually. We've always lived in quite small places so I've never really had much furniture, but they bought me a bookshelf, a wardrobe, *a chest of drawers* for my clothes and things like this. My uncle once bought me a really nice chair actually, *a sort of desk-chair* so I could be more comfortable when I'm studying.

内容亮点

- a chest of drawers 五斗橱
- a sort of desk-chair 一种办公椅
- 示例回答中除了提到父母买的家具之外，还提到了别人送的家具。因此题目中问的 who 并不是只能提到某一人，这是可参考的重要拓展思路。

手写（Handwriting）▶▶▶

话题介绍

　　该话题是 Part 1 中的难点话题，也符合近年来 Part 1 的出题思路，即话题越来越具体化，但是考生依旧可以通过和具体的事件结合来化解难点。例如现在只会在一些特定的情况下手写文字，考生把这个具体的事件讲清楚即可，比如 send a postcard，或者 put your signature to a contract 就是具体事件的体现。同时如果需要和打字的速度进行对比，也可以具体说一分钟可以打多少字，而手写一分钟只能写多少字等。

★ Part 1

1 Do you prefer to write letters by hand or on a computer?

示例回答

I, of course, prefer to write letters by email on the computer. *In recent years* I think my handwriting *has gone downhill* to be honest. I can't *write as nicely as I used to* because I *barely* get any practice apart from perhaps *making lecture notes* or shopping lists or *scrawling down my ideas on paper*. So, if I have to write a letter then I can write faster, clearer and easier on a computer. Computers are way more convenient for writing letters.

内容亮点

- in recent years 近些年来
- have gone downhill 走下坡路
- write as nicely as I used to 写得和以前一样好
- barely ['beəli] *adv.* 几乎不（可替换 seldom 等用法）
- make lecture notes 做课堂笔记
- scrawl down my ideas on paper 把我的想法潦草地写在纸上；scrawl [skrɔːl] *v.* 潦草地写
- 示例回答通过描述仅有的写字场景说明现在手写字的频率很低，是可参考的拓展思路。

2 Do you think computers might one day replace handwriting?

示例回答

I think they already basically have, at least in most communications today – from study, to work, to messages, in almost *every sphere of life*. I think we *type on phones and computers* and *rarely* actually write anything by hand. So, yeah, I think it has already happened that computers have replaced handwriting, *almost entirely*.

内容亮点

- every sphere of life 生活的各个领域；sphere [sfɪə] *n.* 范围；领域
- type on phones and computers 在手机和电脑上打字
- rarely ['reəli] *adv.* 罕有地；不常地（可用于替换 seldom）
- almost entirely 几乎完全

3 How can children today improve or practice their handwriting?

示例回答

Children usually learn to write *Chinese characters* in school. And they learn by practicing a lot, *a process of continual improvement*, until they can write well. Still today this is *learned initially by hand*, so that the children can learn to *recognize Chinese*, and one of the best ways to *imprint the characters in the memory*, is through writing. So, we have *quite a strict education in terms of learning to write*, from a young age. I think this is the main practice that kids get with handwriting today. They have to write a lot in school by hand still, at least *in their early years*.

内容亮点

- Chinese character 汉字
- a process of continual improvement 持续改进的过程

  continual [kən'tɪnjuəl] *adj.* 多次重复的，频繁的
- learn initially by hand 最初通过手写学习
- recognize Chinese 辨认中文
- imprint the characters in the memory 把这些字印在记忆里；imprint [ɪm'prɪnt] *v.* 使铭记
- quite a strict education in terms of learning to write 在学习写字方面的教育很严格

  strict [strɪkt] *adj.* 严厉的；in terms of 在……方面
- in their early years 在他们小的时候
- 示例回答较长，提供了很多参考思路。考生如果觉得有难度，练习时选择"如何在学校进行练习"这一个思路即可。

水上运动（Water sports）▶▶▶

话题介绍

  该话题也是 Part 1 中的难点话题，同样是因为内容比较具体。不过好处是一旦掌握了 water sports 的思路，再去应对其他 sports 的相关话题就容易多了。其他话题例如 weekend 和 leisure activity 也可以从这个话题中获取一些思路。另外考生需要注意的是自己回答时所讲的运动是否属于水上运动，多留意示例回答中关于相关运动的词汇，比如 jet-ski、yachting 等。

★ Part 1

1 Have you ever tried any water sports?

示例回答

I've not really tried many water sports. I've gone swimming many times, of course. I've **been in boats on the river...**emmm, but water sports...not really. I've seen things like **jet-ski racing** on television, and surfing and **yachting**, but I've never **taken part in these kinds of sports myself**.

内容亮点

- be in boats on the river 在河上泛舟
- jet-ski racing 水上摩托车赛
- yachting ['jɒtɪŋ] *n.* 帆船运动
- take part in these kinds of sports myself 自己参与这些运动
- 示例回答中展示了在没怎么参加过 water sports 的情况下也可以使用的拓展思路，即描述"曾经看到过哪些 water sports"。

2 **What kind of water sport have you done?**

示例回答

I have only really gone swimming to be honest. I've taken part in quite a few *swimming competitions* in school and I enjoyed them. I like being in water, and *I have a slightly competitive streak in me*, so I quite like taking part in swimming competitions. But I have not had much chance to *properly train and practice beforehand*.

内容亮点

- swimming competition 游泳比赛
- I have a slightly competitive streak in me 我有点好胜；streak [striːk] *n.* 性格特征
- properly train and practice beforehand 事先进行适当的训练和练习
- 示例回答再次展示在没有相关经验的情况下如何进行回答，即可先承认没有这样的经验，再进行思路拓展。

3 **What kind of water sport would you want to try?**

示例回答

I'd like to try *jet-skiing* to be honest. It looks really cool, *fast-paced* and exciting. Maybe it's a little dangerous, but I think it would be okay if I got some training first. I'd love to try it. I've seen jet-ski races on television and I love how they actually *fly into the air a bit* when they *hit a slightly choppy wave*, and it looks really exciting. So, *I'm very keen to give it a go* if I get the chance.

内容亮点

- jet-skiing ['dʒet skiː] *n.* 水上摩托艇
- fast-paced *adj.* 快节奏的；快速的
- fly into the air a bit 有点飞到空中
- hit a slightly choppy wave 遇到一个小波浪；choppy ['tʃɒpi] *adj.* 波浪起伏的；不平静的
- be very keen to do sth. 非常渴望做某事
- give it a go 试一试
- 示例回答中提到了很多关于具体的 water sports 的细节，如果在回答此类题目时缺少思路，可参考以上回答作为拓展方向。

4 **Are water sports popular in China?**

示例回答

Yes, I think so. I'm not that sure to be honest. I imagine that they are more popular with people living in *warmer coastal areas*, like *down south* or in Hainan. I've only really seen water sports on TV – professional water sports – so I'm not sure if *everyday people like me* get much chance to *get involved in such sports*. Like I said, maybe they do in more coastal areas, I'm not sure.

内容亮点

- warmer coastal area 温暖的沿海地区

- down south 往南；南下

- everyday people like me 像我这样的普通人

- get involved in such sports 参加这些运动

- 示例回答中根据不同的地区进行分类和说明，是可参考的拓展思路。

发型（Haircuts）▶▶▶

话题介绍

　　该话题也是 Part 1 中的难点话题，因为比较具体，也比较难和其他类型的话题进行关联，所以需要单独进行练习。如果觉得具体的发型词汇难度较大，可以选择比较简单的内容，比如男生的 crew cut，或者女生的 long or short hairstyle，然后再补充具体喜欢的原因，比如比较容易清洗或者打理方便等。另外考生还要注意理发店用词的区别，比如 barbershop 指的是专门的男士理发店，而如果是男女通用的理发店则是 hair salon 等。

★ Part 1

1 What's your favourite hairstyle?

示例回答

Oh, this is quite hard to say. It depends if we are talking about the hairstyle, I like the most for myself, or the hairstyle I might like to see on other people. That makes a big difference. For myself I prefer to have a short simple hair style. Very short, actually. But, for other people, like perhaps on a famous female star or something, I like *long hair with a lot of volume*, perhaps *a little bit curly*. For a man, I admire men who have *swept back grey hair* that looks natural. I think it *looks dignified* and cool!

内容亮点

- long hair with a lot of volume 蓬松的长发；volume ['vɒljuːm] adj. 大量地（尤指头发的厚，多）

- a little bit curly 有一点卷曲；curly ['kɜːli] adj. 卷曲的

- sweep back grey hair 向后梳的灰白头发

- look dignified 看起来端庄；dignified ['dɪɡnɪfaɪd] adj. 庄重的；庄严的；有尊严的

- 示例回答展示了如果不知道如何表达具体的发型，只形容大致的头发风格即可，这是较容易回答的拓展思路。

2 How often do you have your haircut?

示例回答

I *have my hair cut* about once every one or two months. I *go to a hairdresser* near to my workplace and the same woman cuts my hair each time. It's a nice place. They wash my hair before and after cutting it, and once every six months *I have waves put in my hair*. I like to have *slightly wavy hair*. The service is excellent there and it's not too expensive.

内容亮点

- have my hair cut 去理发（注意不要说 cut my hair）
- go to a hairdresser 去理发店；hairdresser ['heədresə] *n.* 美发师
- have waves put in my hair 头发带点卷
- slightly wavy hair 轻微的卷发
- 示例回答描述了频次之后，还补充了 who 以及 where 等相关细节信息，均是可参考的拓展思路。

3 **Do you often change your haircut?**

示例回答

No, I've *kept the same hair style* for many, many years. Some of my female friends change their hairstyle quite often, *getting their hair cut shorter* in summer and *letting it grow longer* in winter, for example. But I keep mine pretty much the same.

内容亮点

- keep the same hair style 保持发型不变
- get their hair cut shorter 把她们的头发剪短
- let it grow longer 让它长得更长
- 示例回答展示如果自己并不会经常做出改变，可以和他人进行对比，这也是重要的拓展思路。

色彩（Colours）▶▶▶

话题介绍

　　该话题是 Part 1 中的难点话题，但如果进行一些简单的联想之后会发现，其实并不难进行拓展。比如绿色可以和自然或者森林相结合，蓝色可以和海边或者海洋结合。接下来可以说喜欢这些颜色的原因或者看到这些颜色之后有什么感受，例如能帮助你放松下来，即 help me unwind 等。

★ Part 1

1 **What's your favourite colour and why?**

示例回答

Green. *Most definitely* green. I love the colour green as *it reminds me of nature*, the countryside, trees, *valleys of lush vegetation*, mountains and forests. Green, *all shades of green*, makes me think of *the wonders of the natural world*.

内容亮点

- most definitely 明确地；最肯定地
- it reminds me of nature 它让我想起了大自然
- valleys of lush vegetation 郁郁葱葱的山谷

  lush [lʌʃ] *adj.* 茂盛的，郁郁葱葱的；vegetation [ˌvedʒə'teɪʃn] *n.* 植物，植被
- all shades of green 各式各样的绿色
- the wonders of the natural world 自然世界的奇迹
- 示例回答中把颜色和其他事物联系起来说明喜欢的原因，是可以参考的拓展思路。

2 What colours are the walls of the rooms in your home?

示例回答

The walls of my home are *fairly simple*, really. They are *a sort of cream colour*, just *off-white*. They look attractive though, because there's a lot of *framed pictures* on them. I think this is the best way to decorate a fairly simple small *city flat*, really. *Plain walls and tasteful pictures*.

内容亮点

- fairly simple 相当简洁
- a sort of cream colour 一种奶油色
- off-white *adj.* 灰白色的，米黄色的，米色的
- framed picture 镶框的图片
- city flat 城市公寓
- plain walls and tasteful pictures 朴素的墙壁和雅致的图画
- 示例回答展示缺乏思路时，也可以把颜色和房间内的其他装饰品相结合，是可参考的拓展思路。

3 Do you prefer dark colours or bright colours?

示例回答

For the home, I definitely prefer lighter and brighter colours. I think they make a space look larger and more *uplifting*. But for certain types of places, I think *rich, dark colours* can be very attractive, like an old restaurant or a cinema or places like this where you want to *feel the walls closing in around you more* and *a really strong and perhaps elegant emotional atmosphere*. But generally, I prefer bright colours for a home, that's for sure.

内容亮点

- uplifting [ˌʌp'lɪftɪŋ] *adj.* 令人振奋的；使人开心的
- rich, dark colours 丰富，深色的颜色
- feel the walls closing in around you more 感觉墙离你更近
- a really strong and perhaps elegant emotional atmosphere 一个真正强烈的，甚至有些优雅的情感氛围

  elegant ['elɪgənt] *adj.* 优美的；文雅的

4 Do some colours have a special meaning in your culture?

示例回答

I think red has always been a special colour in China. From the days of ancient China and *the dragon symbols* to *the modern-day China*, red has always been *a symbol of strength*, *prosperity*, *hope and honour* for the Chinese. Most definitely red and gold are colours which have a very special meaning in my culture and *deep cultural roots*.

内容亮点

• the dragon symbols 龙的象征

• the modern-day China 现代中国

• a symbol of strength, prosperity, hope and honour 象征着力量、繁荣、希望和荣誉

  strength [streŋθ] *n.* 力量；prosperity [prɒ'sperəti] *n.* 繁荣

• deep cultural root 深层的文化根源

• 除了示例回答中提到的思路之外，考生还可以结合红色和传统节日进行解释举例，这也是比较容易回答的一个思路。

植物（Plants）▶▶▶

话题介绍

　　该话题是 Part 1 中的难点话题，因为植物本身的细节不容易描述。我们依旧可以和具体的事件场景相结合，比如喜欢养植物就可以说在家里有一个专门的区域、植物对健康有益等；不喜欢的话可以说照料植物很花费时间等。这个话题请考生务必熟悉，因为也可以和 flowers 或 trees 等话题进行关联。

★ Part 1

1 Have you ever planted trees?

示例回答

Actually, no. I've never planted a tree myself. But I've seen and helped people plant trees. My uncle planted a tree on his balcony in a large pot, and I helped *pack the soil around the roots of the tree* and water it. That was a long time ago, though!

内容亮点

• pack the soil around the roots of the tree 把土埋在树根周围

• 示例回答展示在自己没有相关经验的时候，可以提及其他有类似相关经历的人，这是可参考的重要拓展思路。

2 Where did you plant trees?

示例回答

As I said before, it was on my uncle's balcony. *Come to think of it*, I've helped my mother too. She planted a number of plants which I guess you could call "trees" because they were quite large and had *branches and leaves*. That was also on the balcony, where we very often have plants and small trees.

内容亮点

- as I said before 正如我之前所说的

  重要连接词，需要重复上文提到的内容时可使用。

- come to think of it 细想一下

- branches and leaves 枝叶

3 Do you like plants?

示例回答

Yeah, I have lots of *leafy green plants* at home because they *promote health and well-being*. I mean they *help me with stress and anxiety*. Also, it's so cool to plant something in the ground, then *fertilise*, water, and take care of it *while watching it grow and bloom*.

内容亮点

- leafy green plant 多叶的绿色植物

- promote health and well-being 促进健康和福祉

- help me with stress and anxiety 帮助我缓解压力和焦虑；help me with sth. 帮我做某事

- fertilise ['fɜːtəlaɪz] *v.* 施肥

- while watch it grow and bloom 看着它生长开花；bloom *v.* 开花；绽放

4 Do you keep plants at home?

示例回答

Yes, I like plants. My home is quite small so I have *small house plants* that *come into flower* about once or twice a year. I live quite near to *a flower market* so I enjoy occasionally going to buy *a nice pot plant* for my kitchen window or balcony.

内容亮点

- small house plant 小型室内盆栽

- come into flower 开花

- a flower market 一家花市

- a nice pot plant 一盆漂亮的盆栽

- 示例回答除了描述具体种植的植物之外，还结合 where 和 when 进行拓展，是可参考的拓展思路。

5 **Do you know anything about growing plants?**

示例回答

I know a little about growing plants. In school we used to plant seeds and water them and watch them grow – I really found this very exciting when I was a child. You know, planting the seeds, watching them *sprout*, and then *nurturing* them by watering them and *putting them in the sunshine*.

内容亮点

- sprout [spraʊt] *v.* 发芽
- nurture ['nɜːtʃə] *v.* 养育
- put them in the sunshine 把它们放在阳光下
- 示例回答提及了具体的种植方式，这种把抽象问题具体化的展开回答，是可参考的重要拓展思路。

野生动物（Wild animals）▶▶▶

话题介绍

　　该话题是 Part 1 中的难点话题，因为不只是提问 animals or pets，而是直接把内容限制在了野生动物这个范围内。如果考生没有近距离见过野生动物（see wild animals up close），可以说在一些纪录片中见过，然后补充有什么感受、是否好奇、有机会想去哪里看这些动物等内容。

★ Part 1

1 **Do you like to watch TV programs about wild animals?**

示例回答

I love *wildlife documentaries*, actually. I find it *soothing* and informative to watch them. I particularly like the British ones with David Attenborough, as I love his voice. I think voices are important, and I find the way he talks very relaxing.

内容亮点

- wildlife documentary 野生动物纪录片
- soothing ['suːðɪŋ] *adj.* 安慰的，使人平静的
- 考生如果不熟悉具体的节目内容，可以谈论和节目相关的其他信息，例如示例回答中就只谈论了与 wild animal 相关的节目主持人。

2 **Did you learn something about wild animals at school?**

示例回答

Not so much. But yes, *we did have classes of biology*, and in those classes, we learned about animals and *how they relate to humans*, *human evolution*, *animal biology* and things like this. I enjoyed these kinds of lessons to be honest.

内容亮点

- we did have classes of biology 我们确实上过生物课

  注意使用过去时的时候可以用 did 强调，表示"我们的确上过"。

- how they relate to humans 它们与人类的关系如何

- human evolution 人类进化

- animal biology 动物生物学

3 **Where can you see wild animals?**

示例回答

In the zoo of course! The main place to see wild animals is in the zoo, *unless* you live on the *plains or jungles* in Africa or the Amazon! I go to the zoo occasionally, usually during the holidays with my nephew and niece.

内容亮点

- unless *conj.* 除非

- plains or jungles 平原或丛林

- 示例回答使用 unless 条件句说明了特殊情况，同时也补充了会和谁一起去看动物，均是可参考的拓展思路。

4 **In which country do you think you can see many wild animals?**

示例回答

I think several countries in Africa are famous for wild animals. I've never been to Africa, but my brother was in an African country – the name I forget – and he *went on safari*, where you *drive the car through the areas* where you see *wild rhinos*, elephants, tigers, *giraffes* and all sorts of other animals. It's a fantastic experience, *apparently*, and I'd love to do it, to be honest.

内容亮点

- go on safari 去考察野生动物

- drive the car through the areas 开车穿过这些区域

- wild rhinos 野生犀牛；rhino ['raɪnəʊ] *n.* 犀牛

- giraffe [dʒə'rɑːf] *n.* 长颈鹿

- apparently [ə'pærəntli] *adv.* 据说；显然；似乎，好像

- 在自己没有相关经验的情况下，可以尝试讨论其他有相关经验的人的经历，这是可参考的拓展思路。

天空（Sky and stars）▶▶▶

话题介绍

　　该话题是 Part 1 中的难点话题。除了描述具体的场景之外，还可以结合环保类的问题进行拓展。比如白天的天空是 crystal-clear 的，晚上的天空也很少有 light pollution，所以很适合仰望天空或者星空。基于这一点，这个话题也可以和 relaxation 等相关话题结合，因为仰望天空也是一种休息或者休闲方式。

★ Part 1

1 **Do you like to look at the sky?**

示例回答

Yes, I certainly do. I enjoy looking at the night sky *in particular*. The stars have always *fascinated* me, and you can get an especially good view of the night sky from my grandmother's home which is out in the countryside.

内容亮点

• in particular 尤其；特别

• fascinate ['fæsɪneɪt] *v.* 深深吸引

• 示例回答补充了看天空的具体地点，这也是可参考的拓展思路。

2 **Can you see the moon and stars at night from where you live?**

示例回答

In the big city, no, it's not really a good place to see the moon and stars, but when you *are out of town*, and there is no *light pollution*, then you can see the stars, especially, really clearly in the night sky.

内容亮点

• be out of town 在城外

• light pollution 光污染

• 示例回答提到的光污染，在涉及环保（environmental protection）相关的话题时也可使用。

3 **Do you prefer the sky in the morning or the sky at night?**

示例回答

I definitely prefer the sky at night. I've always loved reading about *astronomy*, *outer space* and things like this. So I *find a certain romanticism* about the night sky, especially the stars and planets, and I often follow *the cycles of moon* on an app on my phone.

内容亮点

- astronomy [əˈstrɒnəmi] *n.* 天文学
- outer space 外太空
- find a certain romanticism 寻找某种浪漫；romanticism [rəʊˈmæntɪsɪzəm] *n.* 浪漫主义；浪漫精神
- the cycles of moon 月亮的周期
- 示例回答通过相关的兴趣说明喜欢看夜空的原因，这是可参考的重要拓展思路。

4 **Is there a good place to look at the sky in the city you live in?**

示例回答

The best places in a city to look at the sky are *the rooftops of high buildings*. Some hotels and even bars and restaurants have lovely *outdoor terraces on the rooftops*. From there you can get a good view of the sky day or night.

内容亮点

- the rooftops of high buildings 高层建筑的屋顶
- outdoor terraces on the rooftops 屋顶上的户外露台；terrace [ˈterəs] *n.* 平台；阳台
- 示例回答展示了具体化描述的方法，在回答时，不要仅仅提及在某个城市，还要说出具体的某个地方。

历史（History） ▶▶▶

话题介绍

该话题是 Part 1 中的难点话题，虽然可以和 museums、films、reading 等话题结合，但是总体还是比较抽象。考生可以结合学习历史知识的具体形式表达自己感兴趣的相关内容。例如，历史老师用讲故事的方式介绍历史人物（historical figures），相比只是让学生阅读文字介绍的方式，讲故事的方式更有吸引力。

★ Part 1

1 **Have you ever been to a history museum?**

示例回答

Yes, I've been to several history museums. Some of them I've found really boring, and some I've found really interesting – it depends on how the *artefacts* are exhibited. I tend to prefer *natural history museums* that *house dinosaur skeletons* and *interactive experiences*. Museums that just have lots *relics*, like *ancient vases* or *jade stones in glass cabinets* with *lots of text to read*, well...I find them pretty boring to be honest. I like museums that have interesting displays that *engage visitors and inspire us to take an interest in history*.

内容亮点

- artefact ['ɑːtɪ,fækt] *n.* （尤指有历史或文化价值的）手工艺品
- natural history museum 自然历史博物馆
- house dinosaur skeleton 存放恐龙骨架

  house *v.* 收藏，存放；skeleton ['skɛlɪtən] *n.* 骨骼
- interactive experience 互动体验
- relic ['relɪk] *n.* 遗物；遗迹
- ancient vase 古老的花瓶
- jade stone 玉石
- in glass cabinet 在玻璃橱柜里；cabinet ['kæbɪnɪt] *n.* 贮藏橱；陈列柜
- lots of text to read 有很多文本要读
- engage visitors and inspire us to take an interest in history 吸引游客和激发我们对历史的兴趣
- 示例回答中的内容在回答和 museum 相关的话题时可以直接使用。

2 **Do you like history?**

示例回答

I enjoy learning about aspects of history, yes. I don't really like studying history in school – it's usually boring and *full of dates and events* that I don't find very interesting. But I do enjoy learning about certain aspects of history – like how different inventions *came about*, or how we *evolved from apes and came to live in caves*, or how the *pyramids* might have been built and why. These types of things are inspiring and interesting to me.

内容亮点

- full of dates and events 满是日期和事件
- come about 发生；产生
- evolve from apes and come to live in caves 从猿类进化而来，然后生活在洞穴里
- pyramid ['pɪrəmɪd] *n.* 金字塔
- 示例回答中的内容依旧可以在回答与 museum 相关的话题时使用。

3 **Have you ever watched historical films?**

示例回答

I have seen a few *history documentaries*, yes. In terms of actual films, movies, I've seen a few historical films, and some of them I enjoy, and some I don't like very much. It really depends. I don't like *war films* very much, films about *kings and emperors* who have huge armies *are tied up in political battles* as well. This is something I find really *tedious*. I like things like *Downton Abbey* and those kinds of more *family-oriented period dramas*. That's my *personal preference* anyway.

- history documentary 历史纪录片

- war film 战争片

- kings and emperors 国王和皇帝

- be tied up in political battles 被卷入政治斗争；be tied up in 被捆绑在……

- tedious ['tiːdiəs] *adj.* 冗长的，单调乏味的

- family-oriented period drama 以家庭为中心的时代剧

- personal preference 个人喜好

4 Did you like history when you were young?

示例回答

I didn't really. I liked certain *fun facts*, *like I said earlier*, like how the pyramids were built or about how dinosaurs lived and how they *became extinct*. But history lessons in school and the usual sort of *national and political history* I find *uninteresting and uninspiring*.

内容亮点

- fun facts 有趣的事实

- like I said earlier 就像我之前说的（重要连接词，用于引用上文提及的内容）

- become extinct 灭绝；extinct [ɪk'stɪŋkt] *adj.* 灭绝的；消亡的

- national and political history 国家和政治史

- uninteresting and uninspiring 无趣且毫无新意；uninspiring [ʌnɪn'spaɪərɪŋ] *adj.* 乏味的

5 When was the last time you read about history?

示例回答

The last time I read about something in history was a book I had about *tribes* in Africa. It is fairly interesting actually. I quite like reading about how they hunted animals hundreds of years ago, and how certain tribes *got along well with each other* but badly with others, and things like this. I was very attracted to the *colourful imagery* in the book I was reading – the natural scenery in Africa as well as the way people lived there.

内容亮点

- tribe [traɪb] *n.* 部落；宗族

- get along well with each other 和睦相处；志趣相投

- colourful imagery 彩色图像

- 示例回答中的内容在遇到和 reading 相关的题目时也可参考使用。

广告（Advertisements）▶▶▶

话题介绍

    该话题在口试的 Part 1、Part 2 和 Part 3 中都以不同形式出现过。在 Part 1 中，回答的难点在于广告的内容不好描述，考生可以多描述观看广告之后的感受，比如广告的形式，即 it was really impressive, just like a mini-movie。如果题目涉及看到广告的地点，也可以具体描述广告的投放形式给人们带来的感受，比如 it's usually really annoying 等。

★ Part 1

1 **What kinds of advertisements do you watch?**

示例回答

I *detest adverts* and I *get annoyed* when they come on TV or on apps on my phone. There are all kinds of adverts and I try to *ignore them or skip them* if I can. There are adverts for pretty much any product or service *you can imagine*.

内容亮点

- detest [dɪ'test] *v.* 厌恶；憎恨
- advert ['ædvɜːt] *n.* 广告
- get annoyed 变得气恼；变得生气
- ignore them or skip them 忽略或跳过它们
- you can imagine 你可以想象的
- 示例回答描述了对广告的感受和广告出现的时机，是可以参考的拓展思路。

2 **Where can you see advertisements?**

示例回答

Online, on mobile apps, on websites, on the subway, in elevators. There are adverts pretty much everywhere in our lives when we are in *commercial places*, cities, malls, *transport facilities*, online, everywhere. Today, you can't escape adverts – they're *ubiquitous*!

内容亮点

- commercial place 商业场所
- transport facility 交通设施
- ubiquitous [juːˈbɪkwɪtəs] *adj.* 普遍存在的，无所不在的
- 示例回答提及了很多地点和形式证明广告无处不在，是可参考的重要拓展思路。

3 **Have you ever bought something because of its advertisement?**

示例回答

I guess I have *subconsciously*. That's how advertising works—you *get presented with ideas* when you see adverts, and then they affect the decisions you make. I recall buying lots of *meal deals* because of adverts I've seen online or in the elevator at work on screens.

内容亮点

- subconsciously [ˌsʌbˈkɒnʃəsli] *adv.* 潜意识地
- get presented with ideas 获得各种想法
- meal deal 套餐
- 示例回答描述了被广告影响从而购买该产品的具体事例，是可参考的拓展思路。

4 **Do you watch advertisements from the beginning to the end?**

示例回答

Usually not. As I said before, I try to ignore them or skip them. But if I'm standing in the elevator going to the 18th floor, and there is nothing else to look at, I find myself watching the adverts on the TV screens there, *over and over again*, so I guess I do watch some adverts *from beginning to end*. That's *how the power of advertising works*!

内容亮点

- over and over again 一再地；反复不断地
- from beginning to end 自始至终
- how the power of advertising works 广告的力量是如何发挥作用的
- 示例回答通过描述乘坐电梯的场景，有效地补充了自己的观点，是可参考的拓展思路。

物品类（Objects） ▶▶▶

话题介绍

Part 2 的物品类话题一般可分为两类。一类是描述某件具体的或有形的物品，例如童年的玩具、特别的礼物等。另一类是描述某个较为抽象的或无形的事物，例如节日传统、喜欢的电影等。

该类型话题往往要求考生描述物品的特征及相关内容、如何获得该物品、何时获得该物品、对此件物品是否有特别的情感等相关内容。考生遇到该类话题时，如果没有清晰的思路，或者描述某件物品的特征和内容有明显困难，可尝试多描述该物品对自己生活的影响、带来的改变、该物品的意义等。同时也可尝试和类似的物品进行对比，进而拓展说明自己对该物品的感受。

考生可通过本书中的示例回答，整理物品特征的描述，尤其是描述各种抽象类物品的思路和表达方式。物品类话题在雅思口语 Part 2 题库中占比较大，考生需要预留更多准备和练习时间。回答完 Part 2 之后考官会根据考生的回答进行 Part 3 的提问，该部分是对 Part 2 内容的进一步延伸。

★ Part 2

> **1** Describe a toy you got in your childhood.
> You should say:
> 　　What it was
> 　　When you got it
> 　　How you got it
> And explain how you felt about it.

示例回答

One of my favourite toys was a train set. Actually, I still have it today. Well…I mean, it is still at my parents' house in my hometown. *It's a brand of train set that is called Hornby*, *which is quite famous*. It's not only a toy, actually. Some adults also have Hornby train sets and if they have the space in their homes, they build *an entire landscape of* mountains, trees, sometimes small towns and stations that the train track goes around. *It's* an electric train set *you see*, with different *engines and carriages*. *I'm still very fond of it today*, although it is in its box in pieces and it isn't set up anywhere.

I *got given* the train set for my 11th birthday by my mum and dad. I *remember feeling really excited* when I received it, and my dad and I *spent hours setting it up* in the *attic room* above the house. *I loved playing with it* and *I still have really happy memories of it* to this day. In fact, I was thinking about it recently, and I decided that if I have a child one day, especially a boy, I might give him the train set to *pass this gift down through the generations*.

It's interesting how children's toys have changed over the years, and a lot of these "*old fashioned*" style toys are not popular today, as children are often playing *games on ipads*, *tablets and even smartphones* a lot more. I suppose that is why I might feel especially sentimental about the train set – I tend to believe that these more "*physical*" toys and ways of playing are really good for children, and perhaps nowadays they spend far too much time *staring at screens*. *So, all in all*, I have a lot of positive feelings about my childhood and the kinds of toys we used to play with then.

内容亮点

- One of my favourite toys was a train set. / I still have it today. 注意这两句话的时态变化
- Well...I mean 属于英文中的 filler，适当添加可减少停顿，类似表达有：hmmm、let me see、you know、um、let me think、kind of / sort of、actually。
- It's a brand of train set that is called Hornby, which is quite famous. 连用两个定语从句，补充说明了玩具的名称和品牌知名度
- an entire landscape of... 由……组成的全套景观
- It's...you see 中可使用上升语调，you see 在口语中可拉近与听者的距离感。
- engines and carriages 引擎和车厢
- I'm still very fond of it today 至今我都非常喜欢

  be fond of sth. 表示对某事的喜爱，下文中的 I loved playing with it 表达的喜爱程度更深，I still have really happy memories of it 继续表达了对某物的喜爱。
- got given = was given 得到，收到
- remember feeling really excited 记得当时很兴奋

  remember doing sth. 记得做过某事；remember to do sth. 记得要去做某事
- spent hours setting it up 注意动词和宾语的搭配形式，spend time doing sth. 意为"花时间做某事"。
- attic room 阁楼；顶楼
- pass this gift down through the generations 将这个礼物代代相传
- 最后一段话用对比的方式将 toys 的变迁与作者的感受结合起来。过去的玩具是 old-fashioned and physical，而现在的孩子经常 staring at screens，"玩具"也变为 games on ipads, tablets and even smartphones，由此引出作者对这套 train set 尤为感伤的怀念。
- So, all in all 引出全文结尾

★ Part 3

1 Why do some people think advertising aimed at children should be prohibited?

示例回答

Children are *vulnerable*. They are easily influenced and they *are not mature enough to* think for themselves very well, or understand when someone is *tricking* them or trying to cheat. So, advertising aimed at children should be controlled at least, and possibly *prohibited*, especially if it's for products that can *have a negative impact on* their development or *distract* them too much *from* studies or social interactions with family or friends.

内容亮点

- vulnerable *adj.* (~ to sb. / sth.) weak and easily hurt physically or emotionally （身体上或感情上）脆弱的，易受……伤害的
- be not mature enough to do sth. 在做某事方面不够成熟
- trick *v.* 欺骗

  本句中 trick sb. = cheat sb.，中间用 or 连接，表示两者为并列关系。
- prohibit *v.* [often passive] to stop sth. from being done or used especially by law（尤指以法令）禁止

  作者认为此类广告应该被管控，而从法律层面禁止只是一种可能，所以加了 possibly 表示实现的可能性。
- have a negative impact on... 对……有消极影响
- distract sb. from sth. 转移某人的注意力
- 本回答的亮点之一是使用 and / or 表达同义关系，如 be not mature enough = be easily influenced，trick sb. = try to cheat，think for = understand。

2 Why do you think some parents buy lots of toys for their kids instead of spending more time with them?

示例回答

Some parents think that children should be given everything they want, and also if they do not have much time to spend with their children, they try to *compensate* by buying them gifts all the time. *I also believe that* most parents *genuinely* want the best for their children, and they might feel a sense of pressure not only to make their children happy, but to *compete with* other parents and families and not be seen to be *disadvantaging* their own children. So, there are two levels to this – the desire to contribute to the happiness of their children, and a kind of social pressure to live up to. These are the main reasons why some parents might *feel obligated to* spoil their children.

内容亮点

- compensate *v.* (~ for sth.) to provide sth. good to balance or reduce the bad effects of damage, loss, etc. 补偿；弥补
- I also believe that... 引出作者的第二理由
- genuinely *adv.* 发自内心地
- compete with 与……竞争
- disadvantaging 使处于不利地位（disadvantage 的现在分词形式）
- feel obligated to do sth. 感觉有必要 / 义务做某事
- 示例回答采用分总结构，在给出两个原因之后用 So, there are two levels to this... These are the main reasons why... 进行总结。

3 What are some of the differences between the toys kids play with nowadays and those they used to play with in the past?

示例回答

One of the main differences is that children today play a lot with tablets, phones, you know, mobile devices, *whereas* in the past they did not really have these forms of entertainment. Kids would read more, play with physical toys more, things like this.

内容亮点

- One of the main differences is that... 直接回答问题
- whereas 是连词，用来对比现在和过去的不同。
- 题目中的 nowadays 和 in the past 暗示回答时要使用不同的时态，建议考生多留意示例回答中时态的切换。

4 Are there any kinds of electronic games or computer games that can have educational benefits for young children?

示例回答

Yes, there are lots actually. There are some real benefits to playing games on tablets and some games are quite educational, related to learning vocabulary in foreign languages, or even one's own language, such as number games, *and all sorts of things like this*. Electronic games can be great, but parents must be careful to not allow children to *get* too *attached* or even *addicted to* such devices.

内容亮点

- Yes, there are lots actually. 开篇直接表明态度
- ...and all sorts of things like this = and so on，这是两个常见的替换表达。
- get attached to 非常喜欢……
- get addicted to 沉迷于……
  这个表达的喜欢程度比 get attached to 更深，用 or even 连接两个近义短语形成递进关系。

★ Part 2

2 Describe a gift that took you a lot of time to prepare.
You should say:
    What it was
    Who you gave it to
    How you prepared it
And explain why you spent a lot of time preparing it.

示例回答

A gift that comes to mind that I took a long time to prepare was a photo album I made for my grandfather when he was sick in hospital. I spent a few weeks preparing it, actually. I *went round* my relatives' houses, and wrote to those that didn't live in the same city, and asked them if they had any *physical photos* of my grandfather throughout or at any point in his life. *After a time*, I had gained a collection of about 50 photographs *dating back to* when he was a child, *through to* when he was a teenager, *and then in later life*, in various locations in his hometown, and around China.

It was an interesting historical family research project *in a way*, and I learned a lot as I *compiled* the photos into a book – an album. I had found a really nice-looking *scrap book* with grey pages and a *hardback* red cover. So, I used some glue, and carefully stuck all the photos in each page, *in chronological order*, and wrote in a nice silver ink pen under each photo, a line or two about what the photo was, where it was taken (if I knew) and more or less the date of the photo or occasion. After I *had filled* the entire scrapbook, I *was quite proud of* what I *had done* – it looked great, and was most certainly a great collection of memories of my grandfather's life, from when he was a child to the present day.

Then I went to the hospital where he was and presented it to him. *He was amazed* and *deeply moved* by what I had done. He couldn't believe it and he knew that it *must have taken* a lot of effort to get all these photos together from all the different family members that still had photos of the family, and then put them into one book. I think it was a great idea and a great gift. It had taken a long time to prepare, but was most certainly worth it. I had *gotten the idea from* a TV show that I saw, and *was inspired by* the idea of creating an "old style" photo album, especially in this digital age where everyone seems to *be obsessed with* taking digital photos on their phones! I think it's a great idea that most people should consider doing to an older member of their family.

内容亮点

- A gift that comes to mind that I took a long time to prepare was a photo album I made for my grandfather when he was sick in hospital. 我能想到的花了很长时间准备的一份礼物，是我在祖父生病住院时为他制作的相册。

  这句话使用了三个定语从句，结构紧凑，一气呵成。主句为 A gift was a photo album，第一个定语从句为 that comes to mind，修饰 a gift，意为"我能想到的一份礼物"；第二个定语从句为 that I took a long time to prepare，同样修饰 a gift，意为"我花了很长时间准备的一份礼物"；第三个定语从句为 I made for my grandfather when he was sick in hospital，修饰 a photo album，意为"我在祖父生病住院时为他制作的相册"。

- go round = call round 去拜访

  We went round to Jim's house. 我们去了吉姆家。

- physical photos 意为"纸质照片"，可以对应 digital photos（放在手机或电子设备中的照片）。

- after a time 一段时间后

- date back to..., through to..., and then in later life... 追溯到……，直到……，在他的晚年……

- in a way = in some degree 在某种程度上，相当于

- compile *v.* (to produce a book, list, report, etc.) 编写（书、列表、报告等）

- scrap book 剪贴簿
- hardback *adj.* 精装的；a hardback novel / book 精装书
- in chronological order 按照时间顺序
- After I had filled the entire scrapbook, I was quite proud of what I had done. 一般过去时和过去完成时体现动作的先后顺序
- be amazed = very surprised 非常吃惊
- be deeply moved 被深深地感动了
- must have done sth. 对过去发生事情的肯定推测
- get the idea from... 从……中获得想法
- be inspired by 受到……的启发
- be obsessed with sth. / doing sth. 对……痴迷

★ Part 3

1 To what extent are expensive gifts important when giving presents?

示例回答

In certain countries, people *do* tend to value expensive gifts, sometimes a bit too much. People tend to care about brands and image and things like this. I think it's a bit much. Though I can see *the root of this is to* show respect to others, I think we should be very careful to not be too *materialistic*.

内容亮点

- do 为助动词，放在动词前加强语气。
- the root of this is to...引出原因，root 使用了修辞用法，表示"根源；背景"，常见搭配有 the root of the problem / matter / unhappiness / evil。
- materialistic *adj.* (caring more about money and possessions than anything else) 物质享乐主义的

2 Do you think that gift-giving habits and customs have changed since you were a child?

示例回答

I think that gifts have become generally more fancy and more expensive these days, and people care more about named brands and things like that. *Generally*, it depends on what is *fashionable at the time*. I *do* believe, however, that people have become way too *materialistic* in recent years, and I think this is a *shame*.

内容亮点

- generally *adv.* 普遍来说
- fashionable *adj.* 流行的
- at the time 在那时
- do 为助动词，放在动词前加强语气。
- materialistic *adj.* 物质享乐主义的
- shame *n.* （相当于 pity）令人遗憾的事

3 **Are there any items which are regarded as being inappropriate to give as gifts, and why?**

示例回答

In China, it's not good to give people clocks. Emmm, I can't *think of* anything else really. *Traditionally* people *were superstitious about* clocks because time could *symbolise* death, or time going by too quickly! Something like that. Actually, it's because the word "Zhong" for clock, sounds like the word for "end", like death being the end of life. I think that's the reason. I don't think people are so superstitious these days, *to be honest*.

内容亮点

- think of sth. 想起某事 / 物

- traditionally *adv.* 传统上

- be superstitious about sth. / doing sth. 对某事物 / 做某事心存迷信

  superstitious 是多音节单词，在口语回答时一定要注意其发音 [ˌsuːpəˈstɪʃəs]。

- symbolise = be the symbol of 象征着

- to be honest 意为 "老实说"，在句中的位置灵活。

4 **What kinds of attitudes do people have towards hand-made gifts today in society?**

示例回答

Generally, I think people don't really like receiving handmade gifts here. *I'm not sure* why. *I just think* that's the culture really, at least where I am from. *Perhaps if a child* makes something by hand for a family member or so, then this *will be appreciated* a lot. *But between older people*, giving hand-made gifts isn't really common or appreciated much.

内容亮点

- 示例回答使用了一连串词汇 / 短语表达对某事的不确定：I'm not sure... / I just think... / Perhaps...。

- 当一件事不能用 "Yes or No" 一概而论时，分类讨论是很好的选择。示例回答将问题中的 people 分为两类，用 if a child...和 But between older people...分别描述了不同的人群对于手工制作礼物的态度。

- will be appreciated 会被赏识和感谢

★ Part 2

3 Describe a photo you like which is placed in your room.
You should say:
　　　What it is about
　　　Where it is
　　　How you got it
And explain why you like it.

示例回答

There is a photo I really like and that is the photo of myself with my school mates, *well*, university mates, *I guess you'd say*, ...in Xi'an, *around* 2004. That's where I studied and graduated. Well, I like the photo because it *symbolises* a time in my life that *I see as the happiest I've ever had*. I had a great time in university and *enjoyed most of my classmates' company*.

The photo was taken outside of the main gate of the campus. It's a beautiful entrance way, actually, and we took the photo at the end of our final year, just after graduation. It's a custom that I think is pretty global. I mean most students all over the world do this – take photos of their classmates and with their classmates at the end of their university years. I also like this photo because this was one that my classmates and I took, and not the more formal or official one. It *features* only my best friends and best dorm mates and classmates. This makes it a bit more special and a bit more natural in my opinion. So, this photo is very meaningful to me and *reminds* me *of* a fantastic time in my life and makes me feel closer to my old friends from college.

Today, of course, things have changed quite a bit, because people all have smartphones with really great cameras and store all their photos online. In fact, because we can take so many photos, so easily and so quickly, it means that perhaps we *value* them a lot less than we did in the past, because they're not so precious. *This is one main reason why* I think that the traditional idea of the photo – one that you got printed out at a photo shop after you'd finished the camera roll – is a lot more *sentimental*, a lot more meaningful.

内容亮点

- 在口语表达中经常需要补充或更正信息，第一段首句中 with my school mates, well, university mates 有语气停顿，在 well 后对 school mates 进行更正；I guess you'd say, ...in Xi'an 在回忆中补充了地点，最后 around 2004 补充了时间。

- symbolise = be symbol of 象征着

- I see as the happiest I've ever had.

  描述过往经历或感受的常用句型：最高级/序数词 + I've ever + done，如：This is the second book that he read this month. / This is the best movie I've ever seen.

- enjoyed most of my classmates' company 喜欢和我的同学在一起

  enjoy sb.'s company = enjoy being with sb. 喜欢和某人在一起

  She enjoys her own company / being by herself when she is travelling. 她喜爱独自旅行。

- feature *v.* 以……为特色；由……主演；以……为主要组成

  相当于 have as a feature，常见搭配为 feature sb. / sth. (as sb. / sth.)

  The film features Cary Grant as a professor. 这部电影里卡里·格兰特饰演一位教授。

- remind sb. of sb. / sth. 让某人想起某人/某事；remind sb. to do sth. 提醒某人做某事

  You remind me of your father when you say that. 你说这样的话，使我想起了你的父亲。

  Can you remind me to buy a bottle of wine? 你能提醒我买一瓶葡萄酒吗？

- value (*v.*) = to think that sb. / sth. is important 重视，珍视

  表状态，不用于正在进行时；常见搭配有 value sb. / sth. (as sth.)，value sb. / sth. (for sth.)

  I really value him as a friend. 我真的把他视为好朋友。

- This is one main reason why + 表结果的句子

  类似的句型还有 The reason why + 结果句 + is that + 原因句

  The reason why I was late is that the traffic was terrible this morning.

- sentimental *adj.* 令人伤感的

★ Part 3

1 **What are some of the advantages and disadvantages of taking photos with smartphones compared to traditional cameras?**

示例回答

Well, of course, the convenience that smartphones offer is ***unrivalled***, basically. We can take photos, store them and edit them even. It's just fast, efficient and effortless, almost. I don't know anyone today that uses a "traditional camera" to be honest – maybe ***photographers***...yes, professional photographers usually use a proper camera, actually.

内容亮点

- unrivalled [ʌnˈraɪvld] *adj.* (formal) better or greater than any other 无与伦比的；无双的
- photographer [fəˈtɒɡrəfə(r)] *n.* 摄影师；重音在第二音节

  请对比以下两个词的重音：

  photograph [ˈfəʊtəɡrɑːf] 重音在第一音节

  photographic [ˌfəʊtəˈɡræfɪk] 重音在第三音节

- 本回答的亮点在于使用并列词或并列结构，如动宾并列：take photos, store them and edit them；形容词并列：fast, efficient and effortless。

2 **Some people think that painting and drawing are not important skills for children to learn in school. To what extent do you agree or disagree?**

示例回答

I kind of disagree because I think that creative skills like painting and drawing are very important. Children learn ***hand-eye coordination***, ***creative thinking*** and certain technical things about ***proportion*** and ***dimensions*** and ***perspective***, if they learn to draw or paint. These are important in developing our ***intelligence***, actually. So, I think it is important that children have art classes.

内容亮点

- hand-eye coordination 手眼协调能力
- creative thinking 创造性思维
- sense of proportion = sense of perspective 分寸感，权衡轻重的能力
- dimension *n.* 维度

  in two / three dimensions 二维 / 三维

- intelligence *n.* 智力

  a person of high / average / low intelligence 智力高的 / 一般的 / 低下的人

3 How do people become famous artists? To what extent is it through hard work and skill, and to what extent is it through relationships and connections?

示例回答

Well, to become a famous artist you have to have some talent, *to start with*. And *apart from* talent, to be honest, you need to usually have good *connections*, wealthy connections, important connections and the ability to market yourself... *yes to sell yourself*. Part of being a famous person in any way is how you market yourself.

内容亮点

- to start with 意为"首先"，在口语中可放于句子前，也可以放在句尾，起补充作用。
- apart from 相当于 besides，在回答中表示除了天赋还需要具备其他条件。
- connection = personal tie，意为"人脉，人际关系"，回答提到了"良好的人脉""丰富的人脉"和"重要的人脉"。
- ...yes to sell yourself 用同义替换的方式对前文的 to market yourself 进行了再次确认，常用来补充或强调信息。

★ Part 2

4 Describe a thing you bought and felt pleased about.
You should say:
  What you bought
  Where you bought it
  What it is for
And explain why you felt pleased about it.

示例回答

Something I bought and felt really happy with is a new bike. I love cycling and I'm a member of a cycling club and we go out every weekend outside of the city to the amazing countryside there on long bike rides as a big group. I *used to* have a mountain bike with big tyres which I really liked, *but I recently changed* it for a road bike with a *slimmer* frame and tyres, and it's amazing.

I bought it online, actually, after reading a lot of *reviews* and taking advice from friends. It was from a fairly famous and reliable online site. *I feel really good about this purchase because* it's such a great bike, so much easier to ride and so much better on the roads. It's dark grey and looks quite cool actually. It's also a very good and famous brand of bike, so I am sure it's pretty good quality and will last a really long time. The brakes are *top of the range* and the *gears* are a special type of gears that cyclists use for all sorts of different *terrain*, from steep mountain roads to very flat city streets. It's good to have this level of control when you are cycling on all sorts of different types of roads, in and outside of the city. The seat is also a special design which enables the air to flow through it so you don't sweat or get too hot when you are cycling *uphill*.

Generally speaking, *I am usually pleased with things that I buy because* I almost always put a lot of effort into reading reviews of things, and comparing them, and asking friends, before I actually *take the leap* to buying a product. I think if you *employ* this careful *approach* to purchasing things, you'll usually *end up* being pleased with what you've bought.

So, *all in all*, I'm really pleased with this purchase, and I am happy I took the time and energy and money to invest in a really good quality bike. It makes my weekends with the cycling club a lot more enjoyable, to be honest, and it's always nice to buy new things related to a hobby you have.

内容亮点

- I used to..., but I recently changed...是一个典型的过去和现在对比的表达，前半句的核心短语为 used to ＋动词原型，后半句的时间为 recently（不久前），所以用 change 的过去式表达在不久前发生的动作。
- slim *adj.* thinner than usual 单薄的

  a slim volume of poetry 一本薄薄的诗集
- review *n.* 评论

  a book / play / film / exhibition / music review 书评 / 剧评 / 影评 / 展评 / 乐评
- I feel really good about this purchase because 和下一段 I am usually pleased with things that I buy because 句型相近，都是先表达心情再说出原因。
- top of the range （同类产品中）顶级的，最好的
- gear *n.* 排挡；齿轮；传动装置
- terrain *n.* [地理] 地形，地势

  fertile / infertile terrain 肥沃 / 贫瘠的土地
- uphill *adv.* 朝上坡方向
- take the leap to doing sth. 采取行动

  When you actually take the leap to building your own business, there are other things that you have to consider. 当你真正开始采取行动创业时，你还需要考虑其他一些事情。
- employ...approach 意为"采用这种方法"，回答中 if you employ this careful approach to purchasing things 的意思是"如果你用这种谨慎的方法购买东西"。
- end up doing sth. 意为"以……而告终"，回答中 you'll usually end up being pleased with what you've bought 的意思是"你通常会对你买的东西感到满意"。
- So, all in all 为常用引导词，用于全文收尾总结。

★ Part 3

1 How often do people in your country go shopping?

示例回答

It varies. Some people are *avid shoppers* and spend so much of their free time buying and ordering things online. Others *are not really into* shopping *at all*, and actually dislike it. I'm a bit like this to be honest. Of course, there is also a difference between necessary shopping for the home, *domestic* products, food and things like this, and shopping for clothes or even *accessories*. Some people love both! Especially now things can be bought so easily online and delivered to the home.

内容亮点

- It varies 是频率题的常见开场白，下面可分情况讨论：Some people.... Others...。
- avid shoppers 狂热购物者

  avid 作为形容词通常置于名词前，表达对某事的极度热情，如 an avid reader / collector。
- be into sth. 对某事很有兴趣
- not 后面加 at all 可加强语气，表示完全没兴趣。
- domestic *adj.* 国内的；家庭的

  domestic products 有双重含义，既可以指国产产品，又可以指家庭用品，本文指后者。
- accessory *n.* 配件

  a range of furnishings and accessories for the home 各种各样的家居装饰物及配件

2 Why is online shopping popular?

示例回答

Online shopping *makes the shopping experience much easier*. It's simple to order things online, pay online and receive your shopping *at the door* rather than going around *multiple* stores. Traffic in cities in my country is quite bad, so online shopping helps us avoid the traffic and crowds and *makes life more convenient*. It has become *incredibly* popular in recent years, for these reasons.

内容亮点

- at the door 在门口
- multiple *adj.* 数量多的；多种多样的

  a multiple entry visa 多次入境签证；a multiple birth 多胎产；a multiple pile-up 连环车祸
- 本文出现了两次 make + *n.* + *adj.* 的形式，表达了 online shopping 给人们带来的便利。
- incredibly *adv.* 难以置信地；非常地

3 How should sellers set prices for their products?

示例回答

I don't know to be honest. I don't know much about this side of business management. There are different ways of setting prices for things, *as far as I'm aware*. Proper methods of pricing strategy include *whereby* you compare what other people sell things for, *in terms of* quality, design and price and then you *price* your own products according to the market in order to attempt to be as competitive as possible while still ensuring you *make a profit*.

内容亮点

- 示例回答在一开始就连用 I don't know to be honest. I don't know much about...和...as far as I'm aware

表达自己对定价的方式的确不了解。但在回答雅思口语问题时，最好不要答完不知道就中止对话，可以补充合理的猜测，说出自己的理解。

- whereby *adv.* 凭此；借以；由于

  相当于 by which 和 because of which

- in terms of 依据；在……方面

- price *v.* 给……定价

  常用搭配：price sth. (at sth.)

  The tickets are priced at $100 each. 每张票定价 100 元。

- make a profit 获利；赚钱

4 **Do you think online shopping will replace shopping in real stores?**

示例回答

I think *to a great extent* this has already happened, but I still think that people enjoy going to malls and enjoy the experience of shopping *in a physical setting*, let's say, *compared to* an online one. People still like *browsing* through stores, trying on clothes and accessories and choosing things they see. Also, we often *stop off* at a café or restaurant when out shopping, which *makes it an experience*, *a day out*, you could say. And this is something that is nice to do with others.

内容亮点

- to a great extent 在很大程度上

  同义表达有：to a great degree / to a large extent

- in a physical setting 在现实环境中

- compared to 常用于引出对比对象

  The room was light and lofty compared to the basement. 这个房间与地下室比起来更亮更高。

- browse a store / through stores = to look at a lot of things in a shop / store rather than looking for one particular thing （在商店里）随便看看

- stop off 意为"中途停留"，英文释义为"If you stop off somewhere, you stop for a short time in the middle of a trip."。

- make it an experience 让它成为一种体验

- a day out 一日游

★ Part 2

5 Describe an art or craft activity you have done.

You should say:

　　When this happened

　　What you did in the activity

　　Who you did it with

And explain how you felt about this activity.

示例回答

An art activity that I did that I think is particularly interesting is ***pottery***. I had never done pottery before, until about a year ago, maybe actually just last summer, my friend Adam, who was a young Swedish student studying at Xi'an Normal University, said that he had found ***a craft workshop*** not far from the Big Wild Goose Pagoda, on a street of tea and art shops. I ***went along with*** him, ***thinking it was a bit of a strange idea***, but kind of interesting and fun.

The workshop was full of potter's wheels, and had a few instructors there. A potter's wheel is basically a kind of seat, ***attached to*** a ***fairly*** big ***metal bucket*** with a metal ***disc wheel***. There is ***a pipe of running water*** which you can control to some extent, and you get ***a huge lump of clay*** on the wheel. You use your feet to push the ***pedals*** which then make the wheel ***spin around***. As the wheel spins around, and you are seated on the little seat in front of it, you can ***mould*** the lump of clay into a round shape. That's how you make a vase or a pot or any round ***vessel***. ***It's pretty hard to explain***! Anyway, myself and Adam did this for ***about an hour or so***, with the instructor giving us advice about how to mould the clay, how fast to make the wheel go round and things like this. After we had made a round ball, which was almost ***perfect in form***, he taught us how to use our fingers to create a hole in the middle, and then taught us how to use these small metal tools to shape the designs and patterns into the clay. It was pretty difficult to be honest, and the end result was...***let's say***...a bit ***amateur***.

After that, we painted the pots with ***a clear glaze*** and they then went into a big oven called a ***kiln***. The kiln bakes the pots until they are completely dry and hard. This usually takes a couple of days on a slow heat, so we had to go back later in the week to check our pots. I felt that this was really fun and I'd like to do it again and develop a bit more skill and try to get better results.

内容亮点

- pottery *n.* 陶器（尤指手工制的）
- a craft workshop 一个工艺品店
- 回答的第二句话通过使用大量插入语和定语对主干信息进行了补充。全句主干是 "I had never done pottery before, until my friend Adam said that he had found a craft workshop." 。句中的 about a year ago, maybe actually just last summer 是时间，who was a young Swedish student studying at Xi'an Normal University 补充了 Adam 的身份，not far from the Big Wild Goose Pagoda, on a street of tea and art shops 是工艺品店的位置。
- go along with 赞同；陪……一起
- thinking it was a bit of a strange idea 现在分词 thinking 引导的句子作主句的伴随状语
  a bit of a strange idea 有点奇怪的想法
- be attached to / attach sth. to sth. 把……固定；把……附在……上
- fairly *adv.* 相当地
- mental bucket 金属桶
  bucket 前面可加表用途或材料的词，比如 ice bucket 冰桶、plastic bucket 塑料桶。
- disc wheel 圆盘轮；碟形砂轮
- pipe *n.* 管道

a pipe of running water 一根流水管

- a huge lump of clay 一大块黏土

- pedal *n.* （车辆，乐器的）踏板

- spin *v.* to turn round and round quickly （使）快速旋转

- mould *v.* 塑造 *n.* 模具

- vessel *n.* (a container used for holding liquids, such as a bowl, cup, etc.)（盛液体的）容器，器皿

- It's pretty hard to explain! 这很难解释！

- about an hour or so 大约一小时左右

  about 加在数字前，or so 加在数字后，都有"大约"之意。

- perfect in form 外形完美

- let's say 比如说（用作插入语）

- amateur ['æmətə(r)] *n.* 外行；生手

- a clear glaze 一种透明的釉

- kiln [kɪln] *n.* （砖，石灰等的）窑；炉；干燥炉

★ Part 3

1 What kinds of handicrafts are popular in China?

示例回答

Handicrafts are especially popular at *craft markets* and at tourist sites. Depending on which region of the country or which town you might be in, you'll see different arts and crafts famous in that area. But ones that are common all over the country are *calligraphy works*, *jade jewelry* and *figurines*, traditional paintings, *ink drawings*, *paper cuts*, and *shadow puppets* made of leather...painted...and well, a lot of different things really. These kinds of things, today, *are mainly of interest to* tourists, as *souvenirs*, but there are also a growing number of Chinese people who are *looking back* to the traditional arts with interest, and collecting ancient and traditional crafts and *antiques*.

内容亮点

- handicraft *n.* 手工艺品

- craft market 工艺品市场

- calligraphy work 书法作品

  work 指"著作，作品（a book，piece of music，painting 等）"时，为可数名词。

- jade jewelry 玉石珠宝

- figurine *n.* 雕像；雕刻工艺品

- ink drawing 墨水画

- paper cut 剪纸

- shadow puppet 皮影

- A is / are mainly of interest to B A 主要吸引 B

- souvenir *n.* 纪念品
- look back 意为"回顾，回忆，回想"，英文释义为"If you look back, you think about things that happened in the past."。
- antique *n.* 古玩，古董

② Do many people make handicrafts in China?

示例回答

I think there are still a lot of people in China that make crafts, yes. I'd say there are two types of *craftsmen*: those that make lesser quality crafts for souvenir and tourist markets, and those that make high quality traditional crafts for *discerning* Chinese people who are *collectors or enthusiasts*. An example of the latter would be the people who make the Cha Zhou teapots, *purple clay teapots*. There is *a fine art* to making a perfectly crafted Chinese clay teapot, and the people that make them *pass down* this skill *from generation to generation*. People who *genuinely* love and understand Chinese tea will see the value of a good teapot, not just as an *aesthetically* beautiful item, but a *functional* one, and part of the beauty of preparing and making Chinese tea *in the proper fashion*.

内容亮点

- craftsman *n.* 工匠；手艺人
- discerning *adj.* (able to show good judgement about the quality of sb. / sth.) 有辨识能力的；眼光敏锐的
- collectors or enthusiasts 收藏家和爱好者
- purple clay teapot 紫砂茶壶
- a fine art 一门精致的艺术
- pass down from generation to generation 代代相传
- genuinely *adv.* 真诚地；诚实地
- aesthetically *adv.* 审美地；美学观点上地
- functional *adj.* 实用的
- in the proper fashion 以适当的方式

③ Why do many people send handicrafts as gifts?

示例回答

To be honest, I don't think many people do send handicrafts to people as gifts these days. At least *barely* anyone I know. People I know tend to send people more modern things that they've bought online, technology stuff, *fashion accessories*, things like this. I guess some people might send jewellery or things like this, perhaps items that have been given to them by other family members. I'm unsure, but most people, unless especially into these kinds of crafts, don't really send them to others as gifts.

内容亮点

- 示例回答采用了总分总的结构。先表明态度：现如今人们不怎么将手工艺品作为礼物送人；再给出原因：人们倾向于送其他类型的礼物；最后总结：除了对手工艺品情有独钟的人，大多数人不

会送别人这样的礼物。

- barely *adv.* 几乎不；几乎没有

- fashion accessory 时尚饰品；流行配件

★ Part 2

6 Describe a book you read that you found useful.
You should say:
What it is
When and where you read it
Why you think it is useful
And explain how you feel about this book.

示例回答

A book I found *exceedingly* useful in my studies seems quite a serious book actually, I have to say. It was a book on English grammar, by a man called Michael Swan, a famous *grammarian*. I know it sounds a bit boring, really, but it's been so helpful to me for so many years, I *swear by it* as a key resource in my language study. It was given to me by a foreign teacher at university.

It's a *hugely* useful book, as it is organised and *laid out* in quite a logical way, quite different from other grammar books I've seen. It's really easy to find what you want in it, and the explanations and examples are *incredibly* clear. I used it a lot when I was writing essays, actually, because I was often unsure how to use certain aspects of English grammar, or *in doubt* if I was using them correctly. For example, the use of "would" to be "used to" is something that used to confuse me, so I remember *looking up* "would" in the *index* of the book and finding numerous examples of the usage, not just *the conditional usage*, but its usage in terms of meaning "used to", or "usually" in the past tense. From the examples in the book, I quickly *grasped the difference* in the different uses of "would" in the English language. This is just one example of many times I've used this book to check or *clarify* English language use in my studies. Also, *at times*, the book *verges on* quite humourous explanations which add *a touch of uniqueness*, and helps you to remember some of the grammar points better. I think this technique is very good and *underused* by most writers of grammar explanations and texts.

I feel very happy that my teacher gave me this book as a leaving present when I moved on to another year, and it has helped me *immensely*. I've often lent it to classmates and colleagues and they always say that it's the best grammar book they've seen. It's not cheap to buy though, so I try to look after it and make sure that whoever I lend it to, gives it back to me!

内容亮点

- exceedingly *adv.* 极其地，非常地

  "极其地"表达在文中共出现四次，分别是：exceedingly、hugely、incredibly 和 immensely。

- grammarian *n.* 语法学家

- swear by it 极其信赖，仅用于口语表达

85

- lay out (design of magazines, pages or advertisements) 版面设计

  The volume is attractively designed and laid out. 这卷书的设计排版很吸引人。

- in doubt 不确定

- look up (look sth. up, look up sth.) 查找

- index *n.* 索引；复数形式为 indexes or indices

- the conditional usage 条件（句）用法

- grasp *v.* (to understand sth. completely) 理解；grasped the difference in... 理解……的不同

- clarify *v.* (to make sth. clearer or easier to understand) 使更清晰易懂；澄清

- at times 意为"有时"，通常位于句首或句尾。

- verge on (to be very close to an extreme state or condition) 极接近

  Some of his suggestions verged on the outrageous. 他的一些建议都快到了荒唐的地步。

- a touch of uniqueness 独特之处

  a touch of 有一点，轻微

  She just had a touch of the flu. 她只是有点感冒。

- underused *adj.* not used as much as it could or should be 未充分利用的

★ Part 3

1 **What kind of books do young people like to read nowadays?**

示例回答

Young people tend to read a lot of *adventure stories* I think. Well, it really depends on the age, really. I'm talking about teenagers. I think teenagers like the more modern adventure heroes like the characters in *Marvel Comics* and films. There are *quite a few stories of this nature* which are popular. *Harry Potter* has become internationally hugely famous too, and a lot of young people, young people of all ages, in fact, *have got really into Harry Potter*, both in the original English language versions and also in the Chinese translations. I'd say these probably are the most popular books for young people today. They *capture* all the *elements* young people like: adventure, school drama, magic and *fantasy*!

内容亮点

- adventure story 冒险片
- Marvel Comics 漫威漫画

  Marvel Comics 是一家美国的漫画公司，创建于 1939 年，旗下拥有蜘蛛侠、钢铁侠、美国队长、雷神托尔、绿巨人、神奇四侠、X 战警、恶灵骑士等 8000 多个漫画角色。

- quite a few 不少的，相当多的
- stories of this nature 这类故事
- have got really into 变得非常喜欢
- capture *v.* (to film / record / paint, etc. sb. / sth.) 拍摄；录制；绘制

常用于被动语态：The incident was captured on videotape. 这一事件被拍摄下来。

- element *n.* 元素；要素
- fantasy *n.* 幻想

2 **Some people believe that if children read more books, they may become more successful in the future. What's your opinion?**

示例回答

I think that reading is definitely good for young people as it not only expands their vocabulary in their own language and in a foreign language they're studying, but also helps to improve their understanding of people, *human interactions*, relationships and situations in daily life. Reading is something that also helps to focus the mind, improve concentration and *self-discipline*, and so there are *a combination of reasons* why I think that reading could *contribute to* people becoming more successful *in the long-term*.

内容亮点

- human interaction 人际交往

  相近的表达还有 interpersonal communication
- self-discipline *n.* 自律

  It takes a lot of self-discipline to go jogging in winter. 在冬天跑步需要很强的自律力。
- a combination of reasons 意为 "一系列的原因，种种原因"，combination 本意为 "混合物"。
- contribute to sth. 有助于……
- in the long-term 从长远来看，长期内

  类似的表达还有 in the short-term / medium-term，意为 "短 / 中期内"。long-term、medium-term、short-term 中的连字符可删除，等同于 long term、medium term 和 short term。

3 **What's the value of museums?**

示例回答

It really depends. Museums are useful to a degree. They can be incredibly boring too. I think that if you visit a museum with a group or class from school and you have some tasks to accompany the visit, things to look out for, things to read and do small projects on, then they can be useful and *educational*. *However*, if you just walk around a museum *aimlessly* looking at *artefacts and relics*, it can be quite *tedious*, especially if you have no idea what you're looking at or don't have a guide or *can't be bothered to* read a bit about what you're seeing. I think the greatest value in museums is when they are designed to be interesting, have *interactive exhibits* and make learning about history fun and *entertaining*.

内容亮点

- However 将本题的回答分成了两个部分。前半部分的重点是 educational（有教育意义的），后半部分是 tedious（单调乏味的），最后再用一句话描述了自己心目中有价值的博物馆应有的模样。
- aimlessly *adv.* 漫无目的地

drift along aimlessly 混日子；talk aimlessly 说话东拉西扯

- artefact *n.* （尤指有历史或文化价值的）手工艺品
- relic *n.* 遗迹；遗骸；纪念物
- can't be bothered to do sth. 懒得做某事
- interactive exhibit 互动式展览
- entertaining *adj.* 令人愉快的

  an entertaining speech / evening 妙趣横生的演讲；令人开心的夜晚

4 **Should museums be replaced by the Internet?**

示例回答

Absolutely not. We cannot do everything in our lives online. That actually kills our focus and imagination. Museums are *physical spaces* that we can walk around with other people, and see things directly, not just on a screen. I would always *promote* the improvement of museums and not the replacement of them with online versions. It's important that we keep real artefacts and relics from the history of the world in museums, also to preserve them. And letting *the general public* go in and see these on display is a lot more meaningful than simply putting these things on show online. *However* advanced society becomes, seeing a famous or important historical object in real life is much more interesting than seeing it *in the form of* a photo or video on a website.

内容亮点

- physical space 意为"物理 / 实体空间"，主要对应虚拟空间（virtual space）。
- promote *v.* (to help sth. to happen or develop) 促进；推动

  在本文中与 encourage 的意思相近
- the general public 普通大众
- However 在文中并非表示转折，而是引导状语从句，相当于 no matter how，意思是"无论怎样"。
- in the form of 以……的形式

★ Part 2

7 Describe a film you would like to share with your friends.

You should say:

    Where you watched it

    What it was about

    Who you watched it with

And explain why you want to share it with friends.

示例回答

I watch a lot of films, actually, but the one I want to share with my friends the most is *My Neighbour Totoro*, by Miyazaki, the Japanese director. I love this movie. In fact, I've always enjoyed the film – it **came out** when I was a child and I **used to** watch it with my father at home.

The film is about a father and his two daughters who move to a countryside house **whilst** their mother is in a hospital in a nearby town. The two daughters explore their new home, an old **rickety house**, and the surrounding countryside, fields and **woodlands**, and go to a local school, while the father, who is a university professor, I think, gets the bus every day into the city to teach. One weekend, the girls find an especially large tree in the woodland and a really large cute and magical animal that they call "Totoro". Totoro is a very kind, **sympathetic** and special creature and he lives in a sort of different world to ours, a world that only children can see and interact with.

I love the films of this director and I find the **artwork**, the cartoons, amazingly drawn and of really high quality. The stories are really **touching** and always carry a positive message. They are emotional, and they are **true-to-life** in so many ways, although they **have strong elements of** fantasy and magic in them.

Generally, I watch a lot of films, especially during the holidays. I've always been a big fan of cinema, and not just **animation films** like this one, but a whole range of **genres**. I think that films can teach us a lot about the culture and are often great expressions of human experience – suffering, love, death, relationships and adventure. Films **capture** some of **the real essences of life**, and present them in often exciting and moving ways, usually with a message that we can **take away**, reflect on and learn something from. So, I believe that this film, *My Neighbour Totoro*, **ticks a lot of boxes**. I mean it **fulfills**, at least for me, all the main **criteria** that a good, quality and moving film should fulfill. I'd say this is why I would definitely like to share this film with friends and **recommend** that everyone watch it.

内容亮点

- come out 意为 be produced，与 book、film 或 CD 搭配时，意为"出版，发行"。
- use to do sth. 过去常常做某事
- whilst *conj.* 在……期间

  与 while 的意思和用法相同，较正式
- rickety house 摇摇晃晃的房子

  rickety *adj.* (not strong or well made; likely to break) 不结实的；不稳固的；易折断的
- woodland(s) *n.* 林地

  ancient woodland 原始林区；an area of dense woodland 一片茂密的林区
- sympathetic *adj.* (~ to / towards sb.) 有同情心的
- artwork *n.* （尤指博物馆里的）艺术作品
- touching *adj.* 动人的
- true-to-life *adj.* 自然逼真的

  The naturalness of the dialogue made the book so true to life. 自然逼真的对话使得这本书非常贴近生活。
- have strong elements of 有强烈的……元素

- animation film 动画片
- genres *n.* 流派；种类（genre ['ʒɒrə] 的复数形式）
- capture *v.* 拍摄；录制；to capture sb. / sth. on film / tape 用胶片 / 磁带记录某人 / 某事
- the real essences of life 生命的真正本质
- take away 带走，拿走
- ticks a lot of boxes 字面意思为"打了很多个勾"，延伸意思是"对某事非常满意"。
- fulfill *v.* 满足，与 satisfy 同义
- criteria [kraɪ'tɪəriə] *n.* 标准，条件（criterion 的复数形式）
- recommend *v.* 推荐

  recommend sb. / sth. (to sb.) 向某人推荐某人 / 某事

★ Part 3

1 **Why do you think that older people like different types of films than young people?**

示例回答

Older people *have been brought up* in different times. They, therefore, relate to different things, different types of people, topics, relationships *and so forth*. So, *naturally*, they like different types of films too.

内容亮点

- 首句直接给出原因，之后使用 therefore 和 so 层层推进，引出结果。
- be brought up 意为"被养大"，是 bring up 的被动形式。
- and so forth 意为"等等"，相当于 and so on。
- naturally *adv.* 自然地

2 **Do you think with the advances in computer graphics (CGI), films today are becoming less intelligent, more focused on action and special effects than real stories?**

示例回答

Yes, personally I think that a lot of modern movies are quite weak in terms of *plot and storyline*, because a lot of *emphasis* is placed *on* expensive *graphics* and special effects. We tend to like things that are *a visual sensation* these days, and pay less attention to good stories and dialogue. I think it is *a bit of a shame*.

内容亮点

- CGI (Computer Graphics Interface) 电脑图像界面
- plot and storyline （小说、戏剧、电影等的）故事情节
- emphasis *n.* 重点，强调

  常见搭配有 emphasis on / upon sth.，复数形式为 emphases
- graphics *n.* 图像
- sensation *n.* 感觉，知觉；a visual sensation 视觉感受
- a bit of a shame 有点遗憾

3 **What are the reasons why people might choose to go to watch a film in the cinema rather than at home?**

示例回答

It's obvious! Watching a film in the cinema is a totally different experience than sitting at home watching the TV. There's a huge screen. You're sitting there in the dark, and there is amazing surround sound. You really feel like you are "inside" the movie – it's not only more *realistic*, but also a *dramatic* experience. It's also nicer to go to the cinema with a boyfriend or girlfriend.

内容亮点

- realistic *adj.* 逼真的；a realistic drawing 逼真的绘画
- dramatic *adj.* (exciting and impressive) 激动人心的

4 **What are some of the challenges famous actors might face in public life?**

示例回答

Oh many. In fact, personally, I would not want to be a famous person because public life is basically *non-existent* for them! Haha. What I mean is that everything a famous person does must be *in private*, or *accompanied by* bodyguards. A famous person can't go to bars, restaurants or go shopping like a normal person. People will always bother you, try to take photographs, even *come over* to talk to you or try to touch you.

内容亮点

- non-existent *adj.* 不存在的
- in private 秘密地；私下地
- be accompanied by 由······陪同

  Children under 15 years are free and must be accompanied by an adult. 15 岁以下儿童无须买票，但需在成人的陪同下（参观）。

- come over 走近

  She came over to my desk. 她走到我的桌子旁。

★ Part 2

> **8** Describe an article about health that you have read in a magazine or on the internet.
> You should say:
>> What it was about
>> Where you read it
>> Why you read it
> And explain how you felt about it.

示例回答

I read an article about health on the Internet *fairly recently* actually. It was all about going to the gym. I *paid particular attention to* it because I am thinking of starting to go to the gym. The article was all about different types of training that you can do in the gym, to *develop* different *muscles* in the body as well as get good *cardiovascular exercise* for the heart and blood system. I was sort of interested in what it had to say because I don't really know what to do in a gym, or what the best exercise *regimen* is to suit my needs. I don't really want to develop very strong muscles or anything like that, but I do want to *get more fit*, healthier, and develop some strength in my arms and legs.

Anyway, I talked about the article I read with a friend of mine, whose English name is Troy. He worked many years in a gym as *a personal trainer*, and he said that if you are serious about getting fit and healthy, it's a good idea to get a personal trainer. He also explained that a personal trainer is also a *motivator* – he or she can help you *keep to your routine*, push you harder when you need to be motivated, and advise you how best to use the different machines and equipment in the gym so that you don't injure yourself but exercise your body in the best, most effective way.

So I thought that the article was fairly useful, but frankly, I think that I got better and more useful advice from my friend Troy. Perhaps I could say that the article gave me a good reason to talk to Troy...it *inspired* me *to* talk to Troy... So that was the real benefit of having read this article, actually.

内容亮点

- fairly recently 最近

  fairly *adv.* 用在形容词和副词前，比 very 程度低一些

  a fairly easy book 一本相当浅易的书

  I know him fairly well, but I wouldn't say we were really close friends. 我相当了解他，但并不是说我们是真正的密友。

- pay particular attention to 特别关注

- develop one's muscles 锻炼肌肉

  Already it is known that bones, muscles and nerves develop faster in baby girls. 众所周知，女婴的骨骼、肌肉和神经发育得更快。

- cardiovascular exercise 有氧运动

- regimen *n.* (A regiment is a set of rules about food and exercise that some people follow in order to stay healthy.) 生活规则，养生之道

  exercise regimen 运动方式

- get more fit 变得更健康

- Anyway (well) 在句中被用作副词，无明确意义

  Anyway, let's forget about that for a moment. 好吧，咱们暂时别再提这件事了。

- a personal trainer 一位私人教练

- motivator *n.* 激励者

- keep to one's routine 按常规行事

- inspire sb. to sth. 赋予某人做某事的灵感

★ Part 3

1 **What type of exercise do people in your country often do?**

示例回答

It depends on what types of people you're talking about. People exercise in different ways. Older people often go to the park, do some dancing or use these simple exercise machines in their communities. Young people do all sorts – they go to the gym, they play basketball, football or other *competitive sports*. Other people like to go jogging or cycling. There are lots of popular activities that people do here – pretty much the same as anywhere in the world.

内容亮点

- It depends on what types of people you're talking about. 这取决于你说的是哪种人。
  首句引出下文的分类讨论，将人群划分为 older people 和 young people，年轻人根据兴趣爱好不同，又分成了 some people 和 other people。
- competitive sports 竞技体育

2 **What kind of exercise or physical education do students do in school?**

示例回答

In school, kids learn to do some basic *gym exercises*. They play some football and ball games and they do running. That's pretty much it, really. They don't tend to do a lot of interesting or challenging *physical activities* in schools where I am from, to be honest.

内容亮点

- gym exercises (physical exercises done in a gym, especially at school) 尤指学校的体育活动
- physical activities 体育活动

3 **Do you think children should receive education in school about keeping fit and healthy and eating healthily?**

示例回答

Well, to some extent, yes. I think that they should definitely have *physical education classes* in school, and as a part of those classes, they should also be taught the *basics* of *maintaining a good and healthy diet* and learn about where food comes from and how it's important to avoid eating too many sweets and things like this.

内容亮点

- physical education classes (PE classes) 体育课
- basics *n.* 基本要素（basic 的复数形式）
- maintain a good and healthy diet 保持良好和健康的饮食

4 **What kind of things can the government do to improve health education, awareness and improve the health of the nation in general?**

示例回答

The government should *ensure* that people have at least a basic education about keeping fit and healthy. Also, they should *make sure* that factories that make food, as well as farms and places that produce food, *adhere* very strictly *to* food safety and *hygiene regulations*. Frankly, they have been far too relaxed and perhaps a bit corrupt about this in the past, and I am happy to say that this, I think, is changing – but there is still work to be done and the government should make sure that standards are set and *enforced* more strictly. *The same goes for* the standards of air quality. They need to be stricter about this because cities today are too polluted and the long-term effects of this are not good for people.

内容亮点

- ensure *v.* 担保，保证

  与下文中的 make sure 意思相近

- adhere to sth. 坚持，遵守，遵循（法律、规章、指示、信念等）

  For ten months he adhered to a strict no-fat low-salt diet. 十个月来他严格坚持无脂肪少盐的饮食。

- hygiene *n.* 卫生

  food hygiene 食品卫生；personal hygiene 个人卫生

- regulations 条例，法规（regulation 的复数形式）

- enforce *v.* 强制实施

  常与 law、regulation、policy 搭配使用

- The same goes for... 同样适用于……

★ Part 2

9 Describe a piece of good news you received.

You should say:

When you received it

Where you received it

What the news was about

And explain how you felt about it after you received it.

示例回答

Some good news that I got recently was the news that my grandmother had *recovered* from a fairly serious illness. She has been ill, *on and off*, for a number of years, but this time she was really sick. I do not know exactly what the medical problem was, but it was quite serious and she had to *be admitted to hospital* for over a week. I was really worried because she's pretty old, and as we all know, the older you are, the more difficult it is to deal with serious illness and the harder it is to make a good, *speedy recovery*.

Anyway, after a week or so, she had an *operation*, and the doctors called us to inform us that it had gone really well and she had *healed* better than expected, and she was allowed to come home. This was great news and I *felt massively relieved* too, because, if I'm honest, there was a point when I thought she might die. So, it was a big day when we received this news and it made me really happy.

We prepared a big meal and organised and cleaned the house, and made it as *cozy* as possible for her return. I think hearing the news of a family member's recovery is probably one of the best types of good news a person can receive.

It seems that today we only usually hear bad news or negative news, at least in a lot of media, so I think we should *cherish* every moment that we receive some good news about a friend, family member, a work colleague or some story we have heard that is positive. Good news can help us feel better about life, and *give us faith in ourselves and human nature*. We sometimes forget the positive value of hearing and passing on good news! We really should treasure it!

内容亮点

- recover *v.* 恢复健康；康复；痊愈

  下文的 recovery 是它的名词形式，speedy recovery 意为"快速康复"。
- on and off 断断续续的
- be admitted to hospital 住院

  be admitted to university 被大学录取；be admitted to 获准进入某地
- operation *n.* 手术
- heal *v.* （使）康复，复原；治愈（病人）

  heal the breach / rift 填平裂痕
- feel massively relieved 感到如释重负
- cozy *adj.* 舒适的（也可以写成 cosy）
- cherish *v.* 珍爱；钟爱；爱护
- give us faith in ourselves and human nature 让我们相信自己和人性

★ Part 3

1 **When do companies usually publicise new information to the public?**

示例回答

Companies usually *publicise* new information when they have a new product out. They usually do some kind of *press release* or something like that. It's important that companies maintain a good relationship with the press and media and whenever there is a big change, like an *IPO* or a *new product launch*, or a take-over or a new CEO or something like this, they usually make some kind of *external announcement* to the public. Usually in the form of a *press conference*, an article in a newspaper or even a TV presentation. Apple is quite famous for giving quite big conferences before the launch of the latest model of iPhone or another key product, for example. This is what a lot of big companies usually do today.

内容亮点

- publicise *v.* 宣传，宣扬；公布
- press release / press conference 新闻发布会

  这里的 press 并不是动词按压的意思，而是另外一个比较常用的意思：媒体、新闻界。
- IPO（公司股票的）首次公开发行，上市

  IPO 全称是 Initial Public Offerings，中文释义是首次公开募股，指的是一家企业或公司（股份有限公司）第一次将它的股份向公众出售。
- new product launch 新产品发布；launch *v./n.*（首次）上市，发行
- external announcement 外部公告

② Should companies release news online or in a press conference?

示例回答

Companies should *ideally* do both, as far as I'm aware. It's not a subject I know *an awful lot* about really, because I don't really *follow* much business and tech *news*, but I think that most companies often do both. They have some quite fancy and *elaborate* press conferences and events, as well as sometimes huge *promotions* on and off line. I think there is a lot of *competition* these days, too, which means that companies are increasingly aware that they have to have a range of marketing activities to *keep their brand name high profile* in potential customers' minds. Press conferences are important because that's when lots of journalists from key *media outlets* are invited and then those journalists go off and write articles, accompanied by high quality photos, and that helps to promote a company's activities and new developments to the general public.

内容亮点

- ideally *adv.* 理想地
- awful *adj.* 非常的，很多的

  an awful lot 大量的，很多的
- follow news 关注新闻
- elaborate *adj.* 复杂的；详尽的；精心制作的
- promotion *n.* 促销活动；广告宣传
- competition *n.* 比赛，竞争
- keep their brand name high profile 保持他们的品牌知名度；high profile 高调，高姿态
- media outlet 媒体机构

  outlet *n.* 从事大众媒体行业的公司

③ When do we share good news with friends?

示例回答

People often share good news with friends through *a variety of means. It really depends on entirely what kind of good news it is, when it comes and who it involves*. Some good news is communicated by *text message*, some good news by a phone call. Other people, for example, if they are going to get married or something major like that, might actually arrange a big dinner with friends or family and then make a more formal *announcement* at that dinner – almost as a sort of surprise. This sometimes happens, too. So, it entirely depends on the kind of good news that we're talking about, and how it affects the individuals.

内容亮点

* a variety of means 各种各样的方法
* It really depends on entirely what kind of good news it is, when it comes and who it involves. 这取决于是什么样的好消息、什么时候接到的消息以及与谁有关。
* text message 短信
* announcement *n.* 通知

4 How would you like to receive good news?

示例回答

Again, it depends on the news. I'm a fairly *laid-back* person, so *frankly* I don't really *stand on ceremony* much – I'm happy to receive good news by phone, or by text, but generally I prefer to hear some really good news, especially if it's *sentimental* or romantic, *face-to-face*. *Like for example* when my friend announced his *engagement* – he told me *in person* when we were walking in the park after lunch. It was a nice setting to hear such good news and it was quite *touching*, especially as it was a really sunny day and a beautiful park too. So, I guess if I was made to decide, I'd say that I prefer to receive particularly special good news face-to-face, in person.

内容亮点

* laid-back *adj.* 悠闲的；安详放松的
* frankly *adv.* 直白地，直率地
* stand on ceremony 讲究客套
* sentimental *adj.* 感伤的，多愁善感的
* in person 亲自
  与上一句的 face-to-face 是同样的意思，上下呼应
* Like for example 前面的描述长且抽象，回答使用一个朋友订婚的例子描述了自己得知一则浪漫的新闻的感受，听者瞬间就明白了前面的意思。
* engagement *n.* 订婚
* touching *adj.* 感人的

★ Part 2

> **10** Describe a successful small company.
> You should say:
> What it is
> What it is like
> How you knew it
> And explain how you feel about it.

示例回答

The small company I would like to talk about is a business that my friend Gareth started. It's a consulting company that helps to manage the marketing information and data for other large companies. The company also builds websites and helps to create marketing materials for companies. It's a small company but fairly successful because it has *a stable number of regular clients* as well as all sorts of little side projects.

There are about 10 people in the office and the company culture is warm, friendly and energetic. I first heard about it because Gareth is my friend and he talked a lot about it as he was establishing the company, hiring employees and *renovating* the new office. Actually, I helped him out quite a bit at first and enjoyed watching Gareth's idea and hard work because it's a successful and interesting business.

I feel great to have been involved in it, and although I am now living in another city, I often talk to Gareth and he tells me about how the company is going, and shares his latest ideas with me.

It's not easy to start a company, a small company, and develop it to an extent where it becomes successful. *Working for oneself* is really hard, and you have to multi-task and do lots of jobs at the same time...you know, *fulfill lots of different roles*, at least in a *start-up company*. And I believe that this is exactly what Gareth did to bring his small company to success. So, I always feel *a sense of admiration* for people like Gareth, who set up their own business and manage to build it up to the point where it becomes their main livelihood, and if it becomes really successful and well-known, that's an even greater achievement.

I would like to see more *incentives* for young people to start their own businesses, be more *innovative* and grow their own companies. I think it's a great thing. And knowing Gareth and talking to him about his company and how he set it up and grew it has also *given me a great insight into* business in general, and what being an *entrepreneur* really means.

内容亮点

- a stable number of regular clients 稳定的回头客数量

  regular clients 老主顾，常客，回头客
- renovate *v.* 修复，翻新
- work for oneself 自力更生
- fulfill...roles 扮演……角色
- start-up company 创业公司

- a sense of admiration for sb. 对某人怀有钦佩感
- incentive *n.* 激励；刺激；鼓励
- innovative *adj.* 有创造性的
- give sb. an insight into sth. 让某人对某事有深入的了解
- entrepreneur *n.* 企业家

★ Part 3

1 **Which would you prefer to work for, a family-run firm or bigger national company?**

示例回答

I'd prefer to work for a smaller *family-run company*. Although, in some ways, they are not as *prestigious*, I actually think that smaller companies can offer more interesting and exciting experiences. You may do a wider range of tasks and feel a bit closer to the owners and managers of the company. There is a level of *flexibility* and *warmth* that you don't really get in huge companies.

内容亮点

- family-run company 家族企业
- prestigious *adj.* 有威望的，有声誉的
- flexibility *n.* 灵活度
- warmth *n.* 温暖；warm 的名词形式

2 **What are the important factors in making a company successful?**

示例回答

There are a number of key factors that *contribute to* making a company successful. Firstly, I think the owners, the *founders* or main managers need to *have a sense of vision*, a strong self-confidence and an *ambitious* personality. I also think that a company needs the right kind of employees. The managers need to have a good sense of who to and who not to *recruit*. They also need to treat the employees well, give them *fair salaries* and other benefits and holidays that will ensure they will *be loyal to* the company and work as hard as possible.

内容亮点

- contribute to + doing 有助于，有益于
- founder *n.* 创立者，创始人；co-founder 联合创始人
- have a sense of vision 有远见
- ambitious *adj.* 有志向的，有野心的
- recruit *v.* 招募
- fair salary = decent salary 不错的薪水
- be loyal to 对……忠诚

3 **What kinds of qualities should a successful businessman have?**

示例回答

A successful business person should, to be honest, be quite *assertive*, quite *dominant* in some ways, and know how to talk to a variety of people in the right ways. There are moments to be very *dogmatic* and firm, there are moments to be soft and *diplomatic* – a good business person should be able to *gauge* the different situations and *adopt the correct attitude* to suit what is best for the company. Being decisive is another quality that is important in a business person who wants to succeed and do well. Sometimes you have to make decisions, the best decisions possible, in a very short time – so being able to think fast, evaluate things quickly and be *decisive*, is very important.

内容亮点

- assertive *adj.* 坚定的；assert *v.* 坚称；坚持（权利或权威）
- dominant *adj.* 首要的；占支配地位的
- dogmatic *adj.* 教条的
- diplomatic *adj.* 有手腕的；灵活变通的
- gauge *v.* 判定，判断
- adopt the correct attitude 采取正确的态度
- decisive *adj.* 有决断力的

4 **What emerging industries do you know about at the moment?**

示例回答

The biggest industry that I know about right now is probably the technology field, especially AI – *artificial intelligence*. A lot of money is being invested in *optimising* AI technology and using it in a number of different ways. Some people say that within just a decade, computers will be doing most of the jobs which humans are doing today. I'm not sure if this will really happen, but it's certainly an interesting thing to consider. Secondly, a fairly new industry is the development of *renewable energy resources*. Although people have been researching this for decades, it is only recently that there has been more of a drive to create *alternative forms of energy* and there have been some *significant breakthroughs* in solar power and electric and *hybrid vehicles*.

内容亮点

- artificial intelligence 人工智能
- optimise *v.* 优化
- renewable energy resource 可再生能源
- alternative forms of energy 可替代能源
- significant breakthrough 重大突破
- hybrid vehicle 混合动力车

★ Part 2

> **11** Describe one area of science (medicine, physics and etc.) that sounds interesting to you.
> You should say:
> What it is
> When you knew it
> How you knew it
> And explain why it sounds interesting to you.

示例回答

An area of science that really interests me is *geology*. I mean, I don't have a deep interest in the field, to be honest, but I had a collection of interesting stones when I was a child and I used to *look them up in books* and learn about where they came from, how they were formed and things like this. I *got quite into it* for a time, and I used to read some *National Geographic* magazines, so this led me into finding geography interesting, especially anything related to *volcanoes*. So, I guess you could say I am *mildly* interested in geology and *geography* and the science behind the earth and *plate tectonics* and how physical geography works.

I also watch, occasionally, *documentaries*, with my grandfather, about natural history and *dinosaurs*. I think this kind of knowledge *fits into* the same or a similar area of science really, because we have found a lot of *fossils* of dinosaurs and other creatures from millions or billions of years ago, in stones, mountains, *quarries* and other areas.

So, all in all, I'd say that I'm interested in this field more than any other field really. I've never really had an interest in space, technology, military, science, physics or chemistry really, or the kind of things we learn in school. I don't read about any of these things today – but when it comes to geology and geography, I still have quite an interest.

内容亮点

- geology *n.* 地质学；geography *n.* 地理
- look sth. up in books 在书中查找某个信息
- get quite into sth. 变得对……很着迷，很喜欢
- volcano *n.* 火山

  复数形式为 volcanoes 或 volcanos
- mildly = slightly *adv.* 稍微地

  be mildly interested in sth. 意为"对……有点兴趣"，类似的表达有 mildly surprised / irritated 有点吃惊 / 生气。
- plate tectonic 板块构造
- documentary *n.* 纪录片
- dinosaur *n.* 恐龙
- fit into 与……一致

  短语所在的该句话意思是：我认为这种知识适用于相同或相似的科学领域。

- fossil *n.* 化石
- quarry *n.* 采石场

★ Part 3

1 What kind of qualities should a scientist have?

示例回答

A scientist, I guess, should be very careful about details and have great attention to detail. This is the first thing that comes to my mind anyway. Unlike artists, a scientist should *have a solid foundation* in mathematics and therefore have a strong ability to understand numbers and *complex equations*. This is the very basis of most science. Secondly, I think a scientist needs to be very calm, controlled, and have a strong and long *attention span*. When you are reading specific reports or doing experiments or putting together research papers, you have to concentrate very calmly and *in a very focused manner* – there is no room for error or "*vague* thinking" in science.

内容亮点

- have a solid foundation 有一个扎实的基础
- complex equation 复杂的等式 / 方程式
- attention span 注意力持续时间
- in a very focused manner 注意力非常集中
- vague *adj.* 模糊的

2 Should children be encouraged to learn science?

示例回答

Yes, of course, science is very important and children should be encouraged to have at least a basic knowledge of the physical sciences. And I think teachers and parents should make science interesting for children, show them how it *relates to* the real world and not just force them to learn *endless sums and equations*, but tell how things work in daily life in the home and on earth. How the seas come in tides, how mountains were formed, how crops grow, how the weather works – things like this will inspire interest in children, because they are always asking and wondering why things happen the way they do in life.

内容亮点

- relate to 和……有关
- endless sums and equations 无止境的算术和方程式

3 Can science be applied in life? Can you give me some examples?

示例回答

I think a good example of an area of science which *applies to* life is the use of GPS on *cellphones*. The GPS has a great advantage in enabling us to use *navigation* maps wherever we go. It knows our location and the location of where we want to go to and can plan a route for us. The latest apps that use GPS actually also know where the heavy traffic is, the best *routes* to avoid it, and all sorts of other real-time road conditions.

内容亮点

- apply to 应用于

  The new technology was applied to farming. 这项新技术已应用于农业。

- cellphone *n.* 手机

- navigation *n.* 导航

- route *n.* 路线

4 What influence will international cooperation on technology bring to the society?

示例回答

International cooperation and the sharing of technology, advances and discoveries can help people on the planet *speed up* in terms of developments in all fields. One example is medical science – if we share medical knowledge then more people in the world can *be cured of diseases* or at least develop possible medicines and *vaccinations* much quicker. If the world makes a "team effort" with things like this then it's beneficial to everyone, especially the poorer nations that cannot afford the research and development themselves.

内容亮点

- speed up 加速

- be cured of diseases 疾病被治愈（注意这里的介词用 of）

- vaccination *n.* 疫苗

5 What do you think about unmanned cars?

示例回答

I think they are definitely something that is coming in the future, but we aren't quite there yet. Currently, they are in very early stages of development so there are a lot of issues with potential dangers and accidents, and it's still not clear how *automated cars* will work on busy city roads, places with heavy traffic, quite *disorganised* roads and road systems. For *unmanned cars* to work effectively, we will need to *overhaul* our entire road systems, and this will take many years. So, I think we have a long way to go yet before we can trust such vehicles, but we are slowly getting there. They will certainly bring a lot of advantages when they finally reach the stage when they can be introduced and used *on mass*, but I think we still have a long way to go.

内容亮点

- automated / unmanned cars 无人驾驶车，自动驾驶车

- disorganised 缺乏组织的，杂乱无章的

- overhaul *v.* 彻底检修

- on mass 大规模地

★ Part 2

 Describe a tradition product in your country.
You should say:
    What it is
    When you tried this product for the first time
    What it is made of
And explain how important this product is.

示例回答

A traditional product that I really like, which is very *typical* in China, is tea. I love Chinese tea and *have quite a large collection of* it. I also have a couple of *tea sets*, too. I like tea because it is not only good for the health, the mind and the body, but it is part of an ancient tradition and has its roots way back in our country's history. *It takes me back to a time when* we sat and enjoyed calm *philosophical* and cultural conversations and enjoyed *art and literature* and *discussion and debate*.

Tea and the whole process of making tea and sharing tea, is a very peaceful, almost *spiritual* product. I know quite a bit about the *different varieties of* tea as well, and the slightly different ways of *brewing* them. I *am also really into* the different equipment, *jugs and cups*, *ceramic* tea sets, and all the things *associated with* Chinese tea.

I first tried this product at a fairly young age because my father's brother, my uncle, had a small tea shop in Xiamen. I live in Beijing, so Xiamen is quite far away, but we used to go during the summer holidays. It's really hot there, so we spent a lot of time sitting in the cool tea shop, around the big wooden *polished* table, *sipping* tea and chatting with the locals who came in. It was a wonderful atmosphere in there and I've always held this memory quite close to my heart and tried to recreate it in my own little way at home in Beijing.

内容亮点

- typical *adj.* 典型的；有代表性的
- have quite a large collection of sth. 有一大堆……

  a collection of 相当于 a group of，意思是"一些，许多的"。
- tea set 茶具
- It takes me back to a time when... 意为"它将我带回到……的时候"，when 引导定语从句。
- philosophical *adj.* 哲学的
- art and literature 艺术与文学
- discussion and debate 讨论和辩论
- spiritual *adj.* 精神的
- different varieties of 不同种类的

  variety 意思是"各式各样"，用 different 或 wide 修饰可强调表达效果。
- brew *v.* 沏（茶）；煮（咖啡）

- be really into sth. 非常喜欢……
- jugs and cups 茶壶和茶杯
- ceramic *adj.* 陶瓷的
- (be) associated with 与……有关的
- polished *adj.* 抛光的；擦亮的
- sip *v.* 小口喝；抿

★ Part 3

1 What's the most important tradition in your country?

示例回答

I think one of the most important traditions in my country is something quite simple, but meaningful: it's the tradition of serving people jiao zi, or dumplings, before they go on a long journey, like a plane or train journey to another province or country. At least in my ***extended family***, we always follow this tradition and many of my friends do too. Basically, before you ***set out on*** your trip you eat lots of dumplings – that's it! I am not sure why this tradition is a tradition, but it is! It's meant to be good luck and give you a safe journey. As well as, of course, filling your stomach so you're not hungry!

内容亮点

- extended family 大家庭（几代同堂的家庭）

  与之相对应的是 nuclear family 核心家庭（只包括父母和子女）
- set out on sth. 开始做某事

2 Why should children learn about traditions?

示例回答

It's quite important that children learn about traditions because that's one thing that ***keeps traditions alive*** for generations to come. That's what I was ***alluding to*** earlier really – the fact that so many traditions are getting ***diluted*** these days, as they lose their meaning as they get passed from generation to generation. Young people often have little interest in our own ancient traditions, and as they get older this lack of interest starts to mean that traditions become less meaningful. This is quite a shame. So, I think if children learn about traditions, then it's a good way to keep those traditions alive for the future.

内容亮点

- keep traditions alive 保留传统
- allude to 暗指，提及

  That's what I was alluding to earlier really. 这就是我之前提到的。
- dilute *v.* 削弱；冲淡

  traditions are getting diluted 传统越来越不受重视

105

3 Are there any traditions that have already disappeared in your country?

示例回答

I'm not really sure I know any that have disappeared really, but I am sure there are many. One thing I will say is that traditionally, in history, there were lots of interesting street *parades*, *firework displays* and outdoor activities during spring festival. Whereas in the past 30 or so years, people don't really do much of this – they simply sit and watch a very long *gala* entertainment show on TV, and that's about it. Fireworks have now been banned, because they are noisy and pollute the air. Street parades don't really exist anymore, because basically such gatherings along the roads are not encouraged, and so we are left with a dinner with family and that gala TV show. In a way I think that's a shame. So, I think some traditions have disappeared, or at least they have got *watered down* and are not as exciting or meaningful as they used to be.

内容亮点

- parade *n.* 游行

- firework display 烟花表演

- gala *n.* 庆典，演出

  a charity gala 慈善义演；spring festival gala 春节联欢晚会

- water down 削弱；稀释

  形容词形式为 watered-down，意为"打折扣的；被水冲淡的"。在原文中的意思是一些传统已经消失或者淡化了。

★ Part 2

> **13** Describe a skill that you think you can teach other people.
> You should say:
>> What it is
>> Who you can teach
>> How you can teach others
> And explain how you feel about teaching others.

示例回答

A skill which I think I would be able to teach other people is public speaking and debate. In university, I joined a public speaking and debate society organised by one of our teachers. I bought a couple of books about public speaking, which also, at the time, included some CDs of famous speakers and their speeches. I *became really inspired by* this, and I also enjoyed the debate club. Both of these skills are quite important if you want to enter into the academic world and succeed. Often you have to *reconstruct very logical arguments* based on evidence and support your opinions strongly with examples and *reasoning*.

This is not something that comes naturally to everyone, and I think it takes practice and patience and a certain degree of knowledge and learning. I feel very *enthusiastic* about teaching others and I think it's really exciting when you have a skill that you are confident about ***passing on*** to others. I also believe that in teaching, you also develop yourself too, because you learn a lot about working out the best way to structure classes, workshops and ***seminars***, and through doing so you improve your own skills. I also believe that Chinese students ***have an aptitude for*** public speaking because we have a strong culture of performance and performing in front of others – so I think this really means that students here ***get really engaged*** when it comes to preparing speeches and trying their best when performing for the interest of an audience.

I also believe that in the future, public speaking will become more and more important. In our global and fast-changing society, the importance of communicating ideas and beliefs across cultures, with logic and clear explanation will become greater and greater. So, I think this is not only a skill that I would be able to teach, and enjoy teaching, but also one which is important and very useful.

内容亮点

- become inspired by 被……激励
- reconstruct very logical arguments 重新建立合乎逻辑的论点
- reasoning *n.* 推理
- enthusiastic *adj.* 热情的
- pass on 传递
- seminar *n.* 研讨会
- have an aptitude for 对……有天赋
- get engaged 被……吸引

★ **Part 3**

1 Do you think teachers should be funny when they are teaching?

示例回答

I think that humour is always a good thing in the classroom, in ***moderation*** of course. A teacher who is always ***cracking jokes***, of course, would be a bit ***annoying***, but in the right way, at the right time, in the right place in a lesson, then it can create ***amusement*** and interest, and therefore ***engage*** and motivate the students.

内容亮点

- moderation *n.* 适度，适中
- crack jokes 开玩笑
- annoying *adj.* 使人恼怒的
- amusement *n.* 开心，娱乐
- engage *v.* 吸引（注意力、兴趣）

2 Why do teachers need to be kind to students?

示例回答

Teachers should be kind but *firm* with students, in my view. Being too *harsh* will reduce motivation and cause students to become too *introvert*, too shy and too *averse to* taking risks. Students need to be encouraged to take risks in their learning and in expressing their ideas. So, a kind teacher will be better able to increase student motivation and, in turn, improve student performance. But, as I said, there needs to be a balance of qualities that a teacher *possesses* as well as being kind.

内容亮点

* firm *adj.* 坚定的

  firm 常见的名词释义为"公司"。
* harsh *adj.* 严厉的
* introvert *adj.* 内向的
* be averse to 对……厌恶；不情愿
* possess *v.* 拥有

3 Which one do you think is more important? Practical skills or academic skills?

示例回答

I think both *are of equal importance* really, but it really depends on the path in life a person chooses and their personal *aptitudes* and talents. Ideally, *a blend of* practical skills, good communication and social skills, and academic skills, is the ideal combination in life. A person that combines those skills can often be quite successful in life. For example, someone who is very *academic*, but lacks good communication skills, often doesn't perform very well in their career. And *likewise*, if a person lacks a good, sound academic background, then they will fall behind because they do not have the *logic reasoning* and basis in knowledge to compete, especially in a very competitive society.

内容亮点

* be of equal importance = be equally important 同样重要
* aptitude *n.* 天资
* a blend of ……的融合
* academic *adj.* 学术的
* likewise *adv.* 同样地
* logic reasoning 逻辑推理能力

4 Which age group is the best to learn?

示例回答

I think that young children learn faster and are more willing to learn than older people, frankly. Children, when they *hit about 4 years of age*, reach a stage of quite fast developmental learning, especially in language and understanding the logic of certain basic *concepts*, and if we give them enough attention and focus at that age they can learn really quickly, and *pick up* new things a lot faster than older children or even adults. Early childhood education is an interesting field actually, and if teachers and parents make things fun and *incorporate* games into learning, then kids of this age can develop really fast.

内容亮点

- hit about 4 years of age 长到大约 4 岁的时候
- concept *n.* 概念
- pick up （不费力地）学会
- incorporate *v.* 融入

★ Part 2

14 Describe a perfect job you want to do in the future.
You should say:
What it is
How you can find this job
What you need to prepare for this job
And explain why you want to do this job.

示例回答

I think a perfect job, at least for me, *would* be a *TV presenter* for travel shows. *I'd love* this. I love watching travel shows, you know, *where* a *charismatic* presenter travels to different countries in each *episode*, talks to the locals, sees the main sights, explores a little bit *off the beaten track and so forth*.

I really enjoy these kinds of shows and my mother always says that *I would make a great host or presenter* for these kinds of shows. I am not sure that this is a job that I would be able to achieve getting though. I mean, it's not easy to *get into* this field, even if you feel you have the talent and ability. You have to either study acting and get into the film and television industry this way, and really *excel* in the field, or you have to *have really good connections* in the industry already, or ideally and usually, both!

So, it's easy enough for me to see this as my ideal job, but it's not really a *realistic* goal or anything like this, probably. Perhaps you could say it's more of a *fantasy*, and something that inside I am very confident that I could really do well at, in an ideal world, but not something that I will achieve. Who knows, maybe if I try and explore the possibilities more, there may be a chance, but I don't think *getting one's foot in the door* of this field is an easy task at all, and the competition is *stiff*. Anyway, it's nice to have these dreams and fantasies *from time to time*.

内容亮点

- would 表示假想的愿望：We wish that he would come again! 我们希望他能再来！
- TV presenter 电视节目主持人
- I'd love 的完整写法为 I would love，意为"我喜欢"。
- where 相当于 in which，which 指代 travel shows。

- charismatic *adj.* 有魅力的
- episode *n.* （电视剧或广播剧的）集
- off the beaten track 偏僻的；人迹罕见的
- and so forth 意为"等等"，相当于 and so on。
- I would make a great host or presenter. 我会成为一名优秀的主持人。

  make 在本句中意为"成为"。
- get into 从事
- excel *v.* （在某方面）胜过（或超过）别人
- have really good connections 有丰富的人脉关系
- realistic *adj.* 现实的
- fantasy *n.* 想象，幻想
- get one's foot in the door 迈出第一步
- stiff *adj.* 激烈的

  The company faces stiff competition from its rivals. 公司遇到了来自对手的激烈竞争。
- from time to time 时不时地（一般位于句首或句尾）

★ Part 3

1 What kinds of jobs do children want to do?

示例回答

Children have some wonderful and wild ideas about the things they'd like to do in the future. *Well, some, anyway*. I had friends who wanted to be *astronauts*, top businessmen, technology experts and *entrepreneurs.* All sorts. There are, however, other kids who *are more down-to-earth* and realistic, maybe, and others that just simply want a *fairly* easy and low-pressure job, partly because they realise that being *ambitious* usually means *taking on* big challenges in one's career.

内容亮点

- Well, some, anyway 弱化前文 children 的范围，避免观点过于绝对
- astronaut *n.* 宇航员
- entrepreneur *n.* 企业家
- be down-to-earth 脚踏实地
- fairly *adv.* 相当地
- ambitious *adj.* 有抱负的
- take on 承担

2 What kind of professions are popular in your country?

示例回答

Oh, there's *a whole range of different professions* that are popular in my country today. Many guys like to get into programming. Actually, girls, too. I know a lot of girls and guys who really like IT. Design, *computer graphic design* seems to be quite popular. The field of business is something that some people are very attracted to, because they have this idea that if they can make big business, through online buying or being a *consultant* for a successful company, they can get rich and have a very comfortable and exciting life.

内容亮点

• a whole range of different professions 各种各样的职业

在本句中 a range of 意为 "一系列的，许多的"。

• computer graphic design 电脑图形设计

• consultant *n.* 顾问

3 Why do some people change their ideal jobs from time to time?

示例回答

I think as we go through life, we go through all sorts of changes based on our experiences as well as the people we meet and the things we see in the media. Also, it depends on the advice we get and the changing trends of the market in our country. When we are younger, most of us tend to be less realistic and perhaps *entertain* more ambitious ideas, and as we get older, we realise that high ambitions usually involve a lot of work and luck, so we *end up becoming* a bit more down-to-earth, especially when we are starting to think about starting a family.

内容亮点

• entertain *v.* 怀有（想法、希望、感觉等）

• end up doing sth. 以……而告终

★ Part 2

15 Describe a law or regulation about environmental protection.
You should say:
What it is
How you first learned about it
Who benefits from it
And explain how you feel about this law or regulation.

示例回答

A law relating to environmental pollution that I think is excellent, but should be made even stricter is the law to reduce private cars on the roads by restricting *the number plates* that are allowed on the roads each day. It means that only number plates ending in certain numbers can drive on the roads on certain days. This results in there being much less traffic on the road at any given time, and people have to *alternate* the days they drive, and the days they take public transport.

It's quite a *fair* law really, and means that everyone, rich and poor, must limit the amount of driving they do in the city, which, in turn, means that the air pollution is kept a little lower than it otherwise would be, and of course, helps to *ease* some of the traffic congestion too.

The problem with this law is that rich people who have two cars, end up just changing the car they use each day, so that they are actually driving every day anyway. This is the problem with a lot of laws in my country, and in most countries, actually, if you're really rich you can always find ways around them!

Generally, I am very supportive of all types of environmental laws because I think that *now is the time when* we should all be making a lot of effort to help preserve the natural environment, reduce air pollution and *emissions*, and save water and resources. The planet needs our help *in this regard*, and it benefits us in the long-run, to take care of the planet by *abiding by environmental laws* as well as making our own individual efforts to be responsible – recycle plastic bottles, use less water, try to take public transport more, use fewer plastic bags if we go to the market, things like this.

内容亮点

- the number plate 特指汽车车牌

  本文中的 law or regulation 描述的是汽车限号政策。

- alternate *v.* 交替

  alternate A and / with B 在 A 和 B 之间交替

- fair *adj.* 合理的；相当好的

- ease *v.* 缓解

  类似的表达还有：reduce / alleviate

- now is the time when 现在正是做……的时候

- emission *n.* 排放；排放物

  the emission of carbon dioxide into the atmosphere 向大气排放二氧化碳；emission controls 排放控制

- in this regard 就这一点而言

- abide by the laws 遵守法律

  abide by sth. 中的 sth. 可以是 laws、regulations、an agreement or rules

  You'll have to abide by the rules of the club. 你必须遵守俱乐部的规定。

★ Part 3

1 **What kind of rules do schools in China have?**

示例回答

Schools in China have all sorts of rules. Pretty much like schools anywhere, I guess. Children cannot wear *scruffy* or *outrageous* clothes or fashions, or *dangling earrings* or *dyed hair*, and things like this. Those are *dress-code rules*. There are other rules, too, like you aren't allowed to take mobile phones into the classroom, and you can't run or shout in the *hallways*. I can't think of any more *off the top of my head*, but there are, indeed, lots of little rules to *govern* how students behave on the school *premises*.

内容亮点

- scruffy *adj.* 邋遢的
- outrageous *adj.* 令人惊讶的；outrageous clothes 奇装异服
- dangling earrings 晃来晃去的耳环
- dyed hair 染过的头发
- dress-code rules = dress codes 着装规则
- hallway *n.* 走廊
- off the top of my head （俚语）不假思索
- govern *v.* 统治；管理
- premises *n.* 场所；school premises 校园

2 What should teachers do to make students obey rules?

示例回答

Teachers should set good examples for students, and they should also remind students of the rules, by explaining the context and reasons for them. I think this method works better than simply *scolding* or *bossing* students around. So, the personality and way that a teacher *disciplines* pupils and students is key to getting them to listen, understand and obey rules. If, of course, some especially *unruly* students *persist in breaking the rules*, teachers should *dish out* punishments to *deter* them from breaking the rules again, and deter other students from doing the same.

内容亮点

- scold *v.* 责骂

  常用搭配有 scold sb. for sth. / for doing sth. 责备某人做某事
- boss *v.* 发号施令；bossy *adj.* 爱指挥人的
- discipline *v.* 惩罚；管教

  discipline 作名词除表示"纪律"之外，也有"大学的科目、学科"之意。
- unruly *adj.* 不守规矩的；任性的
- persist in doing sth. 坚持做某事
- break the rules 违反规则
- dish out 给予；dish out punishment 给予惩罚
- deter *v.* 威慑；deterrent *n.* 威慑

3 Are there any laws about education in China?

示例回答

Yes, in most parts of China education is *compulsory* from age six to around age fifteen – there are nine years in total, I think, of compulsory education. There is also a national *curriculum* with a number of compulsory subjects that we must study, and a number of *elective* subjects. We also must do *a certain amount of* physical education and sports, and also learn about good social behavior in *a series of* social studies classes.

So, yes, there are a number of basic laws which govern the education system and how schools should *conform with* national standards of both curriculum and *disciplinary* issues.

内容亮点

- compulsory *adj.* 义务的，强制的
- curriculum *n.* 课程；复数形式为 curricula 或 curriculums
- elective *adj.* 可选择的

  elective subjects 选修课，类似表述还有 optional / selective courses
- a certain amount of 一定数量的
- a series of 一系列的
- conform *v.* 遵守；一致

  常见搭配有：conform with / to sth. 与……保持一致
- disciplinary *adj.* 有关纪律的

人物类（People）▶▶▶

话题介绍

    Part 2 人物类话题一般可分为两类。一类是描述身边的某个人，例如一名家庭成员、一位特别的朋友。另一类是描述一位名人，例如新闻里看到的人或者喜欢的运动员等。

    该类型话题的提示语往往建议考生描述该人物的身份，你如何认识或者知道这个人，你经常和该人物做什么事情，为什么你对该人物感兴趣，你是如何看待该人物等相关内容。考生在谈论该类型话题时，如果没有清晰的思路，可尝试描述该人物和他人的相同或不同之处。比如描述此人和自己的不同点，并按照逻辑继续说明自己对此人的感受或是此人给自己带来的影响。

    考生可通过本书中的示例回答，整理与人物特征和影响有关的思路和表达方式，并结合当季雅思口语题库进行练习。回答完 Part 2 之后考官会根据考生的回答进行 Part 3 的提问，该部分是对 Part 2 内容的进一步延伸。

★ Part 2

1 Describe a family member you spend most time with.
You should say:
    Who this person is
    What kind of person he / she is
    What you usually do together
And explain why you spend most time with him / her.

示例回答

The family member I'd like to talk about is my brother. He's an amusing person, actually, with *a dry and mischievous sense of humour*. He is 5 years younger than me and he works for a company that sell automobiles, a kind of *off-road adventure vehicle* company, I guess you'd call it.

Anyway, to be honest he's a bit lazy, but always seems to be quite lucky in finding good jobs with flexible bosses, great benefits and a fairly high salary! I think maybe it's because of the way he is able to talk confidently to all different types of people, and *command respect*, as well as being an *endearing* person who is pretty well-liked.

I spend most of my free time with him because he lives next door to me and because we help each other out a lot with all sorts of things and on the weekends, we go out for meals, then go to a bar and drink and share stories and discuss family and friends. On Sundays, we *take it in turns to* cook. He enjoys cooking Mexican and *Lebanese* food – it's kind of his hobby really, and I enjoy cooking Chinese and Japanese dishes. So, most Sundays, we invite each other round, along with friends and sometimes other family members, and we eat together.

He's very *sporty*, and I'm not very sporty, so this is the main difference between us really – apart from this we are very similar and have a really good laugh together and share a lot of common interests.

It's interesting when you think about your family members, because there's always usually one uncle or relative that you get on with really well, and you're excited to see. I'm not sure why... I think most people have this experience. Usually, it's the relative that is the funniest, the most interesting and *quirky*, or the one that seems a little different from all the others, and has a strong sense of adventure and fun. At least that's my experience with my brother, and I feel really lucky to have a brother that's really interesting in this way, that I can get along with really well, and spend a lot of time with.

内容亮点

• a dry and mischievous sense of humour 直译是一种干巴巴的、顽皮的幽默感，听起来像是贬义的描述。实际上 dry 在形容幽默时是褒义的，词典的释义为 (of a joke or sense of humor) subtle, expressed in a matter-of-fact way, and having the appearance of being unconscious or unintentional，所以 dry jokes 意为"不露声色的，好像不经意间讲出来的笑话"，往往需要想一想才能发现笑点。a mischievous person 是指 a person who likes to have fun by playing harmless tricks on people，类似于汉语中的"恶搞""皮一下"，有趣但无害。

• off-road adventure vehicle 越野冒险车；off-road *adj.* 越野的

• command respect 使人敬仰

command 是动词，respect 是其宾语

• endearing *adj.* 讨人喜欢的

• take it in turns to do sth. 轮流做某事

• Lebanese *adj.* 黎巴嫩的

• sporty *adj.* 擅长运动的

• quirky *adj.* 古怪的，离奇的

★ Part 3

1 **What are the benefits of younger and older generations living together? How about the drawbacks?**

示例回答

There are a number of practical and emotional advantages to younger and older generations sharing the same home. Firstly, life today is very busy, and often both parents have to go to work – if there are children, then the grandparents can easily *take over* and look after the children during the daytime or when the parents are busy. This is a lot easier if everyone lives together in the same house, especially in big cities where housing is expensive and distances between work and home can involve long *commutes*. The drawbacks, well... there are also a number of drawbacks. You don't get much personal space or private time if you live with other family members, especially grandparents. Sometimes other family members might also *interfere* in your daily business or *poke their nose into* your personal affairs or arguments with your husband or wife. So...everything has its advantages and disadvantages, in life.

内容亮点

- take over 接管
- commute *n.* 上下班路程
- interfere *v.* 干涉

  常用搭配：interfere in sth. 干预某事
- poke one's nose into sth. 干涉，干预，探听，管闲事

  poke 在这里是"伸、探"的意思，这个短语可以直译为"把鼻子插进……"，引申义为"干涉，干预，探听，管闲事"。这个短语带有贬义色彩，通常这种喜欢干预、探听别人事情的人都是不受欢迎的。

2 Which one do you prefer, support from family members or friends?

示例回答

It really depends to be honest. It's impossible to say without a context!! If I want to talk about an emotional problem in a relationship or something, then I prefer to talk to my friends. However, if I want to discuss other issues, perhaps related to other family members, or my work or future, then *I am perhaps more likely to* seek family support and *a listening ear* from my mother and father in particular.

内容亮点

- I am perhaps more likely to do sth. 我更倾向……

  perhaps 和 be more likely 用于加强不确定性。
- a listening ear 一个倾听者

  类似的表达还有：a warm shoulder 温暖的肩膀；a helping hand 援助之手

3 Is it important to visit family members?

示例回答

Of course! It's very important to keep in touch with one's family members and visit them *in person*, as well. Sometimes it's not so easy here in China because it's a big country and cities are very far apart – it takes a long time to travel from place to place and during national holidays, trains and planes are often *over-booked* and crowded. However, everyone in China usually *makes quite a lot of effort* to stay in touch and visit relatives. I think that it's one of the aspects of our culture that we remain fairly traditional about – maintaining a close relationship with the family.

内容亮点

- in person 亲自
- over-booked = overbooked *adj.* 预订超过实际席位的
- make a lot of effort to do sth. 努力做某事

★ Part 2

> **2** Describe an interesting neighbour.
> You should say:
>   Who this person is
>   How you know this person
>   What he or she does
>   And explain why you think this person is interesting.

示例回答

The neighbour I find the most interesting is an old man called Mr. Liu. He has lived next door to my grandparents for as long as I can remember. He's a wise, *talkative* and friendly old man with a lot of interesting stories and *insightful* pieces of advice. He has *a big mop of white hair*. He's fairly tall, and always walks with a decorative wooden walking stick with *a carved bone handle*.

Because the weather is really warm most of the year where I come from, I often see him sitting on the wall outside his home reading novels. I sometimes stop and chat to him and he discusses news, history, the stories he has been reading, or talks about his garden. He enjoys gardening and has a small garden at the back of his house. He is almost always seen with a wooden cage with two birds in it. He's one of those older men you sometimes see in my city who *take their birds in cages out "for a walk"* and talks to them and feeds them in the sunshine.

I think he's a *fascinating* man and I've got a lot of time for him. I think most people in our street feel the same about him. He's also very helpful to the other neighbours and *there was a time I remember quite clearly when* an old lady up the road got sick, he made her soup and bread every day and took it round to her. So, he's popular too and nobody *has a bad word to say about* Mr. Liu.

I think we can learn something from these kinds of experiences, you know, these kind of *encounters* with good neighbours. I always feel that as cities have developed and life has become more fast-paced, many people don't even know their neighbours or pay any real attention to them. So, this is what I have often thought when I think about, reflect on and talk about Mr. Liu – he's one of those special people that's really interesting and I wish it was more common today that we all have more neighbours like him.

内容亮点

- talkative *adj.* 健谈的
- insightful *adj.* 有深刻见解的
- a big mop of white hair 一大团白发

  mop 原意是拖把，a mop of 可以用来形容头发乱糟糟的。

  a mop of unruly hair 一头难梳理的头发；a mop of brown curls 一头蓬乱的棕色卷发
- a carved bone handle 一个骨雕手柄
- take their birds in cages out "for a walk" 遛鸟

- fascinating *adj.* 极有吸引力的
- there was a time I remember quite clearly when... 曾有一段时间我记得很清楚，在那时……
- have a bad word to say about sb. 说某人坏话

  类似表达有：speak ill of sb. / talk behind sb.'s back
- encounter *n.* 经历

★ Part 3

1 Do you have a good relationship with your neighbours?

示例回答

Yes, we have a good relationship with most of our neighbours. But, like a lot of people, I don't think we really have much to do with neighbours. In modern society today, people are quite *estranged from* the people who live near them. Everyone keeps a distance and doesn't really *associate with* them much. It's a shame really. This sense of community has largely been lost, especially in cities.

内容亮点

- estranged *v.* 使疏远

  be estranged from 与……疏远，与 alienate 是近义词
- associate with sb. 与某人交往

2 How can we improve our relationships with neighbours?

示例回答

Generally, I think it's a good idea to have a relationship with the people who live near us, and try to keep it on friendly and *amicable* terms. This can be done by being a little *generous*, *occasionally* giving gifts, or sharing food and *making a point of stopping* to chat when you meet them going in and out of the house.

内容亮点

- amicable *adj.* 友善的
- generous *adj.* 慷慨的
- occasionally *adv.* 偶尔
- make a point of stopping 一定要停下来；make a point of doing sth. 重视做某事

3 Do you think neighbours are important?

示例回答

Yes, of course. Everyone needs to feel *a sense of community* – we are living in a social world, not *isolated in bubbles*! So, neighbours are a normal and important part of daily life. I think it's a good idea to not be too close to neighbours though – maintain a good friendly relationship but not *get* so *involved in* each other's lives or personal life.

内容亮点

- a sense of community 社区感
- be isolated in bubbles 被孤立在气泡中
- get involved in 卷入

4 Do you think people's relationships with their neighbours today is the same as it was in the past?

示例回答

No, I think people are way more distant from their neighbours than they were in the past. Today people tend to live in apartment blocks in cities, and usually they don't want to have that much to do with all the other people living next door to them. Sometimes people are even *suspicious* of each other, to be honest. I think in smaller towns and places in the countryside there is more *closeness* between neighbours, but it seems that as societies develop and *modernise*, there seems to be more distance between people and those that live around them. I'd say it was a sad, but natural consequence of development.

内容亮点

- suspicious *adj.* 不信任的

  常用搭配：be suspicious of / about sb. / sth. 对某人 / 某事不信任
- closeness *n.* 亲密
- modernise *v.* 现代化

★ Part 2

3 Describe a person who is good at his or her job.
You should say:
    Who he or she is
    What he or she does
    What kinds of aspects of the job he or she is good at
And explain why you think he or she is good at the job.

示例回答

I'd like to talk about Elliott. A man, in his mid 40s, from England. He's an old friend and also an *ex-coworker*. In fact, I knew him initially through work, because we worked in the same education company in Beijing. Then after a while we became friends, and started to *hang out* together.

I am not sure what Elliott is doing now, because he left Beijing several years ago, but when we worked together, he was a really incredible work colleague to have. He *was particularly good at* all things related to organisation – he *was excellent at spreadsheets* and technical work using excel for example or managing operations and processes. He was good at helping the technology team with system design, and he *was great at* helping the education team with *proofreading*, editing and writing, sometimes even translating. He was good at project management, setting targets and goals and making sure everyone on his team kept to them.

I imagine he is doing very well in his job in London now. I think he moved to London. It's a shame we *lost touch*, really. I had a great *admiration* for Elliott and his attitude to work and his ability to concentrate and focus on tasks without getting distracted.

I think the people we work with can have a strong influence on how we view the world of work. Elliott most certainly had a big influence on me. Even today while I'm at work in the office and dealing with projects that I find a bit difficult, I always think back to how Elliott used to work, think about how he would *approach the situation*, and it inspires me to try harder and maintain a sense of *professionalism* and work *ethic*.

So, I think he wasn't only good at this job in a purely practical way at the time, but he has had a fairly long-term influence on my attitude to work in general. So, I think this really is a sign of a great worthy employee and someone that has a *lasting* influence on us. If we work with special people who are really good at their jobs, they can have a positive effect on us for the rest of our lives.

内容亮点

- ex-coworker *n.* 前同事

  类似的表达还有 former colleague

- hang out (with sb.) 和某人出去玩

- 该回答中有好几个表达擅长的短语，如 be particularly good at、be excellent at、be great at doing sth.。

- spreadsheet *n.* （计算机）电子表格程序

- proofreading *v.* 校对（proofread 的现在分词）

- lose touch 失联

  其反意表达：keep in touch with sb. 与某人保持联络

- admiration *n.* 钦佩，欣赏

- approach the situation 解决这种处境

  类似的表达有：address the situation / tackle the problems

- professionalism *n.* 专业水平；专业素质

- ethic *n.* 行为准则；work ethic 职业道德

- lasting *adj.* 持久的

★ Part 3

1 **What advice would you give young people going into their first jobs or internships?**

示例回答

*That's an interesting question...well...*I think I would advise anyone new to a job that they should go in on day one and be confident, positive, but also *modest*. I think that *getting along with* bosses and co-workers is really important. And making sure they listen very carefully to advice and instructions, and not be afraid to ask questions.

内容亮点

- That's an interesting question...well... 开头的承接给自己留出思考的时间
- modest *adj.* 谦虚的

  反义词为 immodest，近义词为 humble
- get along with sb. 与……相处

2 **What qualities would you say make someone a good team leader at work?**

示例回答

A leader should be *inclusive* – try to *involve* all members of the team, at least in communicating important information and decisions. A leader should also be patient, but firm when necessary. I also think that we respect and admire leaders that are confident.

内容亮点

- inclusive *adj.* 包容的
- involve *v.* 使参加；加入

  常用搭配：involve sb. in sth. / in doing sth.

  involve all members of the team in communicating important information and decisions 让团队的所有成员参与交流重要信息和决策

3 **Do you agree or disagree that a boss or team leader should be strict in order to motivate a team?**

示例回答

Yes, I think a boss, teacher or a leader should be strict, *to a point*. But it depends on when and how they are strict. I firmly believe in positive *reinforcement* most of the time – I think adults respond to *encouragement* and positive support and understanding. However, sometimes you also need to feel that your boss or leader is a strong, firm person who will not *tolerate slackness*, or laziness or *sloppy* work. As humans we need a bit of both ways I think.

内容亮点

- to a point 在某种程度上

  类似的表达：to some degree / to a reasonable extent
- reinforcement *n.* （尤指通过鼓励或奖赏的）加深
- encouragement *n.* 鼓励
- tolerate *v.* 容忍，相当于 put up with
- slackness *n.* 松弛；懈怠
- sloppy *adj.* 马虎的，粗心的

4 **What ways would you suggest are the best ways to motivate workers to perform better in their jobs?**

示例回答

I think a good *motivator* is giving people *praise*, recognising their strengths and also trying to help people challenge themselves and improve on the things they *are weak at*. I think a good leader or manager should also be a good listener and have the ability to encourage people to work well as individuals and as a team.

内容亮点

- motivator *n.* 激励方式
- praise *n.* 表扬；同义词为 compliment
- be weak at 不擅长

★ Part 2

4 Describe an intelligent person you know.
You should say:
　　Who this person is
　　How you know this person
　　What he or she does
And explain why you think this person is intelligent.

示例回答

An intelligent person I know is my friend Martyn. He's a very academic type, you might say. He's very *knowledgeable* about history, literature and even science, and he also has a very creative and critical mind. I met him when we were in university. In fact, I met him on campus one afternoon. I was new and I couldn't find the café on campus anywhere. Then I *saw this guy reading* on a bench by the lake, and went and asked him for directions. We got chatting about the novel he was reading and we walked to the café together, had a coffee... And we've been friends ever since.

This was about 7 years ago. Now he works at a media company doing writing, editing and some production, I think. He *gets* a bit *frustrated* by his work, so he doesn't talk about it much. But I think that it's common that intelligent people get bored very easily with *repetitive* jobs, and I think he wants and needs something more *challenging*. I think he's intelligent on many levels, actually. He also has an *emotional intelligence* and a good way of understanding other people's situations, their feelings, their *struggles and anxieties*.

So, he's not just *a "booksmart" person*. I think this is a very valuable thing to remember, actually – there are different types of intelligence, and some people are very smart, very intelligent and very fast-thinking, but they can also be *emotionally* very cold and selfish.

I think that Martyn is a good example of the kind of person who is smart in both important ways, and has a rare *integrity* and understanding of people and their emotions, as well as a sharp intellect and academic approach to things with a high degree of critical and reflective thinking. He has been a strong influence on me in recent years and I *hold him in high regard*, as you can see!

内容亮点

- knowledgeable *adj.* 知识渊博的
- see sb. doing sth. 看见某人正在做某事
- get frustrated 感到气馁
- repetitive *adj.* 重复的
- challenging *adj.* 富有挑战的
- emotional intelligence 情商，相当于 Emotional Quotient（EQ）
- struggle and anxiety 纠结和焦虑
- a booksmart person 一个会读书的人
- emotionally *adv.* 情绪上
- integrity *n.* 诚实正直；完整

  回答中 has a rare integrity 是指 Martyn 在读书和理解他人情感方面都做得很好，有罕见的完整性。
- hold sb. in high regard 十分尊敬某人

★ Part 3

1 Would you say you are intelligent or hard-working?

示例回答

I would describe myself as intelligent and hard-working, yes. I think I work better when I'm under pressure and also when I'm doing tasks that I find more interesting. If I get bored, I start to ***stray***, lose interest and ***lose discipline*** and focus. I would say a lot of people are the same, in fact.

内容亮点

- stray *v.* 走神
- lost discipline 失去约束；lose self-discipline 缺乏自律

2 How do people in your country define "intelligent"?

示例回答

It depends on what people you're talking about, but I do think that some people focus a little bit too much on grades to measure intelligence. However, I, personally, view intelligence ***in a broader and deeper sense***. I think people who can solve problems, think critically, ***evaluate*** different opinions and views, and ***come to thoughtful conclusions***, are the real intelligent people in life.

内容亮点

- in a broader and deeper sense 在更广和更深的层面
- evaluate *v.* 评价
- thoughtful *adj.* 深思熟虑的
- come to...conclusions 得出……的结论

3 **Do you think smart people tend to be selfish?**

示例回答

I think sometimes yes, but *not necessarily* in every case. Some smart people can *get* very *absorbed in* things, their own thoughts, hobbies, *obsessions* and interest, *at the expense of* others. So, yes, they can sometimes have a tendency to get selfish.

内容亮点

- not necessarily 未必，不一定
- get absorbed in 聚精会神于
- obsession *n.* 令人着迷的人（或事物）
- at the expense of 以……为代价

4 **Why are some children more intelligent than others?**

示例回答

I think there is a mixture of reasons. Part of the intelligence we have I believe we *inherit* from our parents, from our *genes*. So, it's been proven that intelligence is to some extent *genetic*. However, also it depends on our *upbringing* – whether our parents read to us, talk to us, explain things to us and bring us up to be *thoughtful*, thinking people. So, I think it's *a combination of* genetic factors and upbringing.

内容亮点

- inherit *v.* 继承；inherit sth. from sb. 从某人那里继承某物
- genes *n.* 基因（gene 的复数形式）；genetic *adj.* 基因的
- upbringing *n.* 抚育
- thoughtful *adj.* 体贴的；关心别人的
- a combination of A and B A 和 B 的结合体

5 **Do you think it's true that smart people get more opportunities in their lives?**

示例回答

I'd say so, yes. *In most cases, yes*. Smart people can get things done faster and often talk their ways into better situations that can lead to more opportunities and more *successes*. Also, smart people often have better education and so on, which can lead to better work opportunities.

内容亮点

- In most cases, yes. 在大多数情况下，是的。

  当听到问题的第一反应是 Yes，但转念一想没有这么绝对时，可以用这个句子弱化肯定的程度。

- success *n.* 成功；成功的人或事

  表示"成功"时为不可数名词，常用搭配有：success in sth. / in doing sth.；表示"成功的人或事物"时为可数名词，如："The party was a big success."，其复数形式为 successes。

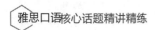

★ Part 2

> **5** Describe a person who is full of energy.
> You should say:
>   Who he or she is
>   What he or she does
>   Why he or she is full of energy
> and explain how you feel about this person.

示例回答

The person I'd like to describe, who is full of energy, is my friend, Mary. She's incredible, actually. I honestly don't know how she has so much energy and manages to do so much with her energy too, and not waste it. As one example, she always gets up early, goes for a run for an hour, comes home and showers, *gets changed*, and then has breakfast and then starts to study. After that she always reads, cooks wonderful food, goes out to parties and a lot of social events in the evenings, and seems to have some time to do all sorts of little hobbies in the meantime.

I have often wondered how she can remain so focused, so active and manage to *fit* so many things *into* one day. I think she must be very healthy, have strong genes, and also perhaps a great sense of confidence, *positivity* and *motivation*, too. I feel great when I am with Mary, because she is always encouraging me to join in new experiences and learn new things, but at the same time I feel quite tired in her company. She never seems to get tired or *run out of* energy and she's always talking. She's so talkative.

I think some people naturally *have a thirst for* experiences and *a strong appetite for* life, and Mary is most certainly one of those people. I feel energised when I'm in her company, but also, she makes me feel that I am a bit lazy, a bit *laid-back* and perhaps don't have much *get-up-and-go* compared to her, so *at times* I feel a bit *inferior*, like something is wrong with me. *In a way* I'd like to be like Mary, but in a way, I also don't think I could *cope with* having such a busy life and maintaining such positivity whilst *juggling* so many different hobbies, activities, studies and *social engagements*.

I'm the type of person that needs more free time alone relaxing and just not thinking that much, or doing so much in my free time. I guess we are all different! But at times these kinds of energetic and active people can be a motivating influence to us all!

内容亮点

- get changed 换衣服；get dressed 穿好衣服
- fit sth. into sth. (to find time to see sb. or to do sth.) 找到时间（见某人、做某事）
- positivity *n.* 积极性（positive 的名词形式）
- motivation *n.* 动力
- run out of 用尽
- have a thirst for 渴望
    类似的表达还有：have a taste / an appetite for 对……有兴趣；have a gift for 对……有天赋

- laid-back *adj.* 懒散的（lazy 的同义词）
- get-up-and-go *n.* (informal) 干劲，雄心
- at times 有时（相当于 sometimes、from time to time）
- inferior *adj.* 较差的，比不上的
- in a way 在某种程度上
- cope with 应付，处理
- juggle *v.* 尽力同时应付（两个或两个以上的重要工作或活动）
- social engagement 社交

★ Part 3

1 What kind of jobs require a lot of energy?

示例回答

Lots of jobs require a lot of energy, in different ways. For example, ***manual jobs*** require a lot of physical energy, ***stamina*** and ***endurance***, whilst ***mental jobs*** like being a lawyer, a CEO or a CFO, require a different kind of energy – you need to have a sharp and fast-thinking mind. So, there are different types of energy required for different kinds of jobs and they are all tiring in their own different ways. Sometimes, for example, doing some physical manual work can be tiring on the body, but ***oddly*** relaxing on the mind. And ***the opposite is true*** of a lot of mentally-tiring jobs, you ***get exhausted*** from thinking so much and thinking of so many things at the same time, but your body doesn't get enough exercise. There are pros and cons of all jobs really.

内容亮点

- manual job 体力工作
- stamina *n.* 耐力
- endurance *n.* 持久力
- mental job 脑力工作
- oddly = surprisingly *adv.* 令人惊奇地
- the opposite is true 反之亦然
- get exhausted 感到筋疲力尽

2 Do you think manual work will all be done by machines in the future?

示例回答

I think most manual work will be done by machines in the future, but this also has some significant downsides. This has been discussed a lot recently as so much factory work, as an example, is done by machines, robots, basically, and this has ***resulted in*** less and less jobs being available to ***lower-skilled workers*** who rely on such manual jobs as their main source of income. So, I would not really like to see so many manual jobs being ***taken over*** by robots, because this means a lot of people will lose their jobs, and if they don't have other skills, they may find it incredibly difficult to find work. These are some of the key issues that ***arise from*** modernization – issues that governments all over the world are needing to ***address*** today, as ***automation*** in the workforce is becoming so ***predominant***.

内容亮点

- result in 导致
- lower-skilled worker 低技能工人

  who rely on such manual jobs as their main source of income 是 workers 的修饰语。原文句子较长，意思是：这一点最近被频繁讨论，例如，大量的工厂工作基本上是由机器和机器人完成的，这导致依赖手工劳动作为主要收入来源的低技能工人可以获得的工作越来越少。

- take over 接管
- arise from 由……引起
- address issues 解决问题
- automation *n.* 自动化
- predominant *adj.* 占主导地位的

3 **Do you think manual workers will earn more in the future?**

示例回答

I am not sure. I don't really understand that much about economics and the ***workforce*** really, but I'd guess that they will because the ***scarcer*** a job is, usually the better paid it becomes. So, say, for example, certain types of factory jobs, perhaps more skilled manual labour, become scarcer, then those that can do those jobs might end up getting paid more.

内容亮点

- workforce *n.* （国家或行业等的）劳动力
- scarcer *adj.* 罕见的（scarce 的比较级）

★ Part 2

6 Describe a person who is very open.
You should say:
　　Who he or she is
　　How you know him or her
　　Why he or she is like this
And explain how you feel about him or her.

示例回答

A person who I'd like to talk about who is very open is my friend Mary. Mary is about 35 years old and she sits near to me in our office. She's kind of my desk mate I guess you'd say. Mary is a curious character because she has lived an ***unconventional*** life compared to many friends I know. Her father is from Australia and her mother is from a city in the south of China. The whole family have travelled and lived in a few countries all over the world, and they have lived a ***fairly*** international lifestyle. I'd say that she is open-minded simply because she has **been exposed to** different cultural and political **perspectives** in the countries she has lived in, and also, she has had a close relationship with her parents on a very mature and open level – almost like friends.

I've spent a bit of time in her house with her family, and it's interesting how they discuss things together like they are good friends, not just parents and daughter. She is not just open-minded, but she is open in the sense that she is quite **extrovert** and honest with her views and her feelings. She is not afraid to say what she thinks about all sorts of issues, even issues which are a bit **controversial**. She likes to share her views and she doesn't mind if people disagree with her or posit different opinions different to hers. She's not very **defensive** about this – so it's possible to have some quite **heated discussions and debates** with her about all sorts of things, without it getting personal or without her taking things personally. I wish more people could be open like Mary.

I find it quite **refreshing** and it always makes for interesting and **stimulating conversations**. However, she can be quite challenging sometimes and I can understand why many of her teachers in university didn't really like her. She, perhaps, sometimes, needs to learn when to be quiet and not be so **expressive** about her emotions and opinions. But she has a good heart and means well – that's just her way – and I wouldn't really want her to change.

内容亮点

- unconventional *adj.* 非常规的；live a unconventional life 过着非常规的生活
- fairly *adv.* 相当地

  用在形容词或副词前，表达的语气较积极，如：a fairly easy book 一本相当浅易的书；a fairly typical reaction 相当典型的反应

- be exposed to 接触；暴露
- perspective *n.* （观察问题的）视角

  常见搭配：different / new / broader / proper / cultural / historical / political / social / theoretical perspective

- extrovert *adj.* 性格外向的

  作名词时指 "性格外向的人"，反义词为 introvert

- controversial *adj.* 有争议的；a highly controversial topic 一个争议极大的话题
- defensive *adj.* 心存戒备的

  defensive 的常见意思是 "防御的"，其名词形式为 defense，在本句中 be defensive about 表示 "对某事心存戒备"。

- heated discussions and debates 激烈的讨论和辩论
- refreshing *adj.* 令人耳目一新的；别具一格的
- stimulating conversation 有启发性的交流
- expressive *adj.* 表现的，表达的

★ Part 3

1 **How do young people express their own feelings nowadays?**

示例回答

Young people are quite expressive about their feelings, I think. Well, I guess it depends on the age we are talking about. I'm not sure if you're referring to children, or teenagers, or young adults, really, but children are usually very open and expressive, at least most kids. Teenagers, too, tend to be quite expressive, and also quite ***stubborn*** and ***opinionated***. Young adults start to learn to be more deferent in their attitudes, especially when talking with teachers or adults or bosses. Some people, however, remain quite expressive throughout their lives, and others are a lot more ***composed*** and keep their feelings inside and don't like sharing their real emotions with others. So, there's quite a variety of types of people in the world, but in general, I'd say that young people, especially children, express themselves more – usually quite ***vocally*** and quite stubbornly, especially when they want something!

内容亮点

- stubborn *adj.* （人）固执的，倔强的

  下文中的 stubbornly 是其副词形式，修饰其行事风格。

- opinionated *adj.* 固执己见的

- composed *adj.* （用在名词前）镇静的

  She seemed outwardly composed. 她表面上好像很镇静。

- vocally *adv.* 口头地；communicate vocally 口头交流

2 **Who are more outspoken? Men or women?**

示例回答

I really can't say. To be honest I've known ***outspoken*** men and outspoken women. It's really a personality thing. In general, I would say that in the home or family women are more outspoken about their feelings when they are upset or angry, and men tend to keep these feelings inside a bit more. But, again, this is a ***generalization***. I also know men who are very outspoken when they are angry, and even more ***unreasonable*** at the same time. I think, especially nowadays, there isn't a huge difference between men and women ***in terms of*** one being more outspoken than another – it ***'s all down to*** individual personalities and one's background, ***upbringing***, and even ***genetics***.

内容亮点

- outspoken *adj.* 坦率的，直言不讳的

- generalization *n.* 概括

- unreasonable *adj.* 不理智的

- in terms of 在……方面

- be down to 归因于

The British Museum's increased popularity is down to its exhibitions. 大英博物馆越来越受欢迎要归功于它的展览（次数或展品丰富）。

- upbringing *n.* 教养
- genetics *n.* 遗传特征

❸ Why do people need to express feelings sometimes?

示例回答

Everyone needs to express their feelings sometimes. In fact, it should be encouraged *to a point*. People who keep all their feelings inside can get quietly *frustrated* and even very *troubled*. It's important to be able to share worries, concerns and anxieties with others. If we express our feelings then we are also *simultaneously* sharing experience with other people in a way that they can also learn from. If more people do this a little more often, then more people will develop *a greater sense of empathy*.

内容亮点

- to a point 在某种程度上

  类似的表达有：to some degree / to a reasonable extent
- frustrated *adj.* 沮丧的
- troubled *adj.* 忧虑的；不安的（同义词为 worried and anxious）
- simultaneously *adv.* 同时地
- a sense of empathy 同理心

  empathy *n.* 同感；共鸣

  常见搭配有：empathy with sb. / sth.、empathy for sb. / sth.、empathy between A and B

❹ Why are people becoming less frank now?

示例回答

I don't think people are becoming less *frank* nowadays, actually. I'd say people are becoming more and more frank, at least young people. More direct, more frank and more honest about their *wants* and needs. Perhaps they are less frank about their feelings towards controversial topics in the society like politics or other areas in which they may have conflicting opinions, but in general, I think young people are pretty frank. It's hard to say, though, again, as I keep saying. It is also down to individual personality, upbringing and background – confident people sometimes can be more frank, and less confident people can be more *introverted*. However, this isn't always the case, either. It depends.

内容亮点

- frank *adj.* 坦率的
- want *n.* 想要的东西

  当表达 sth. that you need or want 时，经常使用其复数形式 wants。
- introverted *adj.* 内向的

★ Part 2

 Describe a person who you think wears unusual clothes.

You should say:

Who this person is

What he or she does

Why you think the clothes he or she wears are unusual

And explain how you feel about this person.

示例回答

A person I know who wears unusual clothes is an artist friend of my father's, who has a studio in ***798 art districts***, Beijing. He also has a workshop on the ***outskirts*** of the city, actually. Anyway, artists usually tend to be quite ***cultured***, and also quite ***eccentric*** in their tastes. He wears very colourful clothes, extremely high quality too, and very ***baggy*** pants. He ***has a collection of*** different pairs of glasses in all sorts of crazy colours and shapes. He also wears a very unusual style of shoe, which is a bit like a ***medieval pointed slipper***. His coats are usually long with high collars and patterns, very unique designs, and he also likes to wear hats. The kind of hats you often see in American films from the 1940s and 1950s.

This man usually spends most of his time sitting in his studio, drinking tea and chatting to visitors when he's not working on a new piece of artwork or sculpture. I feel good about this person. I mean, I always feel good when I'm with him. Sometimes we sit in his studio chatting about art, life, music and things for many hours. He always has interesting views and opinions on things, and I find these ***arty*** people quite fun to be around. They think a bit less ***conventionally*** than most people, and often ***challenge*** generally accepted opinions and notions, and I find this really interesting. He can be quite ***intense***, though, and ***forceful*** in presenting his views. This can be a bit much sometimes, when you're not really in the mood.

It's curious how fashions come and go and change over time. I always quite admire those people who don't really follow the latest fashions but have their own unique personal sense of style. You have to be quite self-confident to ***strike out*** and be different in this way, and I think that it's a good thing really. I really feel that my father's friend is exactly this kind of person, and that makes me feel quite ***inspired*** by him.

内容亮点

• 798 art districts 798 艺术街区（北京一处老厂房改造的创意园区）

• outskirt *n.* 郊区（复数形式为 outskirts）

• cultured *adj.* 有教养的；文雅的

• eccentric *adj.* 古怪的；不同寻常的

• baggy *adj.* 宽松的

• have a collection of sth. 收集某物

• medieval *adj.* 中世纪的

• pointed *adj.* 尖头的；pointed slipper 尖头拖鞋

• arty *adj.* 艺术气息的

- conventionally *adv.* 传统地
- challenge *v.* 质疑；挑战
- intense *adj.* 有强烈感情（或意见、想法）的
- forceful *adj.* （观点、意见等）有说服力的
- strike out (to start being independent) 独立；自立谋生
- inspired *adj.* 受鼓舞的

★ Part 3

1 Do you think online shopping is a good trend?

示例回答

In general yes, I think it's a very good trend, as it's so easy and convenient. However, it sort of takes away the pleasure of actually going into shops, trying things on, looking at things **in person**. I think that this is a shame, as shopping can be fun and interesting and you also get exercise when walking around! It's nice to **grab a coffee** and shop with a friend and chat as you **wander around** a mall or shopping street.

内容亮点

- in person 亲自
- grab a coffee 喝一杯咖啡
- wander around 在……闲逛

2 Are there any differences in men's and women's preferences about clothes?

示例回答

There are certainly differences. Men and women usually have very different fashion tastes. In general, I think women care more about clothes and looks, and image than men. Men tend to be more relaxed about this, prefer **plain colours** and simple designs, whereas women tend to be more **adventurous** in their clothing styles, and also have a wider range of different styles to choose from.

内容亮点

- plain colours 素色
- adventurous *adj.* （指事物、方法、思想）新奇的；有冒险精神的

3 Do you think clothes will influence one's mood?

示例回答

I think clothes can certainly have an influence on how one feels, yes. Sometimes if you wear brighter colours, you tend to feel happier and more positive. If you wear more **somber** and darker colours, you tend to be more serious. I think styles also make us feel different. One obvious example is how you might feel in sporty clothes, compared to very formal clothes, or how a girl may feel in a dress compared to a pair of jeans. So, moods and clothes **are very closely related**, I'd say.

内容亮点

- somber *adj.* 阴沉的；暗淡的
- A and B are very closely related A 和 B 息息相关

★ Part 2

8 Describe the politest person you know.
You should say:
Who this person is
What your relationship with this person is
What he or she likes to do
And explain why you think he or she is the politest.

示例回答

The politest person I know is most certainly a friend of mine called Ian. Ian works in the other department in my company. He is kind, polite and quite formal in the way he interacts with people. He is always ***massively*** helpful to people who are in need, and he is the person that we all ***turn to*** if we have any technical issues with our computers at work, or we need help buying something online or we are not feeling good about an emotional issue. He is polite to everyone, without being ***fake***, if you know what I mean.

His ***politeness comes across*** as quite natural, rather than forced. He seems to have a sense of duty to be nice to people and helpful. I think that his family background is quite interesting: his father is an artist and his mother is a manager for some kind of consulting company that deals with developing poorer areas of the city. So, I think these are quite ***sensitive*** and ***thoughtful*** parents to have, and so they ***passed on*** this to Ian.

A lot of our behaviours are learned from our parents, in my view, so I ***suspect*** that his polite ***manners*** and helpful approach to others and their problems, came directly from his ***upbringing*** as a child. A lot of people I know are a lot less sensitive than Ian, and maybe be polite, yes, but not quite in the same very natural and sensitive way as he is. I am not sure what he likes to do these days. The last time I spoke to him he ***was really into*** music and collecting guitars – that seems to be his main hobby at the moment, though he tends to have different hobbies each time I see him!

内容亮点

- massively *adv.* 大量地

  在本句中相当于副词 very，表达程度。

- turn to sb. 求助某人

  She has nobody she can turn to. 她求助无门。

- fake *adj.* （动作或感情）虚假的

- politeness *n.* 礼貌

- come across 给人……印象

  She comes across well in interviews. 她在面试中常给人留下很好的印象。

- sensitive *adj.* 善解人意的
- thoughtful *adj.* 体贴入微的
- pass on 传递
- suspect *v.* 认为（某事有可能）
- manner *n.* （单数）举止，态度；（复数）礼貌

  常见表达：to have good / bad manners 有 / 没有礼貌

  It is bad manners to talk with your mouth full. 嘴里塞满了东西跟人说话是不礼貌的。
- upbringing *n.* 教养
- be really into sth. 非常喜欢某事

★ Part 3

1 How do people show politeness?

示例回答

In general, I think people's approach to politeness is quite interesting. On the one hand, they are incredibly polite. *Workmates*, for example, are always polite and helpful and usually very concerned about not *offending* others or *prying* into their personal lives. On the other hand, people in public when they deal with strangers, can be quite rude, *invade* your personal space, speak loudly and push and *shove* in crowds. So, it's a bit of a *contradiction* really. I guess because there is such a huge population, you see a bit of everything!

内容亮点

- workmate *n.* 工友，同事（近义词 colleague）
- offend *v.* 冒犯；得罪
- pry *v.* 打探；暗中侦查
- invade *v.* 侵扰；invade one's space / privacy 侵犯个人空间 / 隐私
- shove *v.* 猛推；乱挤
- contradiction *n.* 矛盾

2 Are there any standards to measure one's politeness?

示例回答

I think that like in most cultures, these standards exist but are not written down! I mean, everyone is brought up by their parents and teachers to *conform to* certain rules of politeness, I guess. And there are some standards everyone *tacitly* agrees on. However, it also largely depends on your background and the standards and values of parents and the people you grew up with, and grew up around.

内容亮点

- conform to sth. 遵守
- tacitly *adv.* 心照不宣地

3 **What kinds of behaviors are not polite?**

示例回答

The common *impolite* behaviours that I can think of *off-hand* are not waiting in line patiently, shouting loudly in public, pushing others on the subway, and maybe shouting at waiters and waitresses rudely in restaurants. I don't like to hear richer people being rude to poorer people and staff because they think they're *superior*, and things like this. I think this is very impolite, because they should be educated enough to know better.

内容亮点

- impolite *adj.* 不礼貌的
- off-hand *adv.* 当即，立即
- superior *adj.* （在级别、重要性或职位上）更高的

4 **Do you think politeness is related to one's academic background and family environment?**

示例回答

I think that it is usually related mostly to one's family background and home environment, yes. *Academic background* can influence how polite a person ends up being, maybe. But not usually directly. Usually, there is a *correlation* between people with a good family background and a good educational background, but not always.

内容亮点

- academic background 学术背景
- correlation *n.* 关联

5 **Do you think if there is a country where people there are famous for being polite?**

示例回答

I think there are a few countries where people are famous for being polite, at least *on the surface*. It depends on how you view "being polite" really. On the surface, the Japanese and Germans are very particular about *social interactions* in public and very polite. However, I'm not sure if they really are when you *dig* deeper *below the surface*. Rules of politeness can be quite *complicated* really, and you can look at them on a number of levels depending on the individual situation.

内容亮点

- on the surface 在表面上
- social interaction 社交活动
- dig *v.* 寻找；挖； digger *n.* 挖掘机
- below the surface 在表面之下；实际上
- complicated *adj.* 复杂的

★ Part 2

9 Describe a person you saw in the news you would like to meet.
You should say:
  Who the person was
  When you saw him or her
  What was the news about
And explain how you felt about the person or the news.

示例回答

A person I think I'd like to meet that I've seen in the news is Oprah Winfrey. You may know of her. She's one of the richest women in the world – she's a TV host from the US. I am not sure how often she is on the news, but she has her own talk show, she hosts it, *The Oprah Winfrey Show*, and I've seen it *multiple* times, and I really like her personality, her attitude and *assertive* character and the way she interviews people, listens to them and offers her opinions. I did see her on the news several years ago, in fact.

It was a time when she went into a *high-end* handbag shop and was looking at different bags. The shop assistant did not recognise her and was *apparently* very rude to her by refusing to take down from a high shelf behind her, a very expensive bag that Oprah wanted to see, and Oprah felt that she was treated in this way because she is a black woman – because of *racial prejudice*.

Anyway, I saw this both in the newspaper and on television, because even though Oprah did not reveal which shop it was (because she didn't want to damage the *reputation* of the store), she did openly discuss the *incident* with the media, and then someone in the BBC, I think, managed to *track down* the actual shop, who then gave a public global apology, claiming it was a *misunderstanding*. I think the incident took place in Switzerland, I'm not exactly sure. I am not sure how I felt about this incident. I think it's an interesting story, I'm always interested to see international news stories especially about famous stars like Oprah Winfrey.

内容亮点

- The Oprah Winfrey Show 电视谈话节目《奥普拉脱口秀》
  平均每周吸引 4900 万名观众，并连续多年排在同类节目的首位。在播出了 25 年之后，脱口秀女王奥普拉·温弗瑞的节目《奥普拉脱口秀》于 2011 年 9 月 9 日结束。
- multiple *adj.* 许多的（相当于 several）
- assertive *adj.* 坚定自信的
- high-end *adj.* 高端的，高档的；high-end product 高端产品
- apparently *adv.* 显然；似乎，好像
- racial prejudice 种族偏见
  相近意思的短语还有：racial discrimination，racism
- reputation *n.* 名声
  常见的短语表达有：to earn / establish / build a reputation 赢得 / 确立 / 树立声誉、to have a good / bad reputation 有好 / 坏名声

- incident *n.* (sth. that happens, especially sth. unusual or unpleasant) 发生的事情（尤指不寻常的或讨厌的）
- track down （经过长时间艰难搜索后）找到

  She had spent years trying to track down her parents. 她多年来一直在试图找到她的父母。
- misunderstanding *n.* 误会

★ Part 3

1 What kind of people can be usually seen in the news?

示例回答

Politicians usually *feature in* the news a lot, and some celebrities. And, of course, reporters and *news presenters* who go to different places and different countries to deliver live reports on television.

内容亮点

- politician *n.* 政客
- feature in sth. (to have an important part in sth.) 起重要作用；占重要地位
- news presenter 新闻主持人

2 Do you think famous people, celebrities, can have a big influence on the general public by their behavior?

示例回答

Yes, I think so. Especially on young people. Young people like to have idols and *role models* and they tend to *get* very *passionate about* following famous people sometimes, especially singers, *pop icons*, *sports personalities*, and some actors. So, famous people have a responsibility to behave fairly *decently* in the public eye, so that they do not negatively influence young people, in particular.

内容亮点

- role model 榜样
- get / be passionate about 对某事有热情
- pop icons 流行人物

  icon *n.* (a famous person or thing that people admire and see as a symbol of a particular idea, way of life, etc.) 崇拜对象；偶像
- sports personality 体育明星

  personality 除了表示个性之外，也可以指 a famous person, especially one who works in entertainment or sport，意为"名人，风云人物（尤指娱乐界或体育界的）"，同义词为 celebrity。
- decently *adv.* 合适地，得体地

3 What kind of issues are frequently reported in the news?

示例回答

Oh, lots of things are reported in the news. The news might talk about international events, ***treaties***, conflicts, and major things that are happening in the world between governments. The news might also cover the environment, the economy, business news...things like this.

If there is a natural disaster like a ***hurricane*** or an earthquake or something, this will be reported, and sometimes a reporter will be sent there to do a live report on the event, maybe interview some locals ***and so forth***. For example, only a few weeks ago I heard about the ***eruption*** of a ***volcano*** in New Zealand. Reporters arrived on the scene shortly after the incident and interviewed some of the ***relief crew*** on live television. Things like this are commonly reported on the news, both on television and online.

内容亮点

- treaties *n.* 条约；协定（treaty 的复数）
- hurricane *n.* 飓风；爆发（复数形式为 hurricanes）
- and so forth 等等（相当于 and so on）
- eruption *n.* 喷发；（战争、怒气等的）爆发
- volcano *n.* 火山（复数形式为 volcanoes 或 volcanos）
- relief crew 救援队

4 What's the difference between the news nowadays and the news in the past?

示例回答

The main difference between the news today and the news in the past is that in the past everyone relied on TV and newspapers for news, but today people read most of their news on their smartphones. So, the news is more ***up-to-date*** today than in the past. It's an interesting topic because today there are different opinions about the ***reliability*** of the news. Some people say we can trust the news more today, and some people think we should trust the news less, because there is more ***censorship*** and control of the news. I'm not sure what I think, to be honest, because there are so many more ways of getting news from all over the place. I don't really know whether we can trust it more or less than in the past, but I do know that it's much easier to ***access*** the news and reading news on our phones is certainly a good way to kill time on the subway or in a taxi, or when you're waiting to be served in a restaurant or other times like this.

内容亮点

- up-to-date *adj.* 最新的
- reliability *n.* 可靠性；可信度
- censorship *n.* 审查，检查
- access *v.* (to reach, enter or use sth.) 到达；进入；使用

事件类（Events）▶▶▶

　　Part 2 事件类话题的综合性较强，结合了人物类、地点类、物品类三个话题类型的特征。也正是因为如此，事件类题目有比较多的角度可以拓展。

　　该类型话题的提示语往往建议考生描述具体事件的内容、参与的人物、发生的地点，以及对应的感受等相关内容。考生遇到该类型的话题时，如果没有清晰的思路，可思考并结合事件的特殊性，描述自己的感受。比如是不是第一次尝试某事，或者最后一次和某人做某事的情景等。按照这个逻辑，考生也可以和过往的或是相关的经历相结合，描述自己在此次事件和经历中学到的经验教训，或是给自己带来的影响。

　　考生可通过本书中的示例回答，整理多种与事件感受及影响相关的思路和表达方式。事件类话题在雅思口语题库的 Part 2 中占比较大，请考生多预留准备和练习的时间。回答完 Part 2 之后考官会根据考生的回答进行 Part 3 的提问，该部分是对 Part 2 内容的进一步延伸。

★ Part 2

> **1** Describe a time when you first met someone.
> You should say:
>> Where you met him or her
>> When you met him or her
>> What you talked about
> And explain how you felt about it.

示例回答

I'd like to talk about the time when I first met my friend Alex. *First, I will give you a little background*. I've known Alex now for about 15 years, so we have known each other for a long time. We've been really good friends and although we now live in different cities, we talk regularly online and we meet almost every holiday. I'd say we were kind of soul mates, brothers, maybe.

Right, so we first met in school when we were about 6 or 7 years old. I remember the time very *distinctly*. Alex was introduced to our class by the teacher, because he *joined* about a week later than the rest of us. His family *had only just moved* to Beijing.

My first thought, to be honest, was that Alex was a tall and *strong-looking* boy with *a serious expression* and was surely a bit of a *bully*. I just guessed he was a bully because *he looked so serious and physically strong*, with a sort of *sporty* American football T-shirt. He sat down and I didn't really want to talk to him, but I said a polite, shy hello. We didn't say much to each other at first, and I didn't really feel confident talking to a new person.

Anyway, after sitting next to him in class for a few weeks we began to talk a little bit each day, and after a few months, we discovered that we *had quite a lot in common*. We both liked reading, we enjoyed Japanese cartoon movies and we liked to play the same fantasy computer game on the *PlayStation*. Many years went by and we *have maintained* our friendship *ever since*.

So, I'm happy about this and it also made me think about how we should not judge people or be guided too much by our first impressions. Our first impressions of people are not always accurate or fair.

内容亮点

- First, I will give you a little background. 首先，让我给你一些背景信息。
  作者没有从何时何地认识这位朋友说起，而是通过介绍与这位友人的深厚友谊，展现了为何要选 Alex 而非其他人作为回答的例子。同时这个背景介绍和结尾首尾呼应。
- distinctly *adv.* 清晰地（相当于 clearly）
- join *v.* 成为……的一员；join 后省略了 the class
- had only just moved 用了过去完成时，因为搬家发生在 Alex 来我们班之前。
- strong-looking 和 a serious expression 都是对 Alex 外貌的描写，意为"看起来很强壮""表情很严肃"。
- bully *n.* 横行霸道者；a school bully 学校里的恶霸学生
- he looked so serious and physically strong （上文外貌描述的同义替换）他看上去很严肃，身体健壮
- sporty *adj.* 轻便的，休闲运动的
- (A and B) have quite a lot in common （A 和 B）有很多相同之处
- PlayStation 游戏机
- have maintained...ever since （现在完成时）从那时起友谊一直维持至今

★ Part 3

1 In what ways can people make friends if they move to a new city or country?

示例回答

The best way of making new friends these days is by online apps. This is how a lot of people meet new people...social apps, dating apps, etc. However, I think *it's also a good idea to* join a club or society. If you like sport, you can join a sports club...hmm, *you can also go to* bars and cafés – a lot of people meet new people in bars and cafés too.

内容亮点

- 作者用 The best way of...引出交朋友的第一种方式：网上交友软件；it's also a good idea to 引出第二种方式：参加一个俱乐部或社群；you can also go to...引出第三种方式：去酒吧或咖啡厅。三种方式既有优先排序，结构也整齐统一。

2 **What are your opinions about making friends online or online dating?**

示例回答

I think that making friends online or dating using apps is fine. *Years ago*, I thought it was strange, *but now* it has become completely normal, and also quite a *practical* way of meeting people because you can kind of *vet* them before meeting them.

内容亮点

- Years ago..., but now... 表示过去和现在的想法不同
- practical *adj.* （想法、方法或行动）切实可行的
- vet *v.* 仔细检查，审查（内容、质量等）
  vet 作名词时有"兽医"之意，可以想象兽医在给动物检查身体时，一定是非常仔细的，由此记忆该词作动词时的意思。

3 **How important is it to maintain old friendships? And how can people do this?**

示例回答

I think maintaining old friendships is very important. *Keeping in touch with* friends from school, previous jobs, and perhaps neighbourhood friends is a lot easier today too – we have social media and that's a really good way of keeping in touch with people over a period of years, almost *effortlessly*.

内容亮点

- keep in touch with sb. 与某人保持联络
- effortlessly *adv.* 轻松地，毫不费力地

★ Part 2

2 Describe a situation when you celebrated an achievement.
You should say:
What you achieved
How you celebrated it
Who you celebrated it with
And how you felt about it.

示例回答

The time I remember was only a few years ago. I really wanted to find a job that I liked and, *to be honest*, I kept failing the interviews. *Well*, I'm not sure if I should say "failing", *but*, I didn't get the jobs after the interviews, so maybe I wasn't good enough or they didn't like my personality... *Anyway*, I didn't *succeed in getting the jobs* I wanted, and I felt really *demoralised and depressed*. It isn't *a* very *motivating experience* to keep *getting rejected* like this!

Anyway, I finally got a job interview through a friend in a company that I really felt attracted to, in the CBD. I was excited at the opportunity, but after so many *rejections* and unsuccessful interviews, I wasn't really so confident, but I tried my best to *muster the confidence* and I *felt pretty determined to* get the job.

The interview went really well, I must say, and the interviewer and I *had a sort of connection*, *a chemistry you might say*. We got along well and our personalities connected and I felt good about myself, and started really *coming out of my shell*. I performed really well I must say. And I pretty much knew by the end of the interview that I was going to get the job.

So, two days later I received an email with a job offer and a great salary offer too! I was so happy. I took my family and three of my good friends out to dinner – and we went for drinks at a really cool wine bar near my home.

And I also learned that you just shouldn't lose hope, even after many failed attempts at something, it's important to stay positive and confident.

内容亮点

- 在描述不愉快的经历时，作者用了很多语气衔接词，如 to be honest、well、but、anyway，适当的停顿使听众能够感受到作者当时低落的心情。

- succeed in doing sth. 成功地做某事

- demoralised and depressed 气馁和沮丧的

  morale [məˈrɑːl] *n.* 士气；加否定前缀 de 和动词后缀 ise 之后变为：demoralise *v.* 使泄气

- a motivating experience 一次倍受鼓舞的经历

- get rejected 被拒绝（相当于 be rejected）

- rejection *n.* 拒绝

- muster the confidence 鼓起信心

  muster *v.* 聚集（支持、勇气等）；常与 confidence、courage、strength 等词搭配

- feel pretty determined to do sth. 下定决心做某事

- A and B have a sort of connection, a chemistry you might say. A 和 B 有某种连接，你可以说是一种化学反应。

  这个表达比较抽象，实际上就是个性相通，志趣相投的感觉。

- come out of one's shell 不再羞涩

★ Part 3

1 **What kind of things happen during special occasions, festivals and events in your country?**

示例回答

Oh well...pretty much the same thing to be honest. People basically just get together with their family – their *wider family* – eat lots of food, *usually special food*, have a good time, a good laugh, maybe watch certain entertainment programmes on TV. *That's about it really*.

内容亮点

- 回答中使用了很多短语进行列举，同时用 their wider family 对 family 进行补充，usually special food 对 food 进行补充。

- wider family 意为"其他家庭成员"，一般指 nuclear family 以外的成员。
- That's about it really. 就是这样。

2 **Talking of personal achievements in sport, what are some of the differences between winning as a team in a team sport, and as an individual in an individual sport?**

示例回答

Winning as part of a team is *a great and valuable experience* for a group of people together, as it can also create and help *develop bonds* between the team members. We know that teamwork is important as it involves cooperation – cooperating with others to achieve *a shared result*. It's also a great and valuable experience to win an individual sport, too, like a running race or something, but it's not the same feeling as a team achievement. It's a more personal thing, winning an individual sport.

内容亮点

- 作者对题目中提及的两种情况的评价都是 a great and valuable experience，但又有不同。前者可以 develop bonds and involve co-operation，后者则是 a more personal thing。
- develop bonds 建立良好关系
- a shared result 一个共享的成果

3 **In what ways are birthday celebrations different for young people and older people?**

示例回答

Birthdays are special for young people – they're exciting. In fact, I think they are mainly for younger people. Young people like to have a birthday cake, presents and gifts and maybe go out with family and friends for a special meal. Older people don't like the feeling of getting older, so they don't really enjoy birthdays so much.

内容亮点

- 作者在回答中很好地呼应了三个关键词：birthday celebrations, young people, old people。年轻人庆祝生日时充满了欢乐：exciting, cake, presents and gifts, go out for a special meal，与上了年纪的人形成鲜明对比。

★ Part 2

3 Describe a time when you tried something but was not successful.

You should say:

　　When it was

　　What you tried

　　Why it was not successful

And explain how you felt about it.

示例回答

The one thing I can think of that really was not successful at all...*that I tried once*, was *windsurfing*, when I was on holiday in France with a group of *colleagues* from my company. My company ran some kind of special deal where you can have an extra couple of days for holiday and they would fund a part of your trip, if you could get a group of *workmates* together and book *a package holiday*. There was *a choice of* a few different locations and activities that went with them. A few colleagues and I chose to go on the France trip.

We had the chance to try windsurfing on the beach. There was an *instructor* who was really good, patient and professional, and an amazing windsurfer himself. But despite his patience and continual support, I simply couldn't *balance* on the board at all. I couldn't keep myself from falling in the water each time, just after a few seconds. It was terrible, and also quite *embarrassing* to be honest. The water wasn't very warm either, so it wasn't that pleasant. It wasn't really cold, because it was summer, but it certainly wasn't really nice and warm like in Hainan in the summer! And because I'm from an area of China where it's quite hot in summer, I simply couldn't get used to *shivering* and being cold all the time.

So, all in all, I would say that my attempts at windsurfing were *a dismal failure* – partly because I have no sense of balance and *aptitude* for those kinds of physical activities, and partly because I simply found it unpleasant and *not worth the hassle*. I can imagine it being really exciting if you get good at it, but how long does it take, and *how many times do you have to fall off before you reach that stage on the learning curve*? So, I guess it's not my thing. It was a completely unsuccessful attempt at trying to learn to surf, and now I realise that the idea of windsurfing, at least for me, is much more *appealing*, cool, and *exotic*, than the reality!

内容亮点

- ...that I tried once 我曾尝试过的（在思考时顺便补充的信息）
- windsurfing *n.* 帆板运动；也称作 board sailing
- colleague *n.* 同事；与下文的 workmates 是同义替换词
- a package holiday 跟团旅游（旅行社为旅客预订旅馆、订饭菜、包租飞机等）
- a choice of 一个······的选择
- instructor *n.* 教练；导师；a driving instructor 驾驶教练
- balance *v.* 保持平衡

  常用搭配有：balance on sth. 在······上保持平衡

  How long can you balance on one leg? 你单腿能保持平衡多久？
- embarrassing *adj.* 令人尴尬的

  an embarrassing mistake / question / situation 令人难堪的错误 / 问题 / 处境
- shivering *v.* （因寒冷或害怕而）颤抖（shiver 的现在分词形式）
- a dismal failure 一个令人沮丧的失败

  dismal *adj.* 忧郁的；糟糕的

  dismal conditions / surroundings / weather 糟糕的状况；凄凉的环境；阴沉的天气
- aptitude *n.* 天赋；have / show aptitude for sth. / doing sth. 有干某事的天赋

- not worth the hassle 不值得那么麻烦；hassle *n.* 麻烦（非正式用语）
- how many times do you have to fall off before you reach that stage on the learning curve? 在你到达学习曲线的那个阶段之前，你需要跌倒多少次？
- appealing *adj.* 吸引人的
- exotic *adj.* 奇异的，异国风情的

★ Part 3

1 What's your definition of success?

示例回答

I think success is basically being able to try at something and struggle and go through some hardship, and eventually succeed in doing it. I think that is the best, most *succinct* definition of success. I'd say that some people define success as getting lucky, or having a lot of money or support from family to do whatever they want, but personally, I think real success involves personal effort, struggle, and *a sense of determination*.

内容亮点

- 本回答采用了总分总结构。先给出作者对成功的理解，然后对比传统意义上对成功的定义，最后重申自己的观点。
- succinct *adj.* 简明的；言简意赅的
- a sense of determination 决心

2 What kind of things do children try to succeed in?

示例回答

Children try to succeed in winning games. This is the kind of short-term success that kids like more than anything else – they have a lot of *dedication* to games, especially computer games, and they make a lot of effort with them too. I think they enjoy the challenge of winning and because games are exciting, they are prepared to *make an effort to* win. Also, a lot of computer games slowly *ease* you *into* them, if you're not good at first, then you gradually start to pick up the *tactics* and techniques until the game becomes harder and harder, but by that point, you've already got quite good at it. Games are designed in that way, and I think that's clever, and that's why kids are prepared to put the effort into winning.

内容亮点

- dedication *n.* (the hard work and effort that sb. puts into an activity or purpose because they think it is important)（在某件重要的事情上付诸的）努力
- make an effort to do sth. 努力做某事
- ease sb. into sth. 使熟悉（新事物）
  ease 作为动词最常见的意思是"缓解"，如 ease the pain 意为"缓解疼痛"，但是在文中 ease sb. into sth. 意为"让某人逐渐熟悉某事物"。
- tactics *n.* 战术，策略（tactic 的复数形式）

❸ Which one do you think is more important for people to become successful? Hard work or opportunities?

示例回答

I think that hard work is more difficult, more stressful, ***most certainly***. Opportunities can be ***a combination of*** luck and being at the right place, at the right time with the right attitude and focus. ***I would say that a combination of hard work***, ***and being lucky and keeping an eye open for opportunities is important*** – and having a ***personable***, wise and ***social character*** also helps.

内容亮点

- most certainly 这是肯定的
- a combination of A and B A 和 B 的结合
- I would say that a combination of hard work, and being lucky and keeping an eye open for opportunities is important. 我认为想要成功，努力工作、运气和留意机会都很重要。
- personable *adj.* 品貌兼优的；和蔼可亲的
- social character 善于社交的个性

❹ Do you think people will be happy if they don't have any goals to achieve?

示例回答

I think that most people, though maybe not all people, ***thrive on*** goals, ***milestones***, things that want to achieve, short-term, mid-term and long-term as long as those goals are realistic and achievable with some effort. However, if the goals are too overwhelming, ***unattainable*** or involve too much stress or pressure, then they can have the opposite effect on people's sense of happiness. You have to be able to ***attain the goals***.

内容亮点

- thrive on 以……成长
- milestone *n.* 里程碑；时间表
- unattainable *adj.* 难到达的；an unattainable goal 难以达到的目标
- attain the goal 实现目标；attainable *adj.* 可以实现的

★ Part 2

4 Describe a time when you first talked to others in a foreign language.
You should say:
When this happened
Who you talked to
What you talked about
And explain how you felt about this experience.

The time I remember quite clearly when I spoke in a foreign language for the first time properly *was when* I was introduced to a new foreign teacher in university. I had, to be honest, spoken English, *beforehand*, but this was the first "real" time I had a conversation with a native speaker, so I'd like to talk about this. I *recall* that she was quite friendly and *supportive* and spent the entire first class giving us lots of opportunities to speak and talk about ourselves, our ambitions, our family and all sorts of things like this – personal things.

I found this quite exciting in a way, although I was quite nervous *because* I was not used to her pronunciation, *so* I had to concentrate to listen. But I was *pleasantly surprised* at how much English I could speak when I was asked questions, and *the more* I spoke, *the more* I felt confident about speaking more! She then put us in groups of four and we had little tasks to complete – questions and answers, oral English tasks. She came round to each table and asked us about our answers and chatted to us more. I must say that I quite enjoyed this. Although it wasn't really any different from what my Chinese teachers had done in English lessons, I found it *somehow* more exciting because it was a native speaker. It was like an opportunity to show and test my language skills with someone who really did speak that language as their first language and I really liked this chance.

From this day onwards, I became a lot more confident in speaking English, and I often found this teacher *in her breaktimes* and made an effort to *hang out with her* a bit, spend a bit of time drinking tea with her, showing her the local sights, and using this opportunity to practice my language skills. So, I will always remember this first day when I got to speak English with this native speaker, and *thereafter* becoming good friends with her. So, all in all, I felt great about this whole experience.

内容亮点

- 第一句话回应了题目的第一个要求：When this happened。句子主干为"The time was when I was introduced to a new foreign teacher in university."，这句话的意思是：我清楚地记得，严格来说我第一次说外语是在大学里被介绍给一位新外教的时候。
- beforehand *adv.* 在此之前（近义词为 previously）
- recall *v.* 回想起
  recall 不用于进行时态。注意在本句中，recall 使用了一般现在时，因为是现在回想起过去的事情。
- supportive *adj.* 给予帮助的；支持的
- so 用在了 because 之后，仔细阅读这句话可以发现，原因是 I was not used to her pronunciation，所以 I had to concentrate to listen。
- pleasantly surprised 感到惊喜
- the more...the more... 越……就越……
  这是一个复合句，表示一方的程度随着另一方的变化而变化。前半句是状语从句，后半句是主句。the 用在形容词或副词的比较级前，more 代表形容词或副词的比较级。
- somehow *adv.* 不知道为什么
- From this day onwards 从这一天起（onwards 增加延续感）

- in her breaktimes 在她的休息时间
- hang out with sb. 与……出去玩
- thereafter *adv.* 此后

★ Part 3

1 **Why do some people believe that learning a spoken language is easier than learning a written language?**

示例回答

Well, some people believe this because *it's basically true*! It's a lot easier to learn to speak than to write in a foreign language. *This is partly because* if you are writing, you usually have to control your grammar a lot more strictly than if you are speaking. Sentences in spoken language are usually shorter, less complex, and involve less complicated vocabulary. Also, if you are writing in a language, you usually have to write more formally, and use a different *register* of vocabulary than if you are merely speaking. Written language is often slightly more formal, too, which again, involves a richer and higher range of vocabulary and *lexical* use than if you are just having a spoken conversation. So, in general, *there are a few reasons why people are correct in saying* that it is more difficult to write in another language than speak that language.

内容亮点

- 作者用了总分总结构，第一句 it's basically true 与最后一句 there are a few reasons why people are correct in saying 展现出作者对于这个说法的认同和理解。从细节上来看，作者将口语和书面语在 grammar, sentence structure, range of vocabulary 和 register 等方面进行了对比。
- This is partly because... 部分原因是……
- register *n.* （适合特定场合使用的）语体风格
  The essay suddenly switches from a formal to an informal register. 这篇短文的语体风格突然从正式转为非正式。
- lexical *adj.* 词汇的

2 **What difficulties do young people in your country have in learning foreign languages?**

示例回答

Most of them study pretty hard and are good at grammar and *language in the context of tests*, written tests, reading tests, listening tests, for example. But they find the most difficulty in speaking in natural situations.

内容亮点

- 本回答简短，对问题的回应一针见血。
- language in the context of tests 考试语境中的语言

3 **Is it easier for people to learn a new language when they are young or when they get older?**

示例回答

Definitely when they are younger! At least that is usually the case. Young people have more energy, more *enthusiasm* and generally *pick up new things* faster. *It's as simple as that really*. At least most of the time. However, there are some older people who also learn fast, because they have previous experience they can build on.

内容亮点

- enthusiasm *n.* 热情

  常用搭配：enthusiasm for sth. / for doing sth. 对某事 / 做某事的热情

  He had a real enthusiasm for the work. 他的确热衷于这项工作。

- pick up new things 学会新事物

  pick up 特指不经意间学会，而不是通过训练掌握新技能。

- It's as simple as that really. 就是这么简单。

★ Part 2

5 Describe a dinner that you really enjoyed.
You should say:
  When it was
  What you ate at the dinner
  Who you had dinner with
And explain why you enjoyed the dinner.

示例回答

I had a really enjoyable dinner with my family on my birthday. It was a few months ago, actually. We went for *a buffet meal* at a big hotel not far from where I live. I love seafood, and this buffet *specialises* in great seafood – *lobsters*, *crabs*, *scallops*, all sorts. *Myself*, my mother and father and a friend attended the dinner, and we had a really great time – we ate *a tremendous amount of* food, and also lots of desserts and wine. I was completely full by the end of it, and frankly felt a little bit sick.

I think I had been *way too greedy*, to be honest. But, like I said, I love seafood and this place is excellent for a *stunning* variety of seafood and also has an incredible range of sweets and *pastries* and cakes to finish off with. I'll certainly go back again, perhaps when it's the birthday of one of my friends or family members. Everyone had a fantastic time and said they would certainly like to return again in the future. *It was a little on the expensive side*, but definitely worth it.

I think dinner is a really important thing to share with other people, actually. It is also a really strong element of Asian culture which I really appreciate – you know, sitting around a big round table, with family, friends, or colleagues and sharing food and drink, *letting your hair down a bit*, telling amusing stories and *bonding with* people. It's a very natural human thing to do and I think these things are valuable. So, I have many happy memories of dinners that I've shared with people over the years.

内容亮点

- a buffet meal 一顿自助餐；a buffet lunch / supper 自助午餐 / 晚餐
- specialise *v.* 专门研究（或从事）；常用搭配：specialise in sth.
- lobsters, crabs, scallops 龙虾、蟹、扇贝
- 反身代词在正常情况下不作主语，作者在此用 myself 作主语，表强调。
- a tremendous amount of 大量的（修饰不可数名词）
- be way too + *adj.* = be too + *adj.* way 与介词或副词连用时，意为 "太……"

  This skirt is way too short. 这条裙子太短了。
- stunning *adj.* 令人震惊的（相当于 extremely surprising or shocking）
- pastries *n.* 点心；酥皮糕点（pastry 的复数形式）
- It was a little on the expensive side. 它的价格有点贵。
- let one's hair down a bit 字面意思为 "把你的头发放下来"，引申意为 "让自己放松下来"。
- bond with sb. 增强（与某人的）信任关系

  Mothers who are depressed sometimes fail to bond with their children. 患忧郁症的母亲有时无法和孩子建立亲子关系。

★ Part 3

1 What's the difference between eating at home and eating out on a special occasion?

示例回答

Well, there's a lot of difference! Eating at home is more of *a everyday thing*. And eating out on a special occasion is, well...a lot more special, I guess! I mean, at home we would cook fairly normal *tasty dishes* and sit around and have dinner, maybe watch TV and *chat casually*. Whereas at a formal restaurant you might try much more *exquisite foods*, *intricate dishes*, and things you'd not normally be able to create at home – at least not without a lot of ingredients and preparation. So, there are a few key differences. Another difference is the atmosphere. If you choose a particularly famous or *elegant restaurant*, your dining experience will be a lot more special – have a lot more atmosphere and put you in a totally different mood, than if you were to just sit at home and eat dinner. People also often *dress up* to eat out, which adds an extra element of mood at *ambience*.

内容亮点

- more of a everyday thing 一件更日常的事情
- tasty dishes 可口的菜肴

  tasty *adj.* 美味的；a tasty meal 美味的一餐；tasty to eat 好吃的
- chat casually 随意地聊天
- exquisite foods 精致的食物

- intricate dishes 复杂的菜肴

  intricate *adj.* 复杂精细的；carpets with highly intricate patterns 图案复杂精细的地毯
- elegant restaurant 雅致的餐厅

  elegant *adj.* 雅致的
- dress up 打扮，盛装
- ambience *n.* 环境；气氛；格调

  the relaxed ambience of the city 这座城市轻松的氛围

2 Why do people like to have food on special occasions?

示例回答

Food, in many cultures of the world, is an important thing to share, and dinners are a time when people relax and share food, drinks and conversation. These occasions, *the world over*, are often times when people relax, tell each other stories, *gossip a little*, and let their hair down. It's good to get to know people better, and food is always a good way to get people together – in my culture, it's a very important social occasion and is also something that *underscores* many business relationships too.

内容亮点

- the world over 全世界（等同于 all over the world）
- gossip a little 八卦一下

  gossip 作名词意为"流言蜚语"，作动词意为"八卦，闲聊"，其形容词形式为 gossipy。

  a gossipy letter / neighbour 闲聊式的信；爱说三道四的邻居
- underscore *v.* 突出显示，强调

3 Is a country's identity associated with its culinary culture?

示例回答

Most definitely, some countries more than others, of course. In my culture it most certainly is. We have a large country of many regions and *regional variations* in *cuisine*. I think quite a few countries are the same actually. So, it's not only about a country's culture, but also the culture of different regions of a country. Food also goes beyond *cultural barriers* and isn't really related to politics or anything people may have *contentious* differences about. It's a sort of *unifying* thing having dinner with people, rather than something that divides people. I think this is the positive thing about coming from a country where food is such an important part of our *cultural heritage*.

内容亮点

- regional variations 地域差异
- cuisine *n.* 烹饪，风味；饭菜
- cultural barrier 文化障碍

  常与 go beyond / overcome / remove 等动词搭配，表示"跨越 / 克服 / 消除"文化障碍
- contentious *adj.* 有争议的

- unifying 意为"使统一",是 unify 的 ing 形式。这句话的意思是:与人共进晚餐是一种团结的事情,而不是分裂人们的事情。

- cultural heritage 文化遗产

★ Part 2

> **6** Describe a time when you first ate a kind of food.
> You should say:
> When it happened
> Where it happened
> What food you ate
> And explain how you felt about this kind of food.

示例回答

The time I'd like to describe to you is the time when I first ate a burger. I don't mean a Macdonald's burger or a fast-food burger. I mean a "real" burger *in a proper burger and steakhouse*. I was invited there by an American friend at university who insisted that I must try a really good quality proper burger. So, I agreed, and we went to this *fairly well-known* burger and steakhouse not far from campus. This friend of mine was really excited about the experience, and to be honest I was expecting something absolutely fantastic by the way he was talking.

At this time in my life, I had not yet learned that Americans tend to talk "big" about almost everything and *massively exaggerate*! So, I really believed that this would be an incredible experience. Well, in actual fact it was a nice meal, and certainly a lot better than any *fast-food joint* I'd ever eaten in. But, to be honest, I didn't think the burger was that great. I mean, after all, it's just a piece of meat inside a bread bun...with some fried onions and things on top! It was good, yes, but I *was left with the impression that* perhaps burgers were a bit *overrated* compared to loads of other types of food and way more interesting foods too. What I did enjoy were the fries and the dessert! Though I didn't want to tell this friend that I thought the burger was *just so-so*, but the fries and dessert were amazing!

So, it was an interesting and fun experience *on a few levels* really! I always think this is what is really good about those years when you are becoming an adult, *so to speak*, growing up and getting more independent – when you start trying new things, *experimenting* a bit *with* different things you've never tried before, and deciding what you like or dislike for yourself. So, I think I grew up during an interesting time when my city became much more international, with a lot of interesting new things to *indulge in* and *sample*. This story is just one example of when I tried something new and how I felt about it.

内容亮点

- in a proper burger and steakhouse 在一家像样的汉堡牛排店
- fairly well-known 非常有名的;fairly *adv.* 相当地
  表达程度的副词还有 quite、pretty、considerably、rather 等不同的词汇,这些词表达的程度和使用的场合各有不同。

- at this time in my life 在这个时候
- massively exaggerate 极大地夸大
- fast-food joint 快餐店

  joint 指公共场所，尤指价格低廉的饮食和娱乐场所。
- be left with the impression that... 留下了……的印象
- overrated *v.* 对……评价过高（overrate 的过去分词）
- just so-so 一般（口语表达）
- on a few levels 在某些程度上（相当于 to some extent）
- so to speak 可以说；打个比方
- experiment with sth. 尝试；试用某物

  常见的另一个搭配：experiment on sb. / sth. 在……上做实验

  Some people feel that experimenting on animals is wrong. 有人觉得利用动物做试验是错误的。
- 本句中 indulge in 不能简单理解为"沉溺于"，它的意思是 to satisfy a particular desire, interest, etc.，即"满足（欲望、兴趣等）"，紧跟着的动词 sample 指"体验、品尝"。这句话的意思是：城市里有很多新鲜的事物去满足（人们的）兴趣，让人们去体验。

★ Part 3

1 Do you think young people are more open to new food compared with old people?

示例回答

I think as a general rule this is true because young people are *inherently* more curious and interested in *exploring new things*. A lot of my Chinese friends, though they often prefer to eat Chinese food, *are really open to* trying different *cuisines*, and *have quite a varied taste*. I think this is perhaps because Chinese food is incredibly varied, anyway, so they *are accustomed to* a very wide variety of tastes, and therefore willing to try new foods from all over the world, just *out of interest*. Older people are not so interested, but certainly are usually willing to try new foods from time to time, even if they generally prefer to *stick to* what they know and what is familiar.

内容亮点

- inherently *adv.* 内在地；固有地
- explore new things 探索新事物
- be open to sth. / doing sth. 对……开放；愿接受的
- cuisine *n.* 烹饪，风味；饭菜
- have quite a varied taste 有各种不同的口味
- be accustomed to sth. 习惯于
- out of interest 出于兴趣

  out of + *n.* 出于……的理由
- stick to sth. / doing sth. 坚持做某事

2 **Do you think parents and teachers should teach children how to cook?**

示例回答

I think parents should. I am not sure about teachers. Teachers already have to teach children a lot of the important basic studies for academic life, so I don't think cooking is one of the *priorities*, or should be, in school education. I think cooking is *an enjoyable pursuit* that children can learn at home through watching their parents cook, and *helping out from time to time*.

内容亮点

- priority *n.* 优先事项，最重要的事
- an enjoyable pursuit 一个令人愉快的业余爱好

  类似的搭配还有：an enjoyable weekend / experience 令人愉快的周末 / 经历
- help out / help sb. out 帮助……做事
- from time to time 时不时地

3 **What kinds of foreign food are popular in your country?**

示例回答

When it comes to foreign food, I think we tend to lean more towards other Asian cuisines, really. *Thai food* is to some extent popular, *Japanese food* certainly has its place, especially seafood, and maybe occasionally people might enjoy *a Korean barbecue*. Western food is popular more as a fast-food snack or a meal if we go out for drinks with friends, but we don't really go to proper western restaurants as a general rule, as it's not such a *communal* dining experience compared to the Asian eating culture.

内容亮点

- 作者讲到 foreign food 时举了不少例子，Thai food、Japanese food、a Korean barbecue 都各有特点，最后详细讲了 western food。
- communal *adj.* （尤指居住在一起的人）共享的

  其近义词为 shared；a communal dining experience 公共就餐体验

4 **Why do people like food from their hometown?**

示例回答

People always enjoy food from their hometown, especially if they live elsewhere and miss home. It's because it's familiar, and it's what we were *brought up* eating, so it gives us *a degree of comfort* too. People always like to turn to familiar things from time to time and food from our hometown or cities, especially food cooked by our parents, is something that almost always makes us feel good, welcomed and satisfied. Humans are *essentially* quite *nostalgic creatures* at heart, so home-cooked food always makes us feel good!

内容亮点

- bring up 养育

  It's what we were brought up eating. 我们从小就吃这个。

- a degree of comfort 一种舒适度
- essentially *adv.* 本质上
- nostalgic creature 怀旧的生物

nostalgic *adj.* 怀旧的

Many people were nostalgic for the good old days. 很多人都怀念过去的好时光。

★ Part 2

> **7** Describe a time when you missed an appointment.
> You should say:
>   When you missed it
>   Who you were with
>   Why you missed it
> And explain how you felt about it.

示例回答

There are a few times I missed appointments actually. The reason is that the traffic in my city is so bad. It's common that you arrive late for things, even if you *set off* from home on time. The last appointment I missed was *a dental appointment*, I had to *reschedule* it. It was easy to reschedule, but was really annoying to go all the way there to find I was too late for my *slot* and had to go all the way home again. *On this particular occasion*, I had left home about 20 minutes early, at least I had *calculated* it as such, and I tried to order a taxi. However, all the taxis were busy and I stood there at the side of the road *getting* increasingly *frustrated with* the situation. I was completely alone, actually. Nobody was with me.

Eventually, I *gave up* trying to *get a cab* and walked to the nearest bus stop. I took 3 different buses and eventually arrived at *the dental clinic* more than one hour late. Of course, they had given my slot to someone else – they couldn't wait all day for me, and *dentists* were really busy in my time too. So, I talked to the *receptionist*, rescheduled the appointment for another day, and went all the way back home, yes, by the same awkward *bus route* as I had come. I felt really annoyed, frustrated and disappointed that I had wasted so much time simply because all the taxis were *booked up*.

The one thing we learn from missing appointments, especially important ones, is that we should always *be highly organised* and attempt to plan for *the unexpected*, or plan for the *worst-case scenario*, especially if we are living in a place that has *horrific* traffic, or where it's really not easy to *get around for one reason or another*. You have to learn to *pre-empt eventualities* and plan *in advance*. It's a good lesson in life, and it reduces a lot of everyday stress.

内容亮点

- set off 动身

常用表达：to set off on a journey 动身上路；to set off to do sth. 出发做某事

- a dental appointment 牙医预约

I've got a dental appointment at 3 o'clock. 我约了 3 点看牙。

- reschedule *v.* 将……改期

- slot *n.* （为某事安排的）时间，空档

- on this particular occasion 在那个特定的情况下

- calculate *v.* 计算；估计

- get frustrated with 对……感到沮丧

- give up doing sth. 放弃做某事

- get a cab 叫出租车（与上文 order a taxi 呼应）

- the dental clinic 牙科诊所

- dentist *n.* 牙医

- receptionist *n.* 接待员

- bus route 公共汽车运行路线

- book up sth. / book sth. up 把……预订一空（常与 hotel、restaurant、plane 等词搭配）

- be highly organised 非常有组织

- the unexpected 无法预料的事

  the + 形容词 / 分词，表示一类人、一类事或一个抽象概念。

  the rich 有钱人；the unemployed 失业的人；the unknown 未知的事；the good 善良的人

- worst-case scenario 最坏的情况

  scenario [sə'nɑːriəu] *n.* 设想；方案；预测

- horrific *adj.* 极差的；很不愉快的

  We had a horrific trip. 我们的旅行糟糕透顶。

- get around 到处走走

- for one reason or another 出于种种原因

- pre-empt *v.* 抢在……之前行动

  She was just about to apologise when he pre-empted her. 她正想道歉，他却抢先说了。

- eventualities *n.* 可能出现的情况（eventuality 的复数形式）

- in advance *adv.* 预先，提前

★ Part 3

1 Is it important to have a daily plan?

示例回答

I believe so, yes. I'm a pretty organised person, to be honest. Admittedly sometimes on weekends I might *let myself go* and become quite *disorganised*, go out late with friends, and forget about plans and organisation entirely. But that's only when I'm free or attending a special occasion. The rest of the time, especially *regarding* work or family, I like to be on time, I like to be organised, I like to *deliver projects* on time and I enjoy being *on top of* things. I think that's a good way to be.

内容亮点

- let oneself go 放松

  Come on, enjoy yourself, let yourself go! 来吧，尽情地玩，玩个痛快吧！

- disorganised *adj.* 缺乏组织的；杂乱无章的

- regarding *prep.* 关于

- deliver project 交付项目

- be / get on top of sth. 设法驾驭；处理

  I enjoy being on top of things. 我喜欢掌控一切。

2 **What kind of things need to be planned very carefully?**

示例回答

For me, the things I need to plan carefully are my work projects and studies. You see I have a full-time job, but I'm also studying a course. So, I have to be very organised and plan my time around my family as well. So, I plan my work tasks and my studies pretty carefully and always make notes and timetables for myself to help me.

内容亮点

- 作者认为工作和学业兼顾就要做好计划。考生们还可以想想其他情况，比如：making plans for a trip、a study plan before an important exam、a birthday party or celebration of special days 等。

3 **Are there some things in life that cannot be planned for?**

示例回答

Yes, there are always things *cropping up* in life that you can't plan for or plan easily. I can't really think of an example right now *off the top of my head* though...emmm...maybe, things like traffic jams, accidents, things completely unexpected and out of our control can't easily be planned for. We can sometimes pre-empt likely *stumbling blocks and hurdles*, but there are always things out of our control and we cannot really plan for or plan around.

内容亮点

- crop up 意外出现；突然发生

- off the top of my head 不假思索（俚语）

  It was the best I could think of off the top of my head. 这是我能马上想出的最好办法。

- stumbling blocks and hurdles 绊脚石和障碍

  We can sometimes pre-empt likely stumbling blocks and hurdles. 我们有时可以预先绕开可能的绊脚石和障碍。

★ Part 2

> **8** Describe a mistake you've made.
> You should say:
>   What it is
>   When it happened
>   How you made it
> And explain how you felt about this experience.

示例回答

A mistake I made, a big mistake, that really stands out in my mind is when I left my mother's handbag on the roof of the car *by mistake*!

You see, she had gone into a store to buy some *groceries*, and took out her handbag and purse. She took her purse with the money in it, and because she needed a free hand to carry the *shopping*, she gave me the handbag and said, "hold this for me while I go into the store." I stood outside the car with the handbag waiting and thinking about nothing in particular. Then I heard my mobile phone ringing in my pocket. So, I put the handbag on the car roof right next to me to take my phone from my pocket and answer the phone. I chatted to my friend for a while, until my mother returned from the store with the shopping. We put the shopping in the *boot* of the car, got in, and we *drove off*. It was only when we were *halfway home* that she said to me "You have the handbag, yeah?" And suddenly my face went white with the realisation that I had actually put it down on top of the car to answer the phone and forgot.

I told her, in sudden shock, to stop the car. But it was too late, we looked all over the road where we had just been, but it was busy with traffic and impossible to see... also we were quite far from the store at this point so it must have fallen off miles away. She was really really angry with me, and I felt *guilty*. It was an *innocent* mistake, but it was very careless of me. I really regret this even today. I feel really stupid and irresponsible about it.

内容亮点

- by mistake 错误地
- groceries *n.* 杂货；食品；生活用品
- shopping *n.* 从商店采买的东西（shopping 除了做动词，还可以用作名词）
- boot *n.* 汽车后备厢
- drive off 开车驶离
- halfway home 回家的路走了一半（halfway 意为在中途）
- guilty *adj.* 有罪的，愧疚的
- innocent *adj.* 无辜的，无恶意的

★ Part 3

1 Do you think people can learn from mistakes?

示例回答

Of course. In fact, many *psychologists* say that one of the key ways we learn is from making mistakes and solving problems ourselves, with some guidance *occasionally*. Children learn a lot of *trial and error* – doing something, *getting it wrong*, thinking about why it went wrong and trying another method. So, most definitely, we learn a lot from our mistakes.

内容亮点

- psychologist *n.* 心理学家
- occasionally *adv.* 偶尔地
- trial and error 反复试验
- get sb. / sth. wrong 误解某人或某事

2 Do children make mistakes very often?

示例回答

Yes, we all make mistakes often, but especially at the early-learning stages of life, children continuously make mistakes and require some guidance from adults. A combination of *self-directed learning* and adult guidance is best to help young learners develop *at a good rate*, so I understand.

内容亮点

- self-directed learning 自主学习

  我们平时所说的"自学"可以用这个词组来表达，self-directed 的意思是"自我导向的"。

- at a good rate 以很快的速度

  原句的意思是：孩子们有自主学习的能力，再加上成年人的帮助 / 指引，两者结合可以帮助自身快速发展。

3 What would parents do if their children make mistakes?

示例回答

Parents should be *supportive* and encouraging of children making mistakes. As we now know, it's an important part of the learning process. If you *discourage people from making* mistakes they will be *intimidated* and scared to *try things out* for themselves, and simply rely on adult instruction, copying peers and *regurgitating* learned materials. It's a good thing that children, and adults to some extent, make mistakes and this should be encouraged not discouraged.

内容亮点

- supportive *adj.* 支持的；同情的；鼓励的
- discourage sb. from doing sth. 阻止某人做某事，使某人泄气

- intimidate *v.* 恐吓，威胁
- try things out 尝试某事
- regurgitate *v.* 照搬，拾人牙慧

  这个词还可以表示"使（咽下的食物）返回到口中"，即反刍。

★ Part 2

9 Describe a time when you had an argument with a friend.
You should say:

    When it happened

    Why you argued

    How you resolved this argument

And explain how you felt about this experience.

示例回答

I remember a time last year when I ***had a big row*** with a friend. I still feel a bit bad about it actually. It was actually a really silly disagreement. We had decided to study together at a specific time on the weekend, in the library. He didn't show up, and I waited for him ***for ages***. Then I went looking for him on campus and saw him playing basketball with some friends. He ***made a really lame excuse*** about his phone not being ***charged up*** and how he had forgotten the time. I was really angry because, firstly, he is always late for things, secondly, he always seems to get distracted with other interests and social activities when we have an important arrangement, and thirdly, I felt offended that he would give such a terrible excuse for this. I ***felt insulted***, to be honest.

So, after he had finished his game, I found him again and ***confronted*** him directly about these three reasons why he upset and annoyed me. He was really ***defensive*** about it and instead of apologizing, he came out with another ***stream*** of very unbelievable excuses. I felt that he should have simply admitted his faults and told me the truth and apologised and suggested he try better next time to be more reliable.

So, the argument went on for a few days, because I would not forgive him. Eventually, after about a week of not speaking to each other, we had dinner together, in fact, he invited me, and ***he made a real effort*** to apologise and said that he was trying to change this terrible habit of his. I felt better then and forgave him. I learned from this that it's important to be honest and ***self-critical*** at times, and this helps to build bridges, especially after ***falling out with*** somebody badly.

内容亮点

- have a big row 大吵一架

  row 常用的意思是"一排，一行，一列"，在回答中的意思是"纠纷，严重分歧"。
- for ages 很多年

  这里的 age 是年代的意思，作者使用夸张的手法形容漫长的等待时间。
- make a really lame excuse

  lame 的原意是"站不住脚的，无说服力的"，在回答中的意思是"无法让人信服的借口"。

- charge up 给（电池）充电；charge up a phone 给手机充电
- feel insulted 感觉受到了侮辱
- confront *v.* 直面；与某人对峙
- defensive *adj.* 自卫的，防守的
- stream *n.* 一连串
- make a real effort 做出切实努力
- self-critical *adj.* 自我批判的
- fall out with 与某人争吵

  本文给出了两种与"争吵"的相关表达：have a row with 和 fall out with。

★ Part 3

1 On what occasions do people have disagreements?

示例回答

People often have disagreements because of different expectations or different ideas about what is polite or impolite. I think it's *rooted in* how we are *brought up*, what we are used to, and how *tolerant* we are. It's important in life to be more tolerant of other people, especially as we are all so different in the things we get upset about and are *sensitive* about.

内容亮点

- be rooted in 植根于
- bring up sb. 抚养某人
- tolerant *adj.* 宽容的
- sensitive *adj.* 敏感的

2 Are people more likely to argue with their friends or family members?

示例回答

People are most certainly more likely to argue with family members, because of two reasons. Firstly, because we often live with them, and that means there are higher *tensions* between people. And secondly, because we argue more often with people we are very familiar with. There is an old English saying "*familiarity breeds contempt*" and I think this is very true. The more familiar you are with people, the more likely it is that you will disagree and *voice your disagreements* with each other.

内容亮点

- tension *n.* 矛盾，对立；紧张气氛
- familiarity breeds contempt 亲密生嫌隙

  breed *v.* 培育；contempt *n.* 轻视，蔑视
- voice your disagreements 表达不同的意见

★ Part 2

10 Describe an enjoyable journey by public transport.

You should say:

Where you were going

Who you were with

What happened during the journey

And explain why it was enjoyable.

示例回答

I made a really interesting journey by public transport, a few years ago. I'd like to talk about this particular journey because it **sticks in my mind** really strongly. I wanted to go to Dali, in Yunnan Province. I set off from Kunming, and I wanted to take the bus so that I could see the countryside and enjoy the scenery along the way. You can easily get a flight from Kunming to Dali, but I didn't want to do this. In fact, I was with two friends, and they tried to convince me that getting a flight there was a better idea, but I didn't want to do it. I **pushed my point** and **insisted** that we go to the bus station and find a bus. So, they agreed.

You see, I'm really into photography and I write my own blog, and I'd heard that there was lots of amazing and varied scenery on the way from Kunming to Dali, mountain views, winding country roads and all sorts. Anyway, we quite easily got a bus at the bus station and **set off** around 7 am. The bus was a small bus and it was really **packed**. There wasn't much room and it wasn't especially comfortable. But it was okay. The weather was nice, and the other passengers were pleasant, so we were lucky. On the way we chatted, ate snacks, and generally enjoyed the scenery as the bus wound through mountain roads and along highways, and through **woodland areas**, **tunnels**, and above **paddy fields**. I loved the scenery. However, my friend started to **get motion sickness**, and we had to stop the bus a couple of times for him to get out and get some fresh air and he was even sick once. The driver was pretty **sympathetic** to all of this actually, and the passengers were kind and patient. I must admit I felt a bit guilty because I was the person wanting to go by bus on this long 10-hour **cross-country journey**, rather than take the plane!

Eventually, we arrived at Dali, we booked into our hotel and had **a light dinner**, some drinks with the owner – a friendly local man with fascinating stories, and we **turned in for the night**. The rooms were really comfortable and decorated in a traditional Yunnan style. I was really happy we made the trip **overland** rather than by plane, but I'm not sure my friend who was car-sick felt the same as I.

内容亮点

- stick in one's mind 久久难忘
- push my point 使别人同意自己的观点
- insist v. 坚持

  insist 后面接宾语从句的时候，如果指尚未发生的动作，从句谓语常用虚拟语气：should+ 动词原形或直接用动词原形。

- set off 出发

- packed *adj.* 拥挤的（相当于 crowded）
- woodland area 林区
- tunnel *n.* 隧道
- paddy field 稻田，水田
- get motion sickness 晕车
- sympathetic *adj.* 有同情心的
- cross-country journey 越野旅行
- a light dinner 简餐
- turn in for the night 上床睡觉
- overland *adv.* 经由陆地

★ Part 3

1 Do you think it's important to go travelling?

示例回答

Travelling is really good for people. Though it can be tiring, and take some ***preparation***, patience and energy, it's a great way to ***expand the mind***, learn about new regions of your own country, or even different countries and cultures. I think that everyone can benefit from travelling.

内容亮点

- preparation *n.* 准备

  常与 make 搭配，make preparation for sth. 意为"为······做准备"

- expand the mind 开拓视野（相当于 broaden one's horizon）

2 Do you think people will go travelling more often in the future?

示例回答

I think that people will travel about the same as now. People are already travelling a lot more than they used to ten years ago, actually. But I think with recent events in the world, people will start to travel less and focus more on staying in their home cities, working more online and travelling to places closer to them.

内容亮点

- 本题作者表示人们外出旅游的次数并不会变多，并解释了原因，这样的答题结构是一个用 explanation 拓展答案的典型例子。

3 What do you think is the best form of public transport?

示例回答

I think the best form of public transport is a pretty hard thing to give an opinion about. I mean, it totally depends on where you are going and the purpose of your trip. For example, if you are going from Beijing to Bangkok, and you're going on a business trip, then, of course, the plane is the best way of travelling there. If you were setting off on a one-month adventure with friends, then maybe you'd enjoy taking the train. I once took a train all the way from Beijing to Vietnam and it was really exciting, but you'd not want to choose this method if you were on a business trip! So, like many things in life, it depends on your aim, your goal, your purpose, and the amount of time you have, as well, of course, as your personality and preferences.

内容亮点

- 本题作者给出了一种中立的回答方式。遇到一些很难直接用 yes or no 回答的问题时，需要分情况讨论。这种答题结构的好处是答案内容会比较丰富。

❹ Do you think technology will make public transport better in the future?

示例回答

Yes, most certainly. We've seen a lot of evidence of this over the past 10 years. Trains now are super-fast and always, almost always on time, and flight times are less and less. Mobile apps have made it easier to book taxis in cities and so on. I imagine that technology will continue to advance and we will see ***constant improvements*** in public transport as a result.

内容亮点

- constant improvement 持续的进步
- 本回答的观点是未来出行方式会变得更加先进，发展得更好。作者给出了两个例子证明自己的观点：第一点是目前火车的速度大幅度提升，飞机飞行的时间也越来越短；第二点是人们现在可以在手机上预约出租车，所以科技的应用促进交通方式的发展是一个必然的趋势。

★ Part 2

> **11** Describe an important journey that has been delayed.
> You should say:
> What it is for
> When and where you planned to go
> Why it was delayed
> And explain how you felt about the delay.

示例回答

Oh, I've been on several journeys and trips that have been delayed. However, the one that really sticks in my mind is a trip to Urumqi in Xinjiang province, to see my grandfather during the National holiday. It takes about 4 hours to get to Xinjiang by plane – it's really far away. And because my grandfather lives in a small city about 2 hours from Urumqi, so it means getting a train after arriving by plane – it's really a ***massively*** long journey ***door to door***, and ***incredibly*** tiring.

Anyway, naturally, it was an important journey for us, not only because my grandfather is old now and we do not see him very often, but because it takes almost 2 days of our holiday to travel there and back, which really ***cuts into our holiday time***. So, I was hugely disappointed and quite ***frustrated***, angry and upset when, at the airport, it was announced that the plane was severely delayed. In fact, it ended up being a really long delay, and all of us got really impatient. Some of the passengers were complaining to the *airport authorities* when they heard that the plane we were to travel on was not even in the airport yet, but stuck in another city down south, hours from Beijing.

Anyway, these things happen in life, and we all *calmed each other down*. The air company gave us some *vouchers* for *a complimentary meal* in one of the restaurants in the *terminal* and eventually we boarded and had a safe trip. All in all, it was ok, and I was happy to see my grandfather, but it was *a real test of nerves and patience*! China is a big country and Xinjiang is really far away, so it can cut half a day from your holiday if you suffer a big delay like this, as well as making you feel quite stressed and *messing up* other people's plans and arrangements at your destination.

内容亮点

- massively *adv.* 巨大地
- door to door 全程

  The journey takes about an hour door to door. 该旅程全程大约要花一个小时。

- incredibly *adv.* 难以置信地

  incredibly 和上文的 massively 一样，副词 + 形容词可以加强效果，替换了考生们常用的 very 等程度副词。

- cut into our holiday time

  句中的 cut into 本意是把某物切成几块，在本文的意思是"缩短假期时间"。

- frustrated *adj.* 令人挫败的
- airport authorities 机场管理者（方）
- calm sb. down 使某人平静下来
- voucher *n.* 代金券，票券
- a complimentary meal 免费的一餐

  complimentary 在这里的意思是"免费的，赠送的"，除此之外，这个词还有"赞美的，表示钦佩的"意思。

- terminal *n.* 航站楼
- a real test of nerves and patience 一场精神和耐心的真正考验
- mess up 扰乱，打乱

★ Part 3

1 What impacts on the natural environment does transport have?

示例回答

This is a common topic today, discussed in the news a lot – the *carbon footprint*, as they call it, of different means of transport. For example, all forms of transport produce emissions that are bad for the environment, which increase the *greenhouse effect* that warms the planet and causes climate change. Airplanes and huge gasoline intense forms of transport create a lot of emissions, and *so do private cars*. A lot of efforts are being made to create *renewable energy sources* and *electric vehicles*, but we still have a long way to go before this can start *reducing the emissions* especially in countries that are expanding and developing fast, and are focusing on developing more than environmental protection.

内容亮点

- carbon footprint 碳足迹（某个时间段内日常活动排放的二氧化碳量）

- greenhouse effect 温室效应

- so do private cars

  这里涉及 so 引导的倒装句，谓语动词 do 是根据主句谓语动词 create 来决定的，意思是私家车"也是"如此，即私家车也产生了很多碳排放。

- renewable energy sources 可再生能源

- electric vehicles 电动车

- reduce the emissions 减少排放

2 How will means of transport improve or develop in the future?

示例回答

I think more transport will be *electric*, and I think more public transport options will *emerge* as well, and less private cars will be encouraged on the roads. I also think that many vehicles will be *self-driving*, especially buses and taxis.

内容亮点

- 对将来的交通方式如何发展这一问题，本题答案给出了三个可能：第一、电动（electric）车增多；第二、出现（emerge）更多种类的公共交通；第三、自动驾驶（self-driving）汽车会越来越多。

3 Will people still choose to drive private cars if the public transport is free?

示例回答

I think there will always be lots of people that want to drive their own cars. Cars are still a *luxury* in many ways and you have *a sense of freedom* if you have a private car. Furthermore, some people *see it as a status symbol*, something necessary to show your friends and colleagues.

内容亮点

- luxury *n.* 奢侈品

- a sense of freedom 自由的感觉

- see it as a status symbol 把它看作社会地位的一种象征

4 How can we develop transportation in the countryside?

示例回答

The countryside is indeed a place where public transport is *sorely lacking*. I think that there should be better, more efficient and generally more buses. Buses are the main form of public transport outside of the cities, apart from trains of course – but trains tend to go between cities, in the countryside people rely on buses – so we need to develop better bus services and make them more *frequent*.

内容亮点

- 作者认为，要想发展乡村地区的交通，首当其冲的是普及公共交通方式。乡村地区交通方式比较落后（sorely *adv.* 极其地，严重地；lacking *adj.* 缺乏的），buses 作为主要的交通手段，需要提升服务频率，变得更加频繁（frequent *adj.* 频繁的）。

★ Part 2

 Describe a change that can improve your local area.
You should say:
　What it is
　How it can be made
　What problem it might bring
And explain how you feel about it.

示例回答

There is one thing that I think would really improve my local area and that is if they planted more trees and *flowerbeds*. In recent years they have made a lot of *renovations* to the community, the buildings, and the streets nearby. However, they have taken away a lot of trees and bushes to widen the roads and *pavements*. I don't really like this. I was thinking about it the other day, and I thought that there are a number of areas where they could plant trees again, put in a few nice flowerbeds and try to put back some of the natural feels the area had before they made these *concrete renovations*. I don't like it when they *prioritise traffic, roads and garages and things like this over nature* – plants and trees are important in any neighbourhood.

Sometimes they do things *in a slapdash way*, they don't plan things properly – someone in the local government has some funds to spend and an idea and they make a quick decision, usually the cheapest decision possible so that they can spend less money on the actual renovations, and more money on maybe hiring a company they *have connections with* to do the work, and it's the everyday people that suffer.

My grandmother was really unhappy because she was really hoping they were going to make the area more beautiful. However, my father said that these changes were necessary because of the huge traffic the city is facing. Anyway, whatever opinion they have, I believe that now they should make some efforts to re-build some of the flowerbeds and create a few more green spaces – I think this is possible if they plan it properly, and I think they've done this in many areas of the city with great success. So, I am hoping this change can come to my area too!

内容亮点

- flowerbed 花坛

- renovation *n.* 翻新，革新

　下文的 concrete renovations 指代新建筑，concrete 本身的意思是"混凝土"。

- pavement *n.* 人行道
- prioritise traffic, roads and garages and things like this over nature

  这个词组里要学习的表达是 prioritise sth. over sth.，该词组的意思是 "把交通、道路以及车库这些基础设施的建设优先于自然环境的保护"。
- in a slapdash way 草率地
- have connections with 与……有关系

★ Part 3

1 Are people where you come from usually friendly with their neighbours?

示例回答

Yes, mostly yes. The majority of people are fairly friendly, and some people are quite *distant*. There aren't really any unfriendly people I know in my neighbourhood. Well, *come to think of it* there is one old man who is really grumpy and quite rude, to be honest. He never opens the front door for you if you meet coming and going from the building, he never greets you *if you end up in the elevator at the same time*, and he is always seen *moaning* to other neighbours about people in the community. He has a dog as well, and if he can avoid it he will not pick up the dog mess after the dog fouls the pavements. So, we don't like him and we find him very unfriendly. However, for the most part, people around where I live are friendly and polite, I must say.

内容亮点

- distant *adj.* 遥远的（回答中用来形容人与人之间的距离感）
- come to think of it 现在想起来
- if you end up in the elevator at the same time 如果你们同时在电梯里

  end up in 后面一般接某种状态。
- moan *v.* 抱怨

  moan to sb. about sth. 向某人抱怨某事

2 What are the popular activities in and around your community?

示例回答

Popular activities...let me think...exercising on the exercise machines and in the *communal outdoor areas...*is mainly what older people do. Young people sometimes just hang around outside in the summer on the grass, and kids enjoy playing outside very much. I see children enjoying the outdoor areas most, to be honest – on *scooters*, *playing hide and seek*. All sorts of things like this.

内容亮点

- communal outdoor area

  本句中 communal 意为 "公共的"，这个词组的意思是公共户外区域。
- scooter *n.* 小型摩托车，儿童滑板车
- play hide and seek 玩捉迷藏

3 **Do people usually like living in residential compounds and communities alongside other people?**

示例回答

I am not sure really. I think so. I think nowadays people don't really interact much with their neighbours, to be honest, so I don't know they like or dislike it. I think in the past, most people had more of a relationship with their neighbours – there was more *a sense of real community*. Perhaps in the hutong streets of Beijing, you can still feel, especially in spring and summer, more of this *community atmosphere* between people living in the same streets or buildings.

内容亮点

- 在回答本题时，作者分了不同的情况讨论：现在与过去对比，大部分的人和生活在胡同里的人对比。community atmosphere 和 a sense of community 分别意为"社区氛围"和"社区感"。

4 **Where do people who live in the same compounds or communities usually meet? Are there any places where people meet socially?**

示例回答

As I said, nowadays they don't really meet as such. Some communities have a café or a gym or a swimming center, but people don't really meet neighbours there, *as such*. They *cross paths* there, maybe, but I've not seen much real *bonding* between neighbours in the places where I or my family have lived over the years.

内容亮点

- as such 就其本身而言（在此更像是随口一说，没有实际用意）
- cross path 相遇
- bonding *n.* 联结，纽带

★ Part 2

 Describe an interesting animal you have ever seen.
You should say:
    What the animal is
    When and where you saw it
    What it looked like
And explain how you felt about the whole experience.

示例回答

The animal I would like to talk about is actually from a cartoon and is not a real animal. I hope that's ok. I want to talk about him because he's my favourite *fictional character*, I think. And he's a *warthog*, a kind of *wild boar*, which is a type of wild pig. He is one of the characters in the Walt Disney film, *The Lion King*. His name is Pumba.

Pumba is a fairly *simple-minded* character in a way, and he is very *endearing*, friendly and *has a positive outlook on life*. Pumba appears in *The Lion King* when Simba, the boy lion, escapes from the evil lion, Scar, and ends up being in the desert, exhausted and asleep and far from home. Pumba, the wild boar, and Timon, the small humourous Meerkat, find Simba and take care of him, take him to their beautiful *jungle* and teach him about *turning his back on troubles* and worries and being positive about life and the future. Pumba is a brown pig, with hair on his back, a big smile, and *tusks*. He can run fast, and he is always friendly.

He also has a slightly modest side to him. Anyway, I enjoyed this film the first time I saw it, and I was really happy when Pumba appeared as a main character. To be honest, he's the best animal in the film and one of my favourite animals in any film, so that's why I've chosen to talk about him today, although he is a fictional animal and not a real animal.

【内容亮点】

- fictional character 虚构角色
- warthog *n.* 非洲野猪 （下文的 wild boar 也是"野猪"的意思）
- simple-minded *adj.* 头脑简单的
- endearing *adj.* 可爱的，讨人喜欢的
- have a positive outlook on life 对待生活有积极乐观的态度
- jungle *n.* 丛林，密林
- turn one's back on troubles 远离烦恼
- tusk *n.* 长牙，尖牙
- He also has a slightly modest side to him. 他（的性格里）也有谦逊的一面。

★ Part 3

1 Do you think animals are important to human life?

【示例回答】

I think animals are important in a variety of different ways. Firstly, and perhaps a little bit sadly, we rely on animals as part of our diet, as food. Secondly, animals are important as part of the *ecosystem*. The natural world would not be able to continue *the way it does* without the circle of life shared by plants and animals on earth. So, animals are part of this chain – and *are* therefore *of great importance* to human life on the planet.

【内容亮点】

- 本题的答题结构采取了总分的形式，先承认动物在很多方面对人类有用，然后解释其重要性。ecosystem 意为"生态系统"；the way it does 的完整表达为 the way in which it does，在英语口语表达中，习惯省略 in which。
- be of great important 相当于 be very important，是"重要性"这个意思较为书面的表达。

2 **Why do you think some people keep pets?**

示例回答

Pets *keep people company* in the home, and also people enjoy the sense of responsibility you get from looking after a pet like a cat or a dog, or even a *turtle* or fish in a *tank* or whatever kind of animal – I think it's a nice experience to feel you are looking after another life and you can also enjoy their company, in a way.

内容亮点

- keep sb. company 陪伴某人
- turtle *n.* 乌龟
- tank *n.* 鱼缸

3 **What are some of the difficulties in raising pets?**

示例回答

Some of the difficulties in *raising pets* might be dealing with them *making a mess* everywhere. Also, another thing is how much exercise some dogs need – if you are a busy family – everyone working or going to school, then you might not get enough time to give a dog the exercise it needs. Dogs need a good amount of exercise every day and it's a bit *cruel*, perhaps, to keep a big dog in a city apartment without it having a lot of walks. So, there are all sorts of difficulties, I've mentioned just a couple of them.

内容亮点

- raising pet 养宠物

  raise 有多个意思，比如筹款、抬升、举起，在本文的意思是"抚养，养育"。
- make a mess 制造混乱
- cruel *adj.* 残忍的

4 **What kinds of pets do most people usually favour?**

示例回答

Well, of course, it's dogs and cats really. These are the common types of pets that most people keep. Some older people in China like to keep birds – and others like to keep fish in a tank. But I think in pretty much every country in the world dogs and cats are the most popular. Cats are more *independent* and less *reliant* on *a master or keeper*, dogs are quite a bit more *dependent*, but a lot more friendly to their owners. So, both the two most popular pets are quite different, but we can see why different people like to keep them as pets.

内容亮点

- reliant *adj.* 依赖的

  和后文的 dependent 为同义词，是前面的 independent 的反义词，independent 意为"独立的"。
- a master or a keeper 养宠物的人，宠物主人

★ Part 2

> **14** Describe a performance you watched recently.
> You should say:
> What it was
> When you watched it
> Who you were with
> And explain why you watched it.

示例回答

I'd like to describe a performance that I was invited to in Beijing recently. It was a type of gala show in a big theatre. I can't remember the name of the theatre now; it was near Qian men. It was a series of performances just before the new year. All of them involved *choreography* – basically a lot of people dancing together – the entire show lasted about 2 hours and told the story of a man and how he came to fall in love with a beautiful young girl.

The lighting was incredible and so were the costumes and the *stage sets*. In fact, it was very impressive indeed, and *it must have taken a very long time* for them to *rehearse* to get to this professional standard. These kinds of large performances are very popular in China, actually, with dance and group choreography, and *acrobatics* and elements of *martial arts* all mixed together. Usually, they are centred around themes of ancient China, too. I quite like these kinds of historical themes. I think they can be a great *source of inspiration* for us.

However, I must say, I'm not so into performances on TV. There are often stage performances on TV in my country and I find these to be a little *tacky* and boring to be honest. I really enjoy watching things live, you know...I really am not a fan of watching performances on TV and they also tend to *overlay* lots of *computer graphics* and images over them, which makes them just far too *fake and inauthentic*.

内容亮点

- choreography *n.* 编舞，舞蹈设计
- stage set 舞台布景
- It must have taken a very long time to do sth. 肯定花了很多时间做某事

  must have done sth. 表示对过去发生的事情进行推测
- rehearse *v.* 排练
- acrobatic *n.* 杂技
- martial arts 武术
- source of inspiration 灵感之源
- tacky *adj.* 低劣的；俗气的
- overlay *v.* 覆盖
- computer graphic 电脑图像
- fake and inauthentic 假的，不真实的

★ Part 3

1 **Are there any traditional cultural performances that are popular in China?**

There are lots, of course. The Chinese like their cultural performances actually, both on stage and the television. Like I was saying earlier, they like **big group formation dancing**, themes of ancient China and stories about love between different **people of different social classes** in history. Chinese are proud of their history and most cultural performances are centred around key periods in Chinese history.

- big group formation dancing 群舞表演
- people of different social classes 不同社会阶层的人

2 **What's the difference between watching performances live and watching them on TV?**

Well, watching performances live is always more exciting. You're there in person, and **close to the action**. It's much more exciting and you can also feel the excitement of the rest of the audience. **The only disadvantage is that** if you don't like the performance you can't turn it off – you can always turn the television off if you get bored, are not in the mood, or don't enjoy what you're watching.

- 回答一开始提到了观看现场表演的好处：close to the action（身临其境）。The only disadvantage is that 引出后半部分，即观看现场表演的不足之处：不能像看电视那样，如果不喜欢表演就直接关掉。

3 **How can children benefit from taking part in these performances?**

Children can learn a lot from getting involved in performances. They learn a range of skills involving **cooperation**, **teamwork**, **coordination**, as well as dance, acting, and being confident on stage in front of a large audience. **Show business** is a wonderful field to gain these skills.

- cooperation *n.* 合作
- teamwork *n.* 团队协作
- coordination *n.* 协调
- show business 娱乐行业

4 **Should the government provide financial support to promote traditional performances?**

Yes, I think so. I think the government already does this quite a lot. The show that I went to recently was *sponsored* by the Haidian *municipal government labour bureau*, in fact. This kind of thing is quite common, as China is trying to *revive its traditional culture* more and more these years.

内容亮点

- sponsor *v.* 赞助

  be sponsored by 由……赞助

- municipal government 市镇政府

- labour bureau 劳动局

- revive traditional culture 复兴传统文化

★ Part 2

15 Describe an experience when you enjoyed an indoor game.
You should say:
What the indoor game was
Who you played it with
Where you played it
And explain how you felt about it.

示例回答

I haven't played any indoor games for ages, actually. But...I *recall* one game that I played with a group of friends to celebrate one friend's birthday. We went to an indoor swimming pool and leisure center, not far from the centre of Beijing. *It's a huge complex* with lots of areas outside where people can sit, eat snacks, chat with friends and take part in different sports – there's tennis courts, basketball courts, *indoor hockey* and even an *ice rink*.

The time we went there were about 15 of us...old school friends mainly. After about an hour in the swimming pool, one of the groups suggested we go to the *beach volleyball* area. There was a large complex of about 4 volleyball *courts*, and they actually had sand on the floor like on a real beach. Because there were about 15 of us, it was easy to divide into 2 teams. We didn't *take the game really seriously*, but we *more or less played by the rules* and it was really fun. It was much more fun than playing volleyball normally – somehow the sand makes it more exciting and a bit more challenging. We played for a couple of hours and kept changing team members and taking breaks for snacks in the local *eateries* in the leisure centre.

I don't think I've ever been to a leisure centre that was so big with such a wide variety of things to do inside. I'd say that I wish there were more leisure centres in my city, to be honest. I think that the advantage of indoor sports is that you can play them in all weathers, in all seasons, and that's especially important if you live in an area of the country where the climate is not really favourable for outdoor activities.

I hope that in the future there will be more sports centres and indoor sports facilities in my city, because I think it would also encourage people to get involved in more healthy activities in their spare time. I know that I would certainly do more sport if these options were more available.

内容亮点

- recall *v.* 回忆
- It's a huge complex... 这是一个很大的建筑群

  complex 常作为形容词，表示"复杂的"，在本句中作为名词，意为"建筑群"。

  a sports complex 综合体育场；an industrial complex (= a site with many factories) 工业建筑群
- indoor hockey *n.* 室内曲棍球
- ice rink *n.* 溜冰场
- beach volleyball 沙滩排球
- court *n.* 场地；tennis court 网球场
- take the game really seriously 严肃认真地对待比赛

  take sth. seriously 严肃认真地对待某事
- more or less 或多或少地
- play by the rules 遵守规则
- eatery *n.* 小吃店

★ Part 3

1 **How have indoor games changed since you were a child?**

示例回答

Indoor games used to be more physical when I was a child. Today, a lot of people play computer games. Still, I have seen recently quite a few people I know going back to the more old-style indoor games – **board games**, games like chess, **backgammon**, and so forth. Also, I've seen in some bars near my home that there are a lot of people **playing darts** both for fun and in competitions. This, at least in my city, is quite a new development. I didn't see this when I was a child.

内容亮点

- board game 桌游
- backgammon 十五子棋戏（两人游戏，棋盘上有楔形小区，掷骰子决定走棋步数）
- play darts 玩飞镖

2 **How can team games be beneficial for young children?**

示例回答

Team games encourage cooperation, teamwork, working on **strategies** with other people, and also, we learn about our **strengths and weaknesses** as individuals. Different members of a sports team might be good at different important skills.

内容亮点

- strategy *n.* 策略
- strength and weakness 优势和劣势

3 What qualities do you think are important in a good team leader?

示例回答

A good team leader needs to understand all the members of the team, their strengths, their weaknesses and their personalities. A team leader should try to make sure that everyone in a team is performing well with the other members and *they are all in positions* in which they can *make the most of their strengths* for the benefit of the whole team. A good leader should be an understanding and intelligent person who has good people skills as well as *strategic awareness* for the game itself.

内容亮点

- they are all in positions 所有人各司其职
- make the most of their strengths 充分利用他们的优点
- strategic awareness 战略意识

4 How has the popularity of phone and computer games changed how people spend their leisure time?

示例回答

Phone and computer games, in my opinion, have totally *dominated* some people's time and caused people to become *antisocial*, not pay enough attention to real *social interactions* – rudely ignoring members of their family or friends during dinners or social events.

内容亮点

- dominate *v.* 支配，控制
- antisocial *adj.* 不爱交际的
- social interaction 社交

★ Part 2

16 Describe a time when you watched the sky.
You should say:
    When it was
    What you watched
    Who you watched it with
And explain how you felt about it.

示例回答

There was a time that I remember very clearly that I watched the sky for a long time. It was the night sky in Spain, from the rooftop of my friend's house. He had recently moved into a lovely old house in the mountains in southern Spain, just outside *Malaga* – I forget the name of the place now – but it was a small little village in the mountains, with very few neighbours. There's almost no *light pollution* there, so you can see the sky perfectly, all the stars, and even some planets.

The night I really watched the sky was after dinner with some wine. We went outside and sat under the trees, and then my friend suggested we go up onto the **terrace**, on the rooftop basically. And we lay down silently and looked at the sky for what seemed like a long long time. Maybe it was an hour or so, but it seemed forever, and it was such a peaceful feeling. I'll never forget it. It means so much to me because I usually live in a city, where it's not only noisy, but you can't really see the stars in the sky because of the light pollution – all the city lights and traffic lights and so on. So, this was a very **memorable** moment for me.

I think when you live in a big city, you tend to forget about nature a bit – and you forget how **calming** it is, as well as how powerful and important it is. Looking at the sky, especially in a countryside place free from light, noise and air pollution, is a brilliant way of connecting with nature again, and incredibly good for the soul. As you can see, I felt incredibly moved by this experience and most certainly would like to do it more often – **if only** I could live more closely to nature and have such views of the sky more often! I think I would **be at peace with myself** a lot more **frequently** than I am now.

内容亮点

- Malaga 马拉加省
- light pollution 光污染
- terrace *n.* 露天平台
- memorable *adj.* 值得纪念的
- calming *adj.* 使人镇静的
- if only 要是……就好了

  在虚拟语气里使用这一短语，表达一个不可能实现的愿望或者假设，具体有三种情况：表示与现在事实相反的假设，用一般过去时；表示与过去事实相反的假设，用过去完成时；表示与将来事实相反的假设，用 would + 动词原型。
- be at peace with myself 保持内心的平静
- frequently *adv.* 经常地，频繁地

★ Part 3

1 **Do you think it is useful to learn about the planets and outer space in school?**

示例回答

No, not really, I think that maybe in university, but not in school. In school, children have already enough things to learn about which **have higher priorities than** learning about space or the planets.

内容亮点

- 问题里提到的 school 指的是高中及以下阶段的学校，大学生活不包括在 school life 中，这一点需要注意。
- A has higher priorities than B A 比 B 更重要

2 **Why do some governments believe it is a priority to explore space and other planets?**

示例回答

Well, we learn a lot from *space exploration*. Firstly, we learn to develop powerful technology that can help develop our abilities as a nation, and secondly, we may discover new and important things in space or on other planets – perhaps one day we might be able to live on other planets.

内容亮点

- 这个回答采用了总分结构。太空探索（space exploration）重要的原因有两点：第一、有助于提升综合国力；第二、帮助我们寻找第二个家园。

3 **Why do you think some people think the stars and space are romantic?**

示例回答

Stars are so far away and they *shine at night*. Already this is a very romantic notion. Plus, they look beautiful on a silent, dark night when the sky is clear. They are the subject of a lot of romantic poems, *works of art and literature*.

内容亮点

- shine at night 在夜晚闪耀
- works of art and literature 艺术和文学作品

★ Part 2

17 Describe an occasion when you wore your best clothes.
You should say:
　　When it happened
　　Where it happened
　　What kind of clothes you wore
And explain why you wore it.

示例回答

The last time I wore my best clothes was at *a company annual dinner and gala*. They're really big occasions in my country, at least in my company. It was before the spring festival around the start of January, and it was held on a Thursday night. It took place in a big hotel just outside of the centre of the city. It was a *grandiose* occasion and a number of us from each department had rehearsed dance performances and *comedy acts* for the stage show.

So, in fact, I *dressed up* twice, in my best long *ball gown and high heels* for the dinner, and in a sporty sort of *dance outfit* for the stage show. I enjoy dressing up in nice dresses and heels and things like this, and I think they really suit me. It's nice to have these opportunities to wear one's best clothes and for people to *compliment you about* how attractive you look. I think most people enjoy these kinds of occasions. On this occasion, I was really happy because I'd spent a lot of time choosing the dress and a matching pair of heels and a handbag.

My friends also dressed up really *smartly*. The boys wore grey suits and ties and their best shoes, and everyone looked fantastic. This created a really cool atmosphere and I could tell that everyone felt proud to work in our company and enjoyed drinking and chatting and getting to know each other *in a different context to the office* in which we normally see each other.

I think it's really good to have opportunities to wear your best clothes, and to dress up a bit – like I mentioned before, it can make you feel more attractive and confident, and *you can tell that other people around you feel the same way*, so it creates a really good atmosphere and *social dynamic* on special occasions. I think these are quite important things when it comes to *team building* and special occasions and help to create a sense of community which is more interesting than everyday life might usually be.

内容亮点

- a company annual dinner and gala 公司年度晚宴和庆典
- grandiose *adj.* 宏大的；浮夸的
- comedy acts 喜剧表演
- dress up 盛装打扮
- ball gown and high heels 舞会长裙和高跟鞋；下一句的 dance outfit 指舞蹈服
- compliment sb. about sth. 为……称赞某人
- smartly *adv.* 利落地；时髦地
- in a different context to the office 和办公室的环境完全不一样
- you can tell that other people around you feel the same way 中 tell 的意思不是"告诉"，而是"辨别"。
- social dynamic 社交动力
- team building 团队建设

★ Part 3

1 Do you think people should wear formal clothes in the workplace?

示例回答

I think that it depends on your type of work. We are not *a client-facing company* so we tend to *dress quite casually* in the office. If you work in a client-facing company, or in the *service industry* then maybe you have to dress in more formal clothes, or even a uniform, when in the office.

内容亮点

- a client-facing company 一个面向客户的公司（意思是直接和客户打交道）
- dress quite casually 打扮很休闲

  casually *adv.* 休闲地，随意地
- service industry 服务业

2 **Why do some people like to wear traditional clothes?**

示例回答

There's a rising trend nowadays of people starting to dress in traditional Chinese clothes or hanfu. I am not sure if people do it for fun, or whether they want to *hark back to their roots*, but it can be quite nice to see people in traditional clothing. It helps us remember our roots and our past.

内容亮点

- There's a rising trend nowadays of people doing sth. 现如今，做某事的人越来越多了
- hark back to their roots 追忆过去

3 **Do you think traditional clothes will disappear in the future?**

示例回答

No, I don't. I think there will always be some people who like to wear traditional clothes that remind them of their *cultural heritage*. I think it's becoming something people *are* a bit more *aware of* today than maybe a few years ago, even.

内容亮点

- cultural heritage 文化遗产
- be aware of 意识到

4 **Do old people often change their dress style?**

示例回答

Usually, old people stick to the same types and styles of clothes as they wore back in their time. There are some really *hip and modern* older people, however, that like to *move with the times* and wear more modern fashions, and some of them really look good. It depends on their personality, their background and how important they think it is to *keep their finger on the pulse with trends and fashions*.

内容亮点

- hip and modern （衣服、音乐等方面）时髦的
- keep their finger on the pulse with trends and fashions 追赶时尚潮流
  这个词组和前文的 move with the times 可以作为同义词组互换。

地点类（Places）▶▶▶

话题介绍

　　Part 2 地点类话题一般可分为两类。一类是描述某个想去的国家或去过的城市，另一类是描述生活中的某个特定场所，比如某个拥挤的地方、某幢新的建筑物等。

　　在该类型话题的提示语中，往往建议考生描述此地的位置、该地的样子、如何了解到此地、前往的频率、一般和谁同往，或是会在那做哪些事情等相关内容。考生在该类型的话题中，如果没有清晰的思路，可尝试描述在此处会做的事情，说明你被此地吸引的原因及对应的感受。同时，也可尝试和其他类似的地点进行对比，突出说明你喜欢该地点的原因。

　　考生可通过本书中的示例回答，整理对于地点特征和对应感受的相关思路和表达方式，并结合当季雅思口语题库进行练习。回答完 Part 2 之后考官会根据考生的回答进行 Part 3 的提问，该部分是对 Part 2 内容的进一步延伸。

★ Part 2

1 Describe a foreign country (culture) you want to know more about.
You should say:
　　What it is
　　Where it is
　　How you know it
And explain why you want to know more about it.

示例回答

I'd like to learn more about ***Mexico***. ***I've been watching*** a TV series set in Mexico recently, ***and I'm really drawn to*** the way they speak, their ***sense of humour*** and the amazing ***countryside*** of the country. It's a country in South America. So, I know about it mainly from that TV series. I've also been to a few Mexican restaurants in Beijing, which I really enjoy. So, ***I'm quite drawn to*** the food as well as the impression I have of the place from the TV series. I've also heard that it's quite a dangerous country though, unfortunately, with ***a lot of drug problems***, ***violent gangs and crime***.

So, I guess certain areas of the country are not very safe for travelling, but I am sure there are areas that are fairly safe, because I've seen quite a few holidays and travel programmes about the place. I'd like to go to Mexico one day, and they speak Spanish, which is a language I am really drawn to, so I would quite like to go there and perhaps study Spanish for a year or two and maybe even find a job with some connection between Mexico and China. I believe there might be ***increasingly close trade ties*** between the countries and this could mean jobs might require Spanish-speaking Chinese business people to ***help establish and maintain such relationships***. So, there are a number of reasons, a mixture of reasons. I think that Mexico is an interesting country I would like to learn more about.

Generally speaking, I think that having the opportunity in life to learn about and visit foreign countries, either on holiday or with work, is a really good thing for people. It can help *open our minds to* new and different ideas, different ways of thinking or doing things, and can be *quite inspiring and educational* as well. We can learn a lot from the good things and bad things about diverse countries, the ways they are run, the problems they have, the social habits and customs. There is a whole range of things we can learn from *being exposed to other cultures*. *All in all*, it's a great thing, especially for people who aim to *work in international fields* in the future and build stronger relationships between countries.

内容亮点

- Mexico *n.* 墨西哥
- I've been watching..., and I'm really drawn to... 我正在看……，而且我很喜欢……
  注意前后时态的不同。英语句子中的谓语动词都涉及时态问题，需要格外关注。
- sense of humour 幽默感
  常用sense of...表示"……感"，如sense of responsibility 意为"责任感"，sense of achievement 意为"成就感"。
- countryside *n.* 农村，乡村地区
- I'm quite drawn to 我很喜欢……，我被……吸引
- a lot of drug problems, violent gangs and crime 很多毒品问题，暴力团伙和犯罪行为（注意积累话题中的名词）
- increasingly close trade ties 越来越紧密的贸易关系
- help establish and maintain such relationships 有利于建立和维持这样的关系
- generally speaking 总的来说（常用于总体描述）
- open our minds to 开放思想，拓展思想
- quite inspiring and educational 非常具有启发性和教育意义
- be exposed to other cultures 接触其他文化
- All in all 总之（用于总结性的句子）
- work in international fields 在国际领域工作

★ Part 3

1 **What do you think is the best way to learn about a foreign culture?**

示例回答

I think today the internet is *the best way to find out and learn about anything* really. Travel programmes, blogs, websites, there's a lot of ways. Also, through *exploring* their *cuisine* – I think this is a great way to learn about another culture, too – the food. *Getting into the art and music of another country* is a good start – for example, if you're interested in India, you could just go online and search for "Indian Religious Art", or "Indian Music" or "Famous Indian Stars" and loads of articles will come up. So, today it's easy to learn about other cultures, it's a case of having *the right attitude and approach*.

- the best way to find out and learn about anything 找到并学习任何事情的最佳途径

- explore cuisine 探索美食

- get into the art and music of another country 探索另一个国家的艺术和音乐

- the right attitude and approach 正确的态度和方法

② What do you think is the biggest problem when someone works in a foreign country?

示例回答

The biggest problems are usually *communication issues and cultural differences*. Communication can be a real problem and working and living in another language culture *can be really stressful*, especially if you're not good at languages and don't *pick up languages easily*.

内容亮点

- communication issues and cultural differences 沟通问题和文化差异

- can be really stressful 会非常有压力

- pick up languages easily 轻松掌握语言

③ Someone says that reading is the best way to know about a culture. Do you agree with that?

示例回答

I think reading is *definitely a good way*. Much about a culture *is revealed through novels and stories*, as well as perhaps even travel and guide books and online resources. But also there are *travel shows and cooking shows* which can be a good way to learn bits about another culture.

内容亮点

- definitely a good way 绝对是好的方法

- be revealed through novels and stories 通过小说和故事揭示

- travel shows and cooking shows 旅行节目和烹饪节目

★ **Part 2**

> **2** Describe a crowded place you went to.
> You should say:
>> When you went there
>> Who you went there with
>> Why you went there
> And explain how you felt about it.

示例回答

A crowded place I went to that I *didn't actually like*, was the Railway Station. It was *an awful experience*. It was a weekend, I think it was a holiday weekend too, and it was *the most crowded place I've ever been to in my life*. There were so many people there it was almost impossible to even move. I felt *a sense of panic* because I thought that I might *miss my train* because the queues were so long – and you had to *queue up* to get into the station, and then you had to *go through security*, and then you had to find your platform, and everywhere, from outside the entrance to right up to the platform, there were so many people.

On this occasion, I went there because I was going to visit an uncle of mine in another city, down south. He had just bought a new house and he was inviting various family members there to celebrate – it also *coincided with the national holiday* – which was the main reason the station was so crowded – everyone in Beijing seemed to be travelling home to *see relatives* for the holiday. Anyway, so I didn't feel good about this, and I am *quite sensitive to crowds and crowded noisy places*. But when I was on the train it was fine, and actually on the way back the crowds there were much less. You *have to be quite patient* if you want to travel anywhere during the national holidays, you see.

Generally speaking, I'd say that different people are sensitive in different ways to crowds and crowded places. Some people really don't mind being in thick crowds, whilst others *get really agitated* and feel it's an invasion of their personal space. I find it quite curious how people are different these days – *maybe it's all due to their upbringing or what they were used to as a child*. It can be exciting being in crowded busy places, and some people enjoy this, and they find that being in very quiet places is very boring. It's curious how people can be so different in this way.

内容亮点

- didn't actually like 并不喜欢（注意 actually 的用法）

- an awful experience 一次糟糕的经历

- the most crowded place I've ever been to in my life 我一生中去过最拥挤的地方

- a sense of panic 恐慌感

- miss my train 赶不上火车

- queue up 排队等候

- go through security 通过安全检查

- on this occasion 这一次；这种情况下

- coincided with the national holiday 与国庆节是同一天

- see relatives 看望亲戚

- quite sensitive to crowds and crowded noisy places 对人群和拥挤嘈杂的地方很敏感

- have to be quite patient 需要非常有耐心

- get really agitated 变得非常激动

- maybe it's all due to 或许这都是由于

- their upbringing or what they were used to as a child 他们的成长环境或小时候的习惯

★ Part 3

1 Do people like to go to crowded places? Why?

示例回答

I think some people like *certain types of crowded places*. Like...for example *live house* where lots of people are dancing to music – they are quite popular with the younger generation. Some people enjoy *the feeling of being in a busy crowded restaurant* where lots of people are happy, eating and clearly enjoying the company of family or friends. This kind of lively atmosphere makes some people feel they are in a popular place where others are having a good time – and this feeling can be *contagious*. This is why some people like these kinds of crowded places. But I don't think anyone likes *a crowded hospital or a crowded train station* or so.

内容亮点

- certain types of crowded places 某种拥挤的地方
- live house 小型现场演出
- the feeling of being in a busy crowded restaurant 在一个繁忙拥挤的餐馆里的感觉
- contagious *adj.* 传染的，有传染性的
- a crowded hospital or a crowded train station 拥挤的医院或火车站

2 How can the problem of traffic congestion be solved?

示例回答

Problems with traffic in *major cities* are a big concern today. Already the government has made *all sorts of* regulations about the car number plates that can go on the roads on different days. They have also made public transport very cheap and accessible to most people in most areas of major cities. The other thing that could be done is to encourage companies to give their employees better travel allowances – but not for *gasoline receipts* – for taxis and other receipts for public transport.

内容亮点

- major city 大城市
- all sorts of 各种各样的
- gasoline receipt 汽油发票（此处指通过汽车等交通方式产生的开支）

3 Why do people still like to live in big cities even though there are severe traffic jams?

示例回答

Well, big cities have many disadvantages, it's true. There are not only with traffic jams, but pollution, crowds, all sorts of problems like this caused by a large population all living in one place. This can be stressful actually. However, the *job opportunities and social opportunities* are amazing in big cities – at least compared to towns. If you want a good job and to enjoy a rich *social life and cultural life* outside of work and the home, then you've got to live in a big city. In addition, *educational opportunities* are better, *quality of teaching* is better, *quality of hospital facilities* is better, and all sorts of things are *better and more advanced*.

内容亮点

- job opportunities and social opportunities 工作机会和社会机会
- social life and cultural life 社会生活和文化生活
- educational opportunities 教育机会
- quality of teaching 教学质量
- quality of hospital facilities 医院设施的质量
- better and more advanced 更好更先进

4 **What public facilities does your city have?**

示例回答

My city has a lot of *public facilities*. It has major hospitals, three airports, lots of *bus terminals and an extensive subway network*. Everything you can imagine really. It's the capital city of the province so it has to have all of these things. *Not to mention*, *leisure centres*, *art galleries*, museums, all these kinds of public facilities.

内容亮点

- public facilities 公共设施
- bus terminal 公交总站，巴士站点
- an extensive subway network 广泛的地铁网络
- Not to mention 更不用说
- leisure centre 休闲中心
- art gallery 美术馆，画廊

★ Part 2

3 Describe a place where you read and write (not your home).
You should say:
　　　Where it is
　　　How often you go there
　　　Who you go there with
And explain how you feel about this place.

示例回答

I don't read very often these days, but there is one place I go to read sometimes. It is a café near to my home. It's actually *part of a modern hotel*, but the café is public and popular with people having business meetings, travellers, and artistic types. That's partly because *it's located right in the centre of* a really nice area of town, and also has **an art exhibition area**. I often read on my kindle there but sometimes I take **a physical book**. Although the café is a bit expensive, **I don't really mind** because I order one pot of tea and they give you **endless refills**. So, I sit there on the really comfortable sofa and read and study a little.

I usually **go there on my own** but sometimes I meet my friend, Martyn, there, and I stop reading and we sit and chat together for a while. I feel good there. I like the **decor**, I like the fact that it is peaceful, the service is excellent and really polite, and it's just a perfect place to read.

I believe that reading is a really good hobby, and that **in today's more internet-based society**, the world of social media and smartphones removes us from the more traditional habits of sitting quietly with a physical book in a peaceful place and simply **reading**, **digesting**, **taking in what we read** without worrying about the next text message we are going to receive or the next phone call from a friend.

I would say that everyone really needs **a tranquil place** they can spend time in, somewhere away from the **hustle and bustle** of daily life, the crowds, the noise, the traffic and things like this. Especially if we live in a city, it's even more important to find such escapes and safe havens. That's why I like the café I described earlier – it's a social place, but at the same time it's a peaceful place which is **conducive to quiet reflection**. We all need this.

内容亮点

- part of a modern hotel 一个现代酒店的一部分
- it's located right in the centre of... 位于……的中心
- an art exhibition area 一个艺术展区
- a physical book 一本实体书
- I don't really mind 我并不介意
- endless refills 无限续杯
- go there on my own 独自去那里
- decor *n.* 装饰
- in today's more internet-based society 在当今更加互联网化的社会
- reading, digesting, taking in what we read 阅读、消化、理解我们读的内容
- a tranquil place 一个安静的地方
- hustle and bustle 忙忙碌碌
- conducive to quiet reflection 有助于安静地思考

★ Part 3

1 How important is it to read stories to children?

示例回答

It's very important. Children learn a lot from stories and **it's even proven that** a child's vocabulary **increases massively** if an adult reads stories to them **every night before bedtime**.

内容亮点

- it's even proven that 这甚至已经被证实了
- increase massively 大幅度增加
- every night before bedtime 每晚睡前

2 Are there any benefits to teaching children the art of writing?

示例回答

I think so, yes. In life, and in most jobs, we have to write quite a lot. When we are in school, we write, we write at work...emails, reports, and so on. If we have *a good writing style* then *we are better able to* express ourselves, communicate ideas, and *appeal to others*.

内容亮点

- a good writing style 优秀的写作风格
- we are better able to 我们更能够……
- appeal to others 吸引他人

3 Are creative writing skills less important than skills like mathematical ability or computer skills?

示例回答

Emmm, most people might think so, yes. Because they are the *practical skills* needed to get on in life, *basically*...I mean, mathematical skills, computer skills and so on. They are important for work and study and perhaps being more creative, and being able to write creatively is seen as more of *an entertainment skill*, perhaps. A skill that is *indeed useful*, but *not really* for school or work life.

内容亮点

- practical skill 实用技能
- basically *adv.* 基本上，大体上
- an entertainment skill 一项娱乐技能
- indeed useful 十分有用
- not really 不完全是，不见得

★ Part 2

4 Describe a new public building you would like to visit.
You should say:
    Where it is
    What it is like
    How you knew this place
And explain why you would like to visit this place.

There is a new mall in my city...actually it's **more than a mall** because it's a series of buildings, pretty tall buildings, in one particular zone or area. It's called SOHO, because the buildings are dedicated to shops, restaurants, businesses, offices and also there are apartments inside on the upper floors where people can live. So, it's not exactly a mall, as such.

Anyway, the new SOHO in Sanlitun in Beijing is really cool. It also had **water features**, around a sort of garden with grass and trees, an area where young people can **skateboard**, and a lot of different restaurants on the ground floor and lower floor. It's an amazing place – well, according to what my friends say, and what I have read in the local online media.

The buildings themselves are really modern, they **are made of glass and metal**, and are sort of space-age really, because they are designed in **sweeping curves and rounded corners**, rather than **angular or pointy architecture**. It's quite **a fascinating and attractive design**. I am really into art, and I saw that there are two small modern art galleries in this SOHO too, so I am quite interested to go visit with my friends. There's also a lot of international restaurants as well. I enjoy trying food from different countries, so I am quite inspired to go to try out some of these restaurants as well. There's also a cinema, so you can imagine, if you go there you can basically have a day out with family and friends.

In recent years there has been **a marked increase** in new public buildings in my city, and most of them are **office buildings and commercial centres**, but still they usually are built in a very interesting and modern style and they provide quite a few services alongside – like cafés and restaurants, usually on the ground or lower floors. I would say that these kinds of things make life in a city much more interesting, and for those reasons **both interior and exterior design** are important things for the urban development of a city. I am pleased that there has been a great period of development for **civil engineering** and urban planning, and there's a lot of room for more interesting examples of architecture too, as cities grow and change. So, there are quite a few new buildings I'd add to my list of places I would like to visit in the future. That's for sure.

- more than a mall 不只是一个商场
- water features 水景
- skateboard *n.* 滑板
- be made of glass and metal 由玻璃和金属制成
- sweeping curves and rounded corners 弯曲的弧线和圆角
- angular or pointy architecture 有棱角或突起的建筑
- a fascinating and attractive design 令人惊叹并吸引人的设计
- a marked increase 明显的增加
- office buildings and commercial centres 办公楼和商业中心
- both interior and exterior design 室内和外观设计
- civil engineering 土木工程

★ Part 3

1 Do you think that the architecture and designs of public buildings are important for cities?

示例回答

Very important. *I also think that as time goes by*, we should create interesting, innovative, modern buildings to express the *technological and artistic achievements* and trends of our time.

内容亮点

- I also think that 我同样认为……（此处顺着问题继续展开）
- as time goes by 随着时光流逝
- technological and artistic achievement 技术和艺术成就

2 What kind of facilities might a public building have, and which are the most important?

示例回答

Buildings, public buildings, should have *elevators*, *bathrooms*, *a decent lobby*, *a reception area*, things like this. It's also nice if they have features like a small garden or some *artwork or exhibition space*. But most importantly they should have a lot of light and be comfortable, both to the eye and physically.

内容亮点

- elevator *n.* 电梯
- bathroom *n.* 厕所
- a decent lobby 一个气派的大厅
- a reception area 一个接待区
- artwork or exhibition space 艺术品或展览区域

3 To what extent should it be a priority for the government to spend money on preserving old buildings, compared to investing in new ones?

示例回答

It should be *a fairly high priority*, of course, once a city has *basic facilities* like education and healthcare and transportation and decent infrastructure. After these top priority things, then a government should spend time and money *renovating and maintaining old buildings*.

内容亮点

- a fairly high priority 很高的优先级
- basic facilities 基础设施
- renovate and maintain old buildings 翻新和维修老旧建筑

★ Part 2

> **5** Describe a street market you have been to.
> You should say:
> Where it is
> When you went there
> Why you went there
> And explain how you felt about this experience.

示例回答

A street market that I have been to that I really loved was **an indoor street market** in Chengdu. Though it was indoors, the reason I call it a street market is because it was built to look like an old Sichuan town street. It was amazing actually, and featured **all sorts of stalls** selling local produce, souvenirs, snacks and there were also eateries too. The whole indoor "market area" **was divided into different sections**, you see: a vegetable market, a meat market, a fish market, then a **crafts** market, a small **antique** market section, then a street lined with restaurants that specialised in **local snacks** and famous Sichuan dishes. There was also an area where there were small performances – people dressed in **local costumes** and playing instruments and **performing skits**. It was fantastic really, and it isn't just a **tourist site**, it's a great market that the locals also use, at least the locals that live in that central area of that part of the city.

I enjoy the fact that in my city the local governments have spent time and money to design and create these kinds of cultural spaces, which also **have a very practical function**. Usually, street markets are a lot **rougher and dirtier** and not very organised, so this one in Chengdu was especially nice, and I felt I had experienced the real flavour of what old time Chengdu might have been like.

I am quite a fan of street markets, actually, and as I've said, I am quite into traditional things, and the preservation and even the revival of traditional culture. I believe that street markets have always played an important role in Asian culture, so **it's a shame to see** that many have disappeared, although I feel that there are more **sanitised** versions being created these past few years, which give us a real flavour of the past, just with much better **hygiene** and organisation than the rougher and more **disorderly** street markets that I grew up with as a child. I think we shall see an increasing amount of these kinds of street markets and indoor markets in the future – ones which are carefully planned and uniquely designed, just like this one in Chengdu.

内容亮点

- an indoor street market 室内的街市
- all sorts of stalls 各种各样的摊位
- be divided into different sections 被分成不同的部分
- craft *n.* 手工艺品
- antique *n.* 古董，古玩
- local snack 当地小吃

- local costume 当地服饰

- perform skit 表演短剧

- tourist site 旅游景点

- have a very practical function 有非常实用的功能

- rougher and dirtier 更粗糙，更脏的

- it's a shame to see 很遗憾看到……

- sanitised *v.* 改造，净化；给……消毒（sanitise 的过去式和过去分词）

- hygiene *n.* 卫生

- disorderly *adj.* 混乱的，无序的

★ Part 3

① Do you think small markets will disappear in the future?

示例回答

I don't think so. Larger markets and more dirty and unclean markets have indeed been closed down by the government in recent years, as part of hygiene and urban planning *initiatives*. However, now we still see a lot of smaller, much nicer, and *much more organised markets springing up* in designated areas of cities. So, I think that better and well-managed markets will continue to grow, and some of *the sprawling rougher markets* will continue to get closed down.

内容亮点

- initiative *n.* 举措

- much more organised market 更有秩序，组织更好的市场

- spring up 出现，涌现

- the sprawling rougher market 不断扩张的混乱市场

② What factors do people consider before they decide to buy something?

示例回答

Before buying something there are a number of key things a person might consider. Firstly, whether they really need the item they are looking at, or whether it's *just a whim*. Secondly, they might consider which *brand* is the *better quality*, compared to their personal budget, how much they are prepared to pay. And thirdly, the design and look of the item, whether it suits them. For example, if it's a *clothing accessory*, they'd consider if it matches the kinds of colours and clothes they usually wear, like these kinds of things.

内容亮点

- just a whim 只是一时兴起

- brand *n.* 品牌

- better quality 质量更好

- clothing accessory 服装配件

3 **Why do some people prefer to buy things online?**

示例回答

Online purchasing is the most popular way of buying things where I'm from. Everyone does it. It's *quicker and easier*, and you can choose the things you want in the comfort of your own home, on your phone. They get delivered to you sometimes the same day or within a few days, and it's just *all-round more convenient*.

内容亮点

- online purchasing 在线购物

- quicker and easier 更快捷，更简单

- all-round more convenient 各方面来说更加方便

★ Part 2

6 Describe a school you went to in your childhood.
You should say:
    Where it was
    What it looked like
    What you learned there
And explain how you felt about it.

示例回答

When I was a child, the school that really *sticks in my mind* is the one nearest my home that I went to when I was about 7 years old. I think you'd call it a Junior School, in England. Anyway, it was a small school, in a small street not far from the Lama Temple in Beijing. I *have fairly good memories* of my days in this school, although we had to study really hard and it was quite strict. There were about 30 children in each class. Our main teacher was *a very kind*, *but firm woman* who also had a really good sense of humour. We learned to write Chinese characters, do basic mathematics and we learned *a bit of* painting, drawing, history and things like this. We also did physical education – some games and fitness activities in the *playground*. I really have good memories of my days in this school, and I *got on quite well* with my classmates and teachers.

However, *the one thing I didn't like* was the homework – we had way too much homework and I still *resent* the education system here a little bit for *piling so much homework on us* after school time! It was *tiring* and kind of stressful. I think that most people share the same kinds of experiences as me when it comes to schools we went to as children. I'm not sure, maybe it depends where you grew up. I think school life can leave a strong impression on you as a child, and is something that stays with us all our life. And, with that, the teachers we have also *have a big impact on* how we learn, how we feel about education and learning and which subjects we end up being drawn to and good at as we get older and progress on through the school system.

I have seen schools change for the better over the past few years, and I think that kids are maybe encouraged to be *a bit more creative* in class, and I'd say this is a good thing because it engages children more in the learning process and gives them better memories of school, and therefore *much more motivation* as they get older.

内容亮点

- stick in one's mind 令某人印象深刻

- have fairly good memories 有非常好的记忆力

- a very kind, but firm woman 一位非常善良而严格的女性

- a bit of 一点

- playground *n.* （尤指学校或公园中的儿童）操场，游乐场

- get on quite well 相处得很好

- the one thing I didn't like 我不喜欢的一件事

- resent *v.* 不喜欢；怨恨

- pile so much homework on us 给我们布置很多作业

- tiring *adj.* 令人疲惫的

- have a big impact on 对……有很大影响

- a bit more creative 更有创造力

- much more motivation 更多的动力

★ Part 3

1 What are some of the differences between teachers today and teachers in the past?

示例回答

Teachers today tend to be a bit more active than teachers in the past. They usually *incorporate more fun activities into their classes*, and also, they use technology more. I also think that teachers are generally *kinder*, and less strict today. Which can be both good and bad – *it depends*.

内容亮点

- incorporate more fun activities into their classes 在课程中融入更多有趣的活动

- kinder *adj.* 更友善的

- it depends 看情况而定

2 How do you think technology can be used in education?

示例回答

Technology can be used in *a variety of ways*: movies in class, homework assignments online, PowerPoint presentations. All sorts of ways. Today a lot of things are done online, *research projects*, etc. So, I think we are at a stage in history where technology is *an integral part of our lives*, and therefore also, our education experiences.

内容亮点

- a variety of ways 各种方法
- research project 研究项目
- an integral part of our lives 我们生活中不可分割的一部分

3 Do you believe that in the future artificial intelligence will be used to replace teachers?

示例回答

I don't really have that much *faith* in artificial intelligence replacing real people in these kinds of situations. I think that we will always want and need *human interaction* in a classroom or educational environment. Technology and AI might be useful to assist with the learning process or aspects of it, but not *as a replacement of a real teacher*.

内容亮点

- faith *n.* 信念
- human interaction 人类互动
- as a replacement of a real teacher 作为真实老师的替代品

4 What could be the implications of AI on education? Negative or positive?

示例回答

I think the *implications* are *fairly negative*. *I don't like the idea that* people think computers can replace humans and I also think that *overly* relying on computers can cause people to lose the essential social skills that we learn from a lifetime of human interaction and conversations. We feel "real" feelings in life – machines cannot. And feelings are important in education too – they are often the source of our motivations to learn and grow.

内容亮点

- implication *n.* 含义
- fairly negative 非常负面的
- I don't like the idea that 我不喜欢……这一观点
  这句为同位语从句，that 后面的从句是前面 idea 的内容。
- overly *adv.* 过度地

★ Part 2

7 Describe a place you remember well that is full of colors.
You should say:
　　　Where it is
　　　What it is like
　　　What it is used for
And explain why you remember it well.

This is a really interesting question, ***because*** only last week I went to 798, which is ***an art district in Beijing***. I saw an exhibition by a Chinese artist, I can't remember his name ***to be honest***...but anyway, it was a really amazing exhibition – an installation actually.

Basically, you walk into the room or gallery and the entire room is ***the piece of artwork***...how can I explain? It's quite a strange thing to describe, actually. You walk into the room and lots and lots of ***different coloured flowers*** are projected from lights, all over ***the walls***, ***the floor and the ceiling***. The way that the lights are shining and projecting these flower images makes it look 3D, three-dimensional.

So, you walk around the room and the images also ***project onto*** your own body, your face, your arms and so on, and of course, onto the bodies of the other people in the room too. It was really ***a unique and fascinating experience***. Well, I am not sure exactly what this is "used for"... It's a piece of modern art...but I think ***it was designed to express*** the beauty of nature and man's relationship with the natural world.

I went there with ***two of my friends*** from university, and they also ***felt very moved*** by the experience. I think I will ***go back again before the exhibition closes*** and take another one or two of my friends with me to see it. I think it's good to go to see different places in the city where you live, and ***try new experiences***.

内容亮点

- This is a really interesting question, because...引出话题，使用最近的经历来回答问题。

- an art district in Beijing 北京的一个艺术区

- to be honest 坦白讲，说实话

- the piece of artwork 一件艺术品

- different coloured flowers 不同颜色的花

- the walls, the floor and the ceiling 墙壁，地板和天花板（注意积累名词表达）

- project onto 投射到……上

- a unique and fascinating experience 一次独特且令人着迷的经历

- it was designed to express 被设计来表达……

- two of my friends 我的两个朋友

- feel very moved 非常受触动

- go back again before the exhibition closes 在展览结束之前再回来参观一次

- try new experiences 尝试新的体验

★ Part 3

1 Why do some people think textbooks should have pictures, images, diagrams and be colourful?

示例回答

People learn and remember things if they can ***see visual images***. This is a ***psychological fact***, basically. So, if you want kids to learn and remember things in textbooks, then it's better if they have ***relevant*** pictures, images, diagrams and colours. Also, they make books more interesting. And if children have more interesting books, they are more likely to want to study hard.

内容亮点

- see visual images 看到视觉图像
- psychological fact 心理学事实
- relevant *adj.* 相关的

2 How important are colours when decorating a house?

示例回答

Colours are very important in *interior design*. Colours have a great influence on our *moods and feelings*. I believe that we should choose colours in our homes wisely, so that *we feel calm*, *at ease and relaxed*. It's important to be able to feel relaxed at home. So, personally, *I would recommend that* people don't choose colours that are too *bold*. Also strong colours can make rooms look smaller, and lighter colours can make rooms look larger, so we should *bear this in mind*, depending on how we want to feel in our home.

内容亮点

- interior design 室内设计
- mood and feeling 情绪和感觉
- we feel calm, at ease and relaxed 我们感到平静，舒适和轻松
- I would recommend that 我会建议……
- bold *adj.* 大胆的
- bear sth. in mind 牢记某事

3 To what extent does a brand image and its colours influence what we think about a company or product?

示例回答

A *brand identity and brand image* are incredibly important. *After a time*, when a product is popular for long enough, the brand and logo become really valuable, actually. That is because people come to associate the brand with *quality*, *reliability and popularity*. And so that's how a company starts to become really successful – when people see the logo, the brand and think positive things, and want your product.

内容亮点

- brand identity and brand image 品牌标识和品牌形象
- After a time 一段时间以后
- quality, reliability and popularity 质量、可靠性和知名度

★ Part 2

8 Describe an art exhibition you have visited.
You should say:
What it was about
When and where it was held
What you saw in this exhibition
And explain how you felt about this exhibition.

示例回答

I once saw an art exhibition in *the national gallery* in my home city. It was an exhibition by a modern artist from Guizhou. There were several examples of painting, *sculpture*, and a room with a full art installation in it. It really *stands out in my memory* because everything was centred around the concept of light, and lights and patterns in *myriad* colours were projected over the artworks from projectors on the ceilings of the various *exhibition halls*. It was a *stunning* exhibition and quite hard to describe in words really.

It's not easy to describe modern art, even in one's own language, *let alone* in a second language! But, anyway, it was exciting and really made me think. The thing I really enjoy about some of this more abstract, modern art, is that it provokes *a host of* interesting thoughts and *inspirations* about life. I really find that quite *enjoyable* because I'm quite into philosophy and culture, so things that inspire these kinds of thoughts, I get really excited about. I do find some modern art just too abstract or too ridiculous, though, but this particular exhibition was very popular with a lot of people I know, even people who are not so into modern art. The theme of nature and flowers, projected across quite industrial sculptures and paintings, provided a very curious and interesting *contrast* and made me *contemplate* how our daily lives, especially in cities, are quite dominated by machines, and how it's so easy to forget about nature and the importance of the natural world for sustaining our life.

I bought a few *postcards* from the exhibition and even got the chance to *talk a little bit with the artist* who was there at the time being interviewed by several media outlets. There are a few art exhibitions I've enjoyed as much as this one. I found it was particularly special and unique.

I'd say that art is an important part of life, and also an important part of the culture and history of a country, and for these reasons, art galleries should be promoted in cities. I think that some of them, indeed, can be a bit boring, but others are really interesting and reflect a lot of emotions that are difficult to express through other forms or with other experiences. I believe that children should be taken to art galleries and given the chance to *reflect on* the art they see, maybe write about it, talk about it, discuss it in class. We can most certainly learn a lot from such *excursions* and I argue that art plays a much more important role in life and our *mental development* than a lot of people think. So, this art exhibition left me with a lot of reflections and feelings about the role of art in life and education.

内容亮点

- the national gallery 国家美术馆
- sculpture *n.* 雕塑
- stand out in my memory 在我的记忆中留下了深刻的印象
- myriad *adj.* 大量的，无数的
- exhibition hall 展厅
- stunning *adj.* 令人吃惊的
- let alone 更不用说
- a host of 许多，各种各样的
- inspiration *n.* 灵感，启发
- enjoyable *adj.* 令人愉悦的
- contrast *n.* 对比
- contemplate *v.* 沉思；盘算
- postcard *n.* 明信片
- talk a little bit with the artist 和艺术家聊一聊
- reflect on 反思，思考
- excursion *n.* 短途旅行
- mental development 心智发展

★ Part 3

1 How can artwork be influential to children?

示例回答

Art can have a great influence on children, although on the surface many may not see the positive and *enduring* influences of art, and many people may believe that *seemingly* more practical and pragmatic subjects are more important and more influential than art. However, children respond very well to art, both contemporary art and more traditional art. Children think very visually and have lively and active imaginations. The meanings and *metaphors* contained in works of art, as well as the colours, shapes and feelings expressed in art, can have a very *formative* impact on children's mental development and impressions about the world. I am a firm believer in the importance of teaching art, and art history, to young children.

内容亮点

- enduring *adj.* 持续的，持久的
- seemingly *adv.* 看似，好像
- metaphor *n.* 隐喻，比喻
- formative *adj.* 形成的

2 **Why are some artworks expensive?**

示例回答

Some *artwork* is very expensive because they are rare, or gain fame because a painter or artist has become famous, and the market pushes their prices up. I'm not entirely sure exactly how this works, but it is generally, I think, because art is so unique and many pieces of art, especially those done by the hand of a famous artist, cannot be easily replicated or copied. In recent years, the world of modern art has opened up more and more in China, and people have started to develop collections of artworks by famous people. The more collectors *appreciate* certain pieces of art, the more their value increases at *auctions*. I think that's the reason anyway.

内容亮点

- artwork *n.* 艺术作品
- appreciate *v.* 欣赏
- auction *n.* 拍卖

3 **Why do some people enjoy collecting famous paintings?**

示例回答

Some people really enjoy collecting famous paintings because they are so unique, and the older they become, the more their value will increase. It's also *a human instinct* to collect rare items, and artwork is an exciting thing to collect, *for* those that have the money to build up collections, and enjoy seeing their value increase over time. I guess, like anything else in life, people are drawn to things of beauty, and things of value, and the more people *perceive* things to be precious, the more those items will increase in value on the market. This is how *market forces* work!

内容亮点

- a human instinct 一种人类本能
- for 在句中作介词，意思是"对于……"。
- perceive *v.* 认为
- market forces 市场力量

4 **What can art bring to our life?**

示例回答

Art can bring emotion, feeling and philosophical depth to life. Art is something, like music, that is hard to express or explain in words, but often captures feelings and beliefs that are not easily conveyed in the simple practical written or spoken language. *People for millennia* have been drawn to art, for it *represents* beauty and feeling that is beyond the practicalities and struggles of daily life. While the world *is obsessed with* technological advances, machines, cars, houses, and all the things that make up our daily lives, art provides a *sacred space* above and beyond all of these practical things – and people fundamentally need this kind of escape. I believe art has a deeper value than many of us think – and certainly, throughout history, art has been extremely important in human existence.

内容亮点

- people for millennia 人们几千年来
- represent *v.* 代表
- be obsessed with 痴迷于……
- sacred space 神圣的地方

★ Part 2

 Describe a place you visited that has been polluted.
You should say:
Where it is
When you visited this place
What kinds of pollution you saw there
And explain how this place was affected.

示例回答

I once visited a lake. I can't remember the name, but it was on a company *excursion* many years ago when I worked in *a small tech company*. It was a couple of hours outside Beijing past the mountain range to the north of the city. The lake was meant to be an amazing place with *lilies* and incredible *natural scenery*, but I was really disappointed when I arrived because it was quite *murky and oily* in places. You could tell that the place had been used to *dump waste* and not taken care of very well. I noticed there were *a couple of factories nearby* as we approached in the minibus, so I am guessing that the pollution from the factories somehow got into the lake and *the surrounding area*.

It was pretty sad, to be honest, because the area is really rather beautiful, so it was a shame to see it being spoilt in this way. I am sure that there was not much fish in the lake or any other kind of life...at least not healthy lake animals and plants! I really hope that the *local authorities* have enough motivation, time and resources to clean this area up and turn it into *a genuinely nice place* for visitors.

There are a lot of polluted places in the world because human beings consume resources and *inevitably* dump waste in seas, rivers and lakes, as well as into the soil. This is *something that needs to be addressed*, as in the end, we all need nature, not just to enjoy on weekend excursions, but to grow vegetables, obtain clean water, and maintain *a balanced ecosystem*. We learned about this in biology in school, and it's often on the news these days, so I think people are becoming more and more aware of the importance of *taking care of the natural environment*.

内容亮点

- excursion *n.* 游览
- a small tech company 一家小型科技公司

- lily *n.* 百合
- natural scenery 自然风光
- murky and oily 昏暗且油腻的
- dump waste 废料排放
- a couple of factories nearby 附近的几家工厂
- the surrounding area 周边地区
- local authorities 当地政府，地方当局
- a genuinely nice place 一个真正的好地方
- inevitably *adv.* 不可避免地
- sth. that needs to be addressed 需要解决的事情
- a balanced ecosystem 平衡的生态系统
- take care of the natural environment 爱护自然环境

★ Part 3

1 What kinds of pollution are serious in your country?

示例回答

I think the most serious kind of pollution is ***air pollution and water pollution*** maybe. Perhaps air pollution is the worst, from all the ***emissions*** from factories and cars. You see there are a lot of factories, and we produce a lot of goods for the world, so that means there are quite high levels of emissions coming from production. There are measures in place to reduce this, but there needs to be more efforts made to ***enforce these measures***.

内容亮点

- air pollution and water pollution 空气污染和水污染
- emission *n.* 排放
- enforce these measures 实施这些措施

2 What can individuals do to protect our environment?

示例回答

Individuals can do several things to contribute towards looking after the environment. Firstly, trying to use less plastic is an important thing to do because a lot of plastic gets into the rivers and oceans and affects the ***food chain*** as it is consumed by ***marine animals***. Secondly, we can try to take more public transport and reduce private car use to reduce the air pollution in cities. Thirdly, we can try to be more sparing with the amount of water we use at home. These are examples of ***individual contributions*** to the wider environmental cause.

内容亮点

- food chain 食物链
- marine animal 海洋动物
- individual contribution 个人贡献

3 Do you think individuals should be to some extent responsible for pollution?

示例回答

Yes, I do. And I also believe that in schools and universities people should be educated about the basic ways in which we, as individuals, can ***contribute to*** taking care of the environment. All of the small things that we can do to help, especially as we have ***a large population*** – we cannot simply ***rely on*** the government to do everything for us.

内容亮点

- contribute to 有助于
- a large population 人口庞大
- rely on 依赖于，取决于

4 Why is there a need to involve the government in environmental protection?

示例回答

The government has the power to ***put stricter controls on*** traffic, factories and other major sources of pollution. Furthermore, they can put money into research and development of more ***alternative*** and sustainable forms of energy – this is something that needs ***government funding and support*** for scientific researches and technological developments. This is the government's responsibility.

内容亮点

- put stricter controls on 实行更加严格的控制
- alternative *adj.* 可替代的，备选的
- government funding and support 政府资助和支持

第四章 雅思口语补充练习话题

Part 1

1 城市与乡村（Cities and countryside）

- What are the benefits of living in cities?
- Have you ever lived in the countryside?
- Would you like to live in a city or in the countryside in the future?
- What do you usually do in the countryside?

2 与人见面（Meeting people）

- Do you like meeting new people?
- How do you feel when people welcome you?
- Do you often meet new people?
- Can you tell if you like someone when you meet them for the first time?

3 新年（New Year）

- How do you usually celebrate the New Year?
- Is New Year celebration important to you?
- Can you briefly describe your most unforgettable experience about the celebration of the New Year?
- Why do some people believe that New Year is a new start?

4 窗外景色（Window view）

- What scenery can you see from the window of your home?
- Do you like to watch the scenery from your window?
- How do you feel when you can't see any beautiful view from your window?

5 牛仔裤（Jeans）

- Do you like to wear jeans?
- How often do you wear jeans?
- Why do you think jeans are popular in China?

6 疲劳（Tiredness）

- What things make you tired?
- What do you do when you feel tired?
- Who do you prefer to talk to when you feel tired?
- Do you want to talk to strangers when you feel mentally tired?

7 应用程序（App）

- What kinds of apps do you often use?
- What was the first app you used?
- What are the most popular types of apps in your country?
- If you could create an app, what kind would it be?

8 时间管理（Time management）

- Do you make plans every day?
- Do you think it's useful to plan your time?
- What's the biggest difficulty you have when managing time?

9 户外活动（Outdoor activities）

- Do you like outdoor activities?
- Is it important for children to play outdoors?
- Do people in your country prefer to spend time indoors or outdoors?

10 耐心（Patience）

- Would you say you are a patient person?
- Have you ever lost your patience?
- When do people need to be patient?
- Do you think patience is important?

Part 2 & 3

物品类（Objects）▶▶▶

★ Part 2

1 Describe a difficult skill you have learned from an old person.

You should say:

What it is

Why the skill was learned from this old person

How you learned it

And explain how you felt after you learned the skill.

★ Part 3

- What can children learn from parents?

- From whom can children learn more, parents or grandparents?

- What kind of help do you think old people need?

★ Part 2

2 Describe a piece of clothing that someone gave you.

You should say:

What it is

Who gave it to you

When you got it

And explain why this person gave you this piece of clothing.

★ Part 3

- Why do people dress casually in daily life and dress formally at work?

- What are the advantages and disadvantages of wearing a uniform at work and school?

- Why do people from different countries wear different clothes?

★ Part 2

3 Describe a story someone told you and you remember.

You should say:

What the story was about

Who told you this story

Why you remember it

And explain how you feel about it.

★ Part 3

- Do young children like the same stories as older children?

- How has technology changed the way of storytelling?

- Why do children like stories?

★ Part 2

4 Describe a piece of equipment that is important in your home.

You should say:

What it is

How often you use it

Who you use it with

And explain why it is important to your family.

★ Part 3

- What kinds of machines are there in people's homes?

- What are the differences between the young and the old in their attitudes towards machines?

- What kinds of professions require people to use machines?

★ Part 2

5 Describe an ambition that you have had for a long time.

You should say:

What it is

What you can do for it

When you can achieve it

And explain why you have this as an ambition.

★ Part 3

- What kinds of ambitions do people have?

- Why should parents encourage children to have ambitions?

- Should parents interfere with their children's ambitions?

人物类（People）▶▶▶

★ Part 2

1 Describe a band or singer who you like.

You should say:

What style of songs they sing / music they play

When you listen to them

Where you listen to them

And explain why you like this band or singer.

★ Part 3

- What could be the reasons why a lot of young people like pop music more than other types of music?
- What types of music are popular among old people, and why?
- Do you think the best singers are always the ones with most fans – the ones that are the most popular?
- Why do you think clothing fashion and music taste often go hand in hand?

★ Part 2

2 Describe a person you follow on social media.

You should say:

Who he / she is

How you knew him / her

What he / she posts on social media

And explain why you follow him / her on social media.

★ Part 3

- Do you think old people and young people use the same kind of social media app?
- Do old people spend much time on social media?
- What can people do on social media?
- Are television and newspaper still useful?

★ Part 2

3 Describe a person who encouraged you to achieve a goal.

You should say:

Who he or she is

What your goal was

What this person did to encourage you

And explain why this encouragement helped you to achieve the goal.

★ Part 3

• In what ways can a teacher encourage children to try harder in school?

• Are there any occasions that positive encouragement can have a negative impact?

• Do you think encouragement is better than punishment in getting results?

• In what situations and to what extent do you think children need to be punished?

★ Part 2

4 Describe a person you only met once and want to know more about.
You should say:
> Who he / she is
> When you met him / her
> Why you want to know more about him / her
And explain how you feel about him / her.

★ Part 3

• Is it important to have the same hobbies and interests when making friends?

• What qualities make true friends?

• On what occasions do people like to make friends?

★ Part 2

5 Describe a person who helps others in their spare time.
You should say:
> Who this person is
> How often this person helps others
> How and why this person helps others
And explain how you feel about this person.

★ Part 3

• Why are some people willing to help others?

• In what kinds of professions do people help others more?

• Who should teach children to help others? Parents or teachers?

• Do people nowadays help others more than in the past?

事件类（Events）▶▶▶

★ Part 2

1 Describe an experience when you were a member of a team.

You should say:

When it was

What you were working with in the team

What you did in the team

And explain how you felt about the teamwork.

★ Part 3

• Do you think it is important for children to have experience as part of a team?

• What do you think is the most important quality to be a good team member?

• Would disagreement bring heavy impact to a team?

★ Part 2

2 Describe a time when you felt proud of a family member.

You should say:

When it happened

Who the person is

What the person did

And explain why you felt proud of him / her.

★ Part 3

• When would parents feel proud of their children?

• Should parents reward children?

• Is it good to reward children too often?

• On what occasions would adults be proud of themselves?

★ Part 2

3 Describe a good decision you made recently.

You should say:

When it happened

Why you made this decision

What the decision was

And explain how you felt about it.

★ Part 3

• How can parents help children make decisions?

• At what age should children start to make decisions?

• What decisions do people make every day?

• Why are some people afraid of making decisions?

★ Part 2

4 Describe a happy event you organised.

You should say:

     What the event was

     When you had it

     Who helped you to organize it

And explain how you feel about it.

★ Part 3

• How can parents help children to become organized?

• On what occasions do people need to be organized?

• Do people need others' help when organizing things?

★ Part 2

5 Describe a time when you waited for something special to happen.

You should say:

     What you waited for

     Where you waited

     Why it was special

And explain how you felt while you were waiting.

★ Part 3

• On what occasions do people usually need to wait?

• Who behave better when waiting, children or adults?

• Do you think waiting is harder now?

地点类（Places）▶▶▶

★ Part 2

1 Describe a café you like to visit.

You should say:

    Where it is

    What kind of food and drinks they serve there

    What you do there

And explain why you like to visit this place.

★ Part 3

- What kind of people like to go to a café?
- Why do young people like studying in a café instead of at home?
- Do old people like to drink coffee?
- Do Chinese people like to drink coffee?

★ Part 2

2 Describe a part of a city or town that you enjoy visiting.

You should say:

    Where it is

    When was the last time you went there

    Who you like going with

And explain why you like to go there.

★ Part 3

- What public places do old people usually visit?
- Do young people like to go to public places?
- Will more people move to cities in the future?

★ Part 2

3 Describe a place you visited on vacation.

You should say:

    Where it is

    When you went there

    What you did there

And explain why you went there.

★ Part 3

- What are some popular attractions that people like to visit in your country?

- Do old people and young people choose different places to go for vacation?

- Do old people and young people have different considerations regarding their travel plans?

★ Part 2

4 Describe a place where you are able to relax.

You should say:

  Where it is

  What it is like

  How often you go there

And explain how you feel about this place.

★ Part 3

- What activities do employers organize to help employees relax?

- How can students relax?

- Do people nowadays have more ways to relax that they did in the past?

★ Part 2

5 Describe an apartment or a house that you would like to have.

You should say:

  What it is like

  Where it would be

  Why you would like to have such place

And explain how you feel about the place.

★ Part 3

- Is it expensive to buy an apartment in China?

- Do people usually rent or buy an apartment in China? Why?

- What are the differences between the houses that young people and old people like?

- What kinds of factors will influence people to buy an apartment?